HOME
TO ROOST

HOME
TO ROOST

*A Backyard Farmer
Chases Chickens Through the Ages*

Bob Sheasley

THOMAS DUNNE BOOKS
St. Martin's Press
New York

THOMAS DUNNE BOOKS.
An imprint of St. Martin's Press.

HOME TO ROOST. Copyright © 2008 by Bob Sheasley. All rights reserved. Printed in the United States of America. For information, address St. Martin's Press, 175 Fifth Avenue, New York, N.Y. 10010.

www.thomasdunnebooks.com
www.stmartins.com

Design by Kathryn Parise

LIBRARY OF CONGRESS CATALOGING-IN-PUBLICATION DATA

Sheasley, Bob.
Home to roost : a backyard farmer chases chickens through the ages / Bob Sheasley.—1st ed.
    p.   cm.
  ISBN-13: 978-0-312-37364-1
  ISBN-10: 0-312-37364-3
  1. Chickens—Anecdotes.   I. Title.

SF487.3 .S54 2008
636.5—dc22   2008013500

First Edition: July 2008

10 9 8 7 6 5 4 3 2 1

Contents

Acknowledgments

Thank you . . .

. . . to Jake Elwell, my agent,
      for encouragement.

. . . to Peter Joseph, my editor,
      for discernment.

. . . to John Parsley, my editor,
      for enthusiasm.

You're all fine folks just looking for good tales to tell.

And special thanks . . .

. . . to Suzanne, Ross, Gretel, Julia, and Alexandra, my family,
      for love. *We shared a moment in eternity.*

. . . to the *Philadelphia Inquirer* staff, my coworkers,
      for loving good eggs. *And you're all good eggs, too.*

. . . to Ulisse Aldrovandi, my friend,
>   for inspiration. *We'll talk more about this one day.*

. . . and to Sophie, my pig,
>   for not eating the manuscript. *You scattered and chewed it, but I guess it wasn't quite to your taste.*

HOME
TO ROOST

You Come, Too

⚜

A path between two garden gates connects Ulisse Aldrovandi and me. Through pasture and woods it winds away into lands where all time and distances have lost meaning.

At one end is Lilyfield Farm, my Pennsylvania home, where the daylilies spill down the hill to Suzanne's garden of sunflowers and squash, where Sophie the pig wallows by the pear tree, beside the catfish pond. I made the gate to our garden, from old boards adorned with nail holes and knots.

At the other end of the path, a gate of ornate ironwork opens to Aldrovandi's villa Sampolo, in a valley of the Apennines between Bologna and Florence. Sometimes when the light's just right, or I'm tired enough, still draped in dreams, I need only step out from my garden, and I stand in the glory of the Italian Renaissance. Whenever he sees me approach, Aldrovandi beckons to me as he would to a lost friend, home at last.

The old botanist delights in showing me what he's grown, his *pomi d'oro* and other revelations of a dawning age. As we talk, he cradles a hen in his arms. He tells me about the specimens he's spent a lifetime collecting from the New World. They would thrive, I say, at

Lilyfield. In our gardens, the things that I know, and that he knew, mingle under a sometimes pleasant sun.

Come dream with me this morning in my garden, next to our farmhouse on the road to Valley Forge. The sundial says it's early still, though shadows only guess at human time. From his roost in the chicken coop down by the barn, the rooster declares another day coming on, but he can wait.

I built the coop myself, of lumber scraps, an old door, and roofing I scavenged. Suzanne designed it. But I made it, rising early each day to hammer away before heading back to Philadelphia to earn my wage as a newspaperman. Today, half a hundred hens have the run of Lilyfield. They peck in pasture and swale, along the pond and amid the stone ruins of the springhouse, though it's the manure pile they love most, digging deep for the treasures within.

Atop the hill, a weeping cherry shades Suzanne's grandfather. They planted it together long ago, and there she buried his ashes. I see them planting it now; I hear her crying; he rises for a new season. Here, in this garden, I will scatter her ashes one day to nourish the tomatoes. Or will she scatter mine?

Four seasons I've seen spin past six times since Suzanne and I first kissed at midnight under the willow tree on the far shore of the pond. Seventy moons or more we've counted here together. Peeps turn to pullets, the roosters strut, a summer comes and goes, and another, and we marvel each year at the first eggs. I've learned to admire these creatures, as did Aldrovandi, who has taught me more about them than I ever imagined. And, like him, I loved a hen.

Now each day as I head to work, along a crowded path that's far better marked than the one that leads to Aldrovandi's garden, I carry with me a basket of eggs to sell to my newsroom colleagues. Next to me on the seat, the eggs remind me of our lily fields, and of Aldrovandi's villa in Romagna, and of another Pennsylvania farm that I'd thought was lost to me forever.

Come with me today, into the city and home again. Along the way

I'll tell you a story or two. I'll tell you about a rooster that survived the chopping block and became a sideshow curio, a headless wonder fed through an eyedropper. I'll tell you about a perplexed farmer who found a hen floating lifeless in the pond, and the next day another—until, as the body count grew, the farmer finally cracked this serial-killer case.

We'll parse the thirty or more sentences that researchers suggest chickens can say, and translate some of their talk—the peep's lonely call or its trill of terror, the hen's cackle after laying an egg, the rooster's battle cry and the gentle cluck and coo by which he summons his hens.

We'll find out why hot young hens tend to go for those bad broiler cocks at first, until they settle for the family guys from the laying breeds. Man, ever curious, has studied such things.

We'll have questions to ponder: Did an African tribe execute a German explorer in the 1850s near Lake Chad for the crime of eating eggs? Does a rooster have a penis of any consequence? And friend, I will show you hens' teeth, scarce though they are, and a featherless chicken that, praise be, needs no plucking. Science has given us one. It's come to this.

The rooster calls us ever onward to the rush hour. We'll be back at day's end. Suzanne will take us down to the garden to see what's ripe, and we can sit amid the arugula and oxhearts and too many weeds, and laugh as loudly as we want, or let the tears come. We'll watch the chickens finally head home at sunset. Bide with me awhile today, and let's roost tonight at Lilyfield.

"The quickest way to stop a train is to forget your package," warns the sign near the woodstove in the North Wales, Pennsylvania, station. Next to a folded newspaper, a wicker basket of eggs sits unattended on the bench. Returning from the restroom, I find the stationmaster scowling.

I snatch the contraband and scoot out to board the 7:55 into the city, where I work at *The Philadelphia Inquirer* and sell farm-fresh eggs to my fellow editors and reporters. I confess to raising chickens. Forty-eight, last count. We are the creatures of Lilyfield Farm—the chickens and I, my lovely wife, Suzanne, our four children on the cusp of adulthood, Sophie the pig, a few horses, three goats, and a peacock. Our five-acre homestead, two centuries old, is midway between Philadelphia and horse-and-buggy Lancaster County.

A man of hayseed roots long urbanized, my life aswirl, I married a city girl gone country and moved five years ago to her oasis near Valley Forge. So many years distant from the Amish-country enclave of my youth, I'd resigned myself to cities, never dreaming that at forty-six I'd be blessed with life and love anew.

I am "the egg man" now, or so I'm known to the coterie of coworkers who have enjoyed the daily produce of my coop these past four years. Each spring, I add a new brood: Silver-Laced Wyandottes and Barred Rocks, Australorps and Araucanas, Brahmas, Rhode Island Reds, and my latest acquisition: Marans, the French marvels that lay eggs the color of rich chocolate. The others lay brown eggs, mostly, a few white, and some green, or rose, or lavender.

I'm hooked. And so are my customers. These eggs sell themselves. I suppose that's because they come from free-range hens that chase grasshoppers and such. Or because they're hormone-free, a source of omega-3, and quite possibly organic, whatever that may mean. Some folks adore the spectrum of colors; others are lured by the brilliant yellow yolks and the heavenly egginess of their taste.

Grocers and restaurateurs have seen the pattern: People want fresh food, locally grown. Consumers who suspect big producers are cruel to chickens take their business to down-to-earth farmers whom they consider kinder and gentler.

Settling into my window seat on the train, I close my eyes as I often do when it's time to pull away. When next I open them, the world is changing. Outside my window, colors blur as the train slices through rings of suburbia, past old warehouses, new condos, old warehouses becoming new condos, while, sagging in the underbrush, farmhouses molder away as they wait to be bulldozed into profit. Speculators are "developing" old Pennsylvania apace, the countryside underutilized no more.

"Eggs?" asks an overstuffed young woman, a bobbed blonde in black, balancing herself on my seat as she enters the car. She's grinning at my basket, which is taking up a seat to itself. I allow as to how they are eggs.

"Keeping them all in one basket?" she asks, before lurching onward and away.

My fellow travelers come and go, station to station, caught, like me, in the loop of living. We are migrants still: rural to urban to suburban and rural and back, swaying on the track, trying to get home.

"In Milan, first thing we do, see, is get up and go down to the henhouse and suck us a few right there," offers a gentleman across the aisle who clearly has known Italy, his hands enacting this long-ago memory. "We poke the end and suck 'em, right there in front of the hens." He pauses, his eyes in distant mirth, and tells me this again.

A man who carries around a basket of eggs must expect to hear about such egg-sucking exploits and more. There's a coop, it seems, in most everyone's childhood, where we helped a tottering grandpa fetch the eggs on misty mornings; where grandma, apron bespattered, swung her ax wildly in gleeful pursuit of supper.

On the train, as the scenery changes from field to factory, from sprawl to high-rise, I hear how it was once: in Italy or Indiana, in Puerto Rico or Pennsylvania.

And I hear how it is now. I discover others like me, who keep coops: on small farms, in backyards, and even in the city, on rooftops. Speeding through North Philly, I look out upon lines of row houses, or what once were row houses. Next to the El tracks at Eighth and Poplar, a patch of green: A dozen youths have turned an eyesore of trash and tires into a garden of tomatoes and eggplants, lavender and sunflowers, as part of a city program to break through years of encroaching ugliness. I imagine chickens lurking in these neighborhoods, as dispossessed and determined as the greenery amid the rubble.

I lean back and close my eyes again, contemplating other gardens. I think of our patch at Lilyfield—each year we vow to devote the time to tame the weeds, and each year life gets in the way, though the garden blesses us regardless. And I think of Aldrovandi's garden at Sampolo, perfectly arrayed, with a place for everything and paths as organized as his thoughts. He loved the flora of the world he knew and of the new one unfolding across the wild sea. He founded a great botanical garden in Bologna, one of Europe's first.

The man knew a thing or two about chickens, too, and wrote down all that he had heard about them—a good deal of it preposterous, yes, but some of it insightful and wise. I'm sure history will judge a few of our modern ideas absurd as well.

Among the extensive projects he tackled, Aldrovandi set out to record for posterity everything he could learn about birds. The result: his two-thousand-page *Ornithology*, completed in 1600, of which about a tenth deals with chickens. *Aldrovandi on Chickens*, a remarkable 1963 translation into English by L. R. Lind, restores that part to us.[1]

Aldrovandi didn't seem to dare dismiss anything as trivial. Not only do we learn, for example, what chickens are called in many languages, but we get an exhaustive accounting, page after page, of what their various parts are called, in obscure dialects, as well as the many parts of an egg. Many pages are devoted to drawings and descriptions of chicken freaks with four legs or two heads. The world, he believed, needed to note and remember these things—they were part of the larger order.

The master naturalist also collected interesting proverbs about chickens, medical cures, historical anecdotes, and biological findings, to which he added his own insights and musings, as well as the opinions of the great minds of the past.

He understood that chickens are an important part of our natural history, and have long followed wherever people go. Today that can mean a row house roof or suburban backyard. Some coop keepers are recent immigrants who wouldn't dream of giving up their chickens, even if they moved to, say, Philadelphia. Others want to rediscover their rural roots, their inner farmer, to get in touch with something they fear they've lost, or missed. For some, quality is the issue: They want their food wholesome and fresh, not shipped from afar, so they take the "buy local" creed to the next step. Others want ribbons from the fair: Birds of resplendent feather fill exhibition halls as hobbyists follow the lead of Martha Stewart, chicken fancier exemplar, who says she adopted her perfectionist standards from a poultry manual.[2]

Twenty-four billion chickens walk the earth, making them more numerous than any other bird.[3] To wipe them all out, every man, woman, and child would have to gulp down four—in one sitting, lest they multiply. To clear out my coop, my family of six would each have to eat eight.

Some among us would welcome the chance to facilitate chicken extinction. There are those who do not love chickens; who would wring scrawny necks with abandon, given the chance; who cry not over the loss of heirloom breeds. Those urban escapees in the subdivision down the road don't necessarily share a love for predawn cacophonies and acrid scents wafting on the evening breeze. And though country folk will defend their right to keep a coop, they don't necessarily love the processing plant over in the next township—or the new neighbors it has brought in from far away to take jobs nobody local seems to want.

It's no easy matter, introducing the new flock to the old. Any poultry farmer could tell you. To a chicken, the concept is simple, as are all concepts: These are newcomers. They are different from us. We must peck at them. They must keep their place.

In the eight thousand years since chickens were first domesticated from a wild breed called the Red Jungle Fowl of Southeast Asia and India, humans have kept them for many reasons. We never dreamed of a McNugget then, nor the croquette special at Louie's. It wasn't their culinary qualities that first drew our attention. It was their nasty ways. Cockfighting has long been the beloved sport of nobleman and commoner alike. The Greeks made it an Olympic event.

As our ancestors bred roosters to perform gallantly in the ring with razor and spur, so, too, did they perfect the hens' performance back in the coop. Selective breeding created the egg machine that serves us so faithfully even today. In this sense the chicken most certainly came before the egg, for without cockfighting we would not have bred such prolific layers.

Along the way we tossed them on the grill—and today poultry is a world staple. Americans alone eat eight billion chickens a year. The industry boomed in the last century, though the popularity of poultry and eggs has ebbed and flowed with dietary trends. Cholesterol was good, then bad, then both. Atkins dieters redeemed the egg, leading to a new generation of designer varieties considered good for us.

Through our civilized ages, we have fine-tuned our chicken machine to attain economies of production. In the last century, we put the hen on the assembly line, automating its ovum. We helped out the struggling family farmer by concocting a broiler bird that he could get to market more quickly; then Big Chicken took the profits, relegating the farmer to serfdom.

Today, the disassembly line can process eight thousand birds an hour.[4] And prodigious hens such as the White Leghorn, caged nearly motionless over chutes, their heads pumping nonstop into a conveyor of enhanced feed, can plop out their pristine prizes at well over twice the rate they could before we fiddled with them.

In 2006, a typical hen laid 262 eggs a year, a workaday wonder, having steadily increased from 112 in 1925.[5] (My own work year is almost exactly the same as the average hen's: The company pays me for 260 days, though I get 24 of those as vacation when I'm not expected to lay an egg.)

Eggs are cheap, though, and birds don't take days off. Broiler birds grow fat quickly, ready for market in six weeks, bland though they might be. Technology has created the superchicken to serve the masses.

So what need have we now for fine feathers, for the pedigrees of plumage bred lovingly for generations? In the heady days of "hen fever" in the 1800s, when a chicken fancy swept Victorian society, gentleman geneticists crafted an abundance of new breeds. Some rare varieties survive now only due to the diligence of poultry clubs, passionate in their pursuit of perfection for the exhibition hall.

Not only the classic breeds but all of chickendom is in peril, judging by the doomsday predictions in some of the accounts of the avian influenza cases sweeping the Old Country and threatening to migrate to the Americas. The industry began to take a hit as publicity about the disease spread in 2005 and 2006; people shied away from poultry, at least for a while, and various nations imposed restrictions on commerce. Some even scowl at the backyard farmer, whose flock still dares to go outside where it could catch its death. The reports do seem heavily populated with peasants, but it's the factory farm nearby where the virus would likely have more opportunity to mutate. We must, indeed, be vigilant: In 1918, the Spanish flu pandemic killed as many as 100 million people worldwide, one of every sixteen people on earth.[6] We know now that it was an avian flu similar to the one threatening calamity once again.

The chicken had a role in this, but it's hardly out to kill us all—

though some would understand the impulse. To the contrary, chickens have saved countless human lives: Scientists have long used their eggs to culture vaccines to fend off influenza and other diseases. And in antiquity, the chicken was a walking pharmacy.

Aldrovandi praised poultry as the ultimate health food, its flesh so easily digested. Physicians and deep thinkers, he noted, had long recognized every part of the chicken as useful in some way for healing. Among those prescribing the meat for a variety of illnesses was Rhazes, the ninth-century Persian physician and philosopher who profoundly influenced the course of medicine.[7]

Through trial and error, deduction and extrapolation, the ancients put their poultry to the service of medicine. They knew what chicken soup could do. It heals best, Aldrovandi averred, when made from the flesh of an old rooster, chased until he collapsed from exhaustion. Chicken soup cures dysentery, advised the Roman scholar Pliny the Elder. And if a young lady misses her period, Pliny wrote, induce menstruation by slicing three hard-boiled eggs, reheating them on the hearth, and piping the vapors into her uterus.

Hen brains stop nosebleeds, wrote Marcellus Empiricus, one of Rome's great medical minds. And, he pointed out, the dung of a red cock effectively treats boils. Here Aldrovandi drew the line. "I make an exception of their excrement," the wise man wrote.

The ancient Greeks sacrificed roosters to their god of medicine and healing to thank him for good health and to appeal for more. So it was with Socrates, condemned on charges that he had corrupted the youth of Athens by thinking too much. Fading from the hemlock he had quaffed, he called for his old friend. "We owe a cock to Asclepius," he whispered to the tearful Crito. "See that it is paid?"— and spoke no more.

"They are acquainted with the stars," Pliny wrote of the humble chicken, and indeed the ancients believed we had much to learn from these creatures. Namely, who would win the next battle—and for this intelligence, the chicken was compelled to spill its guts. All over the temple floor.

We, too, hold the chicken in high esteem for what it can teach us—though what we wish to learn has more to do with profit margins than war. In 2004, we cracked the genome of the chicken, the first bird so blessed. The feat was tackled by an international team of scientists who, having accomplished this, forged onward to decipher the amoeba.

Taking apart the chicken's genome is a far more fruitful method of learning its secrets than eviscerating it. We discovered, for example, important clues to such maladies as cleft palate and muscular dystrophy.[8] We found that its sense of smell is better than we had thought, and that it has a relatively poor sense of taste. It doesn't know, for example, what bitterness is.

It should. We've given the chicken plenty to be bitter about. Our new insights will let us better manipulate its body to serve us more ef ficiently, and fill our bellies and our pockets more abundantly. We can breed the master chicken race to feed the world, inexpensively. Poultry can be had for a song.

That song would be *The Four Seasons,* by Antonio Vivaldi. The strains of his "Spring," "Summer," "Autumn," and "Winter" are coop favorites, according to a study conducted a generation ago at Cornell University. The researcher found that chickens gained weight faster when exposed to soft music—he chose Vivaldi, explaining that they seemed partial to classical.[9]

Swaying to the music on their roosts, the chickens doubtless believed their keepers had tuned in to their inner need for cultural edification. They'd been had. It wasn't the first time, nor the last.

Spring, summer, fall, and winter. All that mankind has accomplished, Pliny wrote, we owe to the rooster and his crowing, for he rousts our lazy bones each morning lest we sleep our lives away. Before the sundial, the rooster marked our time. And although, some would say, he lacks Vivaldi's sense of song, the rooster does know a thing or two about the four seasons.

"The power of the sun attends the rooster," wrote Aldrovandi, citing the wisdom of the ages. The rooster knows the solar secrets, the philosophers observed; he senses the changes in the air as the sun moves.

The hen, too, is a creature of heavenly rhythms; she orders her life around her clutch of eggs. Like a woman, she is on a monthly calendar. As her cycle begins and ends, she can pop out a few oddballs— some as tiny as quail eggs, some lumpy, some torpedo-shaped, some rubbery, with shells lacking calcium. It happens particularly when she's young and new to this business, but soon she's laying a perfect egg about every other day. She presents it a few minutes later each time until, when the moon has fulfilled all its phases, she begins afresh. Not until the mid-twentieth century did we fully understand how attuned the hen is to seasons and light, and how a farmer could use a timer and lightbulb to coax more eggs from her by fooling her into believing in endless summer.

The rhythms of my daily commute to work are not unlike a chicken's. Each morning as I open the coop door, the chickens burst out in a dash to be first to the manure pile, where they peck the day away till roosting time. They spend their days squabbling, fleeing predators, chasing fluttery things. Puzzled, mostly, they strut and preen.

I check the time. I'm ten minutes from Philadelphia's Market Street Station; from there it's a quarter hour more by foot to the newspaper office, under the big white clock tower between Spring Garden and Callowhill, the finest names two streets could have.

Through the train window, before our descent into subterranean blackness, I look out upon a desolation of chain-link fencing and razor wire. In what passes for a playground, a young man, alone, dunks a basketball through a rusty hoop, swishing the tattered net.

I arrive at Market, where I do my own dash through the crowd, and climb into the sunlight to begin my walk through the old streets with my basket of eggs. I pass the Reading Terminal, once a rail hub but now a cavernous farmers' market where Amish and Italians, Greeks and Asians, and the rest of Philadelphia's pepperpot serve up their best—tandoori chicken and apple dumplings, souvlaki and cheesesteaks, panini and soul food that can make a man weep. I look up at the clock atop the tower of City Hall. My stomach's growling, but there's no time to stop.

I've long lived by deadlines. At *The Philadelphia Inquirer,* I'm a writer of headlines, a polisher of prose. I try to repair grammar. I determine whether "armpit" is one word or two.

For several years, I was an editor of features and arts, with stints on the metro, national/foreign, and business desks. I've loved my job, which, in essence, involves wrestling big ideas into small spaces. And among my coworkers I've found an enthusiastic market for fresh eggs. I sell a dozen or two a day at three dollars a carton.

Several of those customers, some of my best, are gone now, swept away in a round of career-crushing layoffs. Seventy of the *Inquirer*'s most talented editors and reporters disappeared overnight in a concerted effort to improve our lot. I survived.

They asked me to help out on the sports desk.

When my son, Ross, was a wee lad, I took him down to the playground in the Blue Mountain town of Slatington, Pennsylvania, where we lived then, for a test drive on his new tricycle. I brought along a basketball, underinflated from lack of use. On an impulse at the playground's edge, I hurled the ball in a transcendent arc toward the hoop, watching bewondered as it swished the net. A threesome of high-schoolish girls, standing at the corner, applauded, and I bowed.

Then I tried it again. I didn't bow.

It's not that I dislike sports. It's that I didn't grow up with sports. The farmhouse of my childhood heard no hooting in the den on Saturdays. We made hay on Saturdays. Nobody taught me all the rules of play—that is, until third grade, when a crackerjack gym teacher, a master of tact, noticed my deficit and put me with the girls for basic lessons. It can be easier to pretend not to care.

Forty years later, feeling far afield, I found myself on the *Inquirer* sports desk trying to write nightly basketball wraps and craft headlines for the joust du jour. Someone wins, someone loses. It's clear, usually. I do like that. There is a ballistic beauty in perfect bodies excelling, and sportswriting can be a newspaper's best. But this wasn't my dream.

And somewhere, out there beyond the tracks, a determined young man dances on cracked concrete, drives for a layup, and dunks, imagining cheers from the bleachers and the bright lights that will lead him to stardom and anywhere save where he is.

"People say, 'When you make it to the NBA, don't forget about me,'" the teenage athlete William Gates said in *Hoop Dreams,* a 1994 documentary about young inner-city men and those who exploit their desperate hopes. "I feel like telling them, 'Well, if I don't make it, make sure *you* don't forget about *me.*'"

In the dying western Pennsylvania town of Sharon, where I was a cub reporter in the 1970s, I dreamed of an exciting career of Watergate wonders. I moved to city and suburbs, to Washington and New York and Philadelphia. Decades later, I now find my industry fading as sadly as did the steel town I once knew. People are losing the newspaper habit, opting for the Internet.

Each workday evening, I retreat to our farm amid the madly developing suburbia of southeastern Pennsylvania. The pharmaceutical industry thrives in the nearby towns, where the suited masses grab their morning coffees, check their e-mails, shave in the car, bang their BlackBerrys, do most anything but read a morning paper.

Lilyfield Farm is a survivor in a world fast encroaching. I want to see all the vistas of that new world, still, but more and more I want to keep it away, too, and when did that happen? I dream now of making it here, on these few acres, away from the bright lights, tending the chickens and the stables.

"Got to love that Ben Franklin," a gentleman calls to me from the steps of the Pennsylvania Academy of the Fine Arts, where he's sitting with his pal. He stands to intercept me, holding out his left hand while pointing down Broad Street with his right.

I reach out to shake, then notice his bundle, and his coat, too heavy for such a sweet day. It's a coin or two he wants. I doubt even an egg would do. My eyes follow his finger to the celebrated statue atop City Hall.

"You mean Billy Penn?"

He turns slowly and points again, his finger tracing a wide arc back to me, then bows. "Got to love that Bill Penn."

I hand him a dollar, the best-spent alms ever. No longer would he lead our tourists astray. "Say, brother," he says, leaning near, "don't keep 'em all in one basket." His friend on the steps snorts.

My wife is well acquainted with such souls. Suzanne grew up in some less-than-pleasant sections of Philadelphia, moving as an adult to Worcester, thirty miles to the northwest, where she "raised the roof" of a ramshackle stone house, two centuries old. It slumped amid fields choked with wild morning glory and thistle and bane. A massive, gnarled oak tree—one of the county's oldest—graced the lane. It must have stood there, though hardly more than a sapling, when General Washington's men crisscrossed those fields on the way to Germantown, White Marsh, and Valley Forge. Geological layers of manure rose high in the barn stalls. The house showed the weight of its two centuries. But Suzanne set to work and designed the renovation herself, rallying work crews from her church.

I married that girl five years ago, and we combined our separate broods in that yellow farmhouse, reminiscent of the Tuscan countryside.

For years we had been neighbors, living just a few miles apart on opposite sides of the Skippack Creek, each a single parent raising two children. Life had tried to pull us both down. It was time to dream again.

We met in the waning days of August, and in a December blizzard we drove to New Hampshire to visit friends. The next evening, in the mist of the darkling shore of Goose Pond, I asked her to marry me. My two children and I moved across the creek to her farm on Frog Hollow Road. We became a family of six. Ross and Gretel, Julia and Alexandra, and my dear Suzanne—these are the names I wish to have upon my lips when all this fades away someday.

I walk up Broad Street, my stomach competing with the rumble of the subway under the sidewalk grate. Still a few minutes from the *Inquirer*'s brass doors, I stop for a quick McChicken. I set my basket by the register.

"Those eggs," says the cornrowed clerk. He's looking at neither me nor the eggs.

"In one basket," I say, quickly, as I pat my pockets in search of the dollar bill I gave Billy Penn's friend.

Puzzled that I would state the obvious, he repeats himself. "Those eggs."

I want to punctuate him. Was it a question? An observation?

I prefer to think he was having an exclamatory moment, a Philly epiphany, proclaiming throughout all the land: "Brother, got to love those eggs!"

Even after years of knowing cities, I feel like an observer from another world. The places and people I've known have come and gone like the scenes that blur past my window on the R4 line.

During the Depression, my father, at age twenty-one, moved from New York City with his family to an 1870s farmhouse far out in Mercer County, Pennsylvania, on a hundred-acre spread he later fondly described as "the corn among the ragweed."

For sixty years he built his land. He and my uncles and grandparents subsisted, at first, on what they could raise themselves—cows and pigs and chickens, as well as the produce of their garden. It was the 1930s version of sustainable farming, though nobody called it that then. Come the war, my uncles got jobs for a while in Sharon, the nearby factory town on the Shenango River.

In 1988 my father had a stroke while we baled hay as a late July storm swept in. He was seventy-seven. A man of many words—cursing at the cows, reciting long poems, chatting with all comers—he spoke only in labored whispers after that. His life's work eventually slumped into a tangle of joe-pye weeds and briars. He asked my brother and sister and me to sell the farm where we had grown up.

A few years ago the new owner bulldozed the memories. On an August afternoon that throbbed with cicadas—the sound of summer dying—my brother, Jeff, and I walked down the lane to poke around the old homestead as we often had done, exploring the pastures and our past.

The greenery had been rendered rubble. The house was gone, as was the barn that smelled of timothy and old wool, and the pigsty where I played, and what remained of the old coop with its rows of nesting boxes cloaked in cobwebs. We sat silently on the foundation, two men just shy of fifty, and one of us might have wept.

Ours had been one of the last small family operations, a way of life that's fading fast in this age of factory farms. As recently as 1950, in the decade I was born, nearly half of rural Americans lived on farms. Today, it's one of ten.[10]

In 1950, about three-quarters of the farms raised flocks of chickens, and farm families ate 6.6 billion eggs from their own coops, compared to a total 52.2 billion sold. They'd eaten 7 billion in 1925, and well over 8 billion in the depths of the Depression, when thrift was born of desperation.

Of today's remaining farms, fewer than 5 percent even have a coop. Though we're selling 90 billion eggs a year now in America, in 1982 the USDA stopped bothering to count the few we still ate down on the farm.[11]

At Lilyfield, my family and I count ourselves blessed to taste such delights on a crisp Saturday morning, when sizzling essences of egg and bacon mingle. And I still count the eggs—in fact, too diligently, says Suzanne, who has to confiscate enough for her cooking before I whisk them off to market.

Arriving at the *Inquirer,* I join a group of women waiting at the elevator. "I have to ask," says one, pointing at my basket. "Are those—eggs?"

It's a question I hear almost daily. I reassure her. With my farm background, I'm a curiosity at the *Inquirer*—though I regret to say that all newspaper people could soon become a curiosity.

In the newsroom, I double-check my work schedule and take a seat on the national/foreign desk, across the room from my usual haunt on the city/suburban desk. My friend Steve notices I'm out of place.

"What's a hayseed like you doing over on the national/foreign desk?" he asks. "Chickens get loose in Kabul?"

The city desk isn't exactly a pastoral bastion, either, but I don't point this out. "They were down a body today," I explain. They needed some help, the way the sports desk had needed help after the layoffs decimated its ranks. I had spent four months editing sports, surprised that I was sometimes enjoying it, until the bosses figured I'd seen enough of the bright lights and rehired an editor who knew how the games were played.

"Heard you were raised Amish, and came out," another colleague says, then asks me, "Sorry you did it?"

The unadorned truth is that I grew up down the road from Amish farms. We were "English," meaning non-Amish. We harvested crops with our plain neighbors, bartered with them, did commerce with them. They drove their buggies down to our pond to fish. We got along.

"Get awt, I say!" the old man, crouching at his coop, shouted at my father. It was 1965, and we had pulled up in our '56 Ford pickup to buy a few dozen eggs. "These here are fifty cent a dussin, and I'll not be cheated by the likes of ye! Now get awt!"

His son-in-law Albert rushed from the farmhouse to escort his wife's pappy inside, closing the door gently as a bonneted figure within led the poor codger muttering into the darkness.

"He's taken a stroke, Burt," Albert explained to my father. "Don't mind what he says, they're still thirty cent a dussin." Albert, a farmer and wheelwright, had met and befriended my father, the rookie from Brooklyn, years before.

As the facts are hollered down the pipe, I've been rendered Amish. Such is the way information often spreads, as journalists know. I may not be one of the plain people, but I'm forever a farmer by virtue of birth. And when I tally my life someday, I'll be proud to have called myself a farmer and a newspaperman, even as technology transforms both pursuits almost beyond recognition. On the farm and in the office, I have shoveled my share of manure and spread it wide over the fertile earth. The smell, I confess, can be potent, but what seems at first unpleasant often turns, with time, to good.

You come, too, as I make my rounds through pastures and streets, sunshine and shadow, the here and now and the heretofore. I want to tell you what I've learned in my few seasons. We'll crack us a few eggs today and at nightfall chase the chickens to the coop.

SPRING

A Season to Sow

With a hearty *buon giorno* and a kiss to my cheeks, Ulisse Aldrovandi greeted me in his garden. I heard a soft *braawk* as a hen fluttered into the old man's arms, studied me suspiciously, then buried her head in the fur of his tunic. He stroked her with a fingertip.

"She's a darling," I said. My interest pleased him. He smiled, and his eyes smiled, too—round eyes, and kindly.

"So gentle and mild," he said. Some hens are warm and social, he told me; others are peckish and eat their own eggs. His was a hen of the companionable sort. She seemed, however, not to care for the company of other chickens, staying near her master. She would sleep only among his books, when he was nearby, he told me. If he shooed her away, she would lie upon her back—heaven knows why.

The Renaissance man and the neurotic chicken—perfect together.[1]

"She reminds me of one of my own favorites," I said. "A little Blue Cochin, with feathers on her legs, who comes all the way from China. I call her Blue. We ordered her at the Agway this spring, and dozens more—breeds from Egypt and Holland. France, too."

Aldrovandi seemed dumbfounded. "Such specimens must have cost a fortune," he said.

"Just a few dollars each," I said. "Blue, she follows me around, and roosts on my foot when I'm lying down in the hammock with a book. She's not exactly tops in the pecking order, that girl. Maybe it's those feathers; she looks like she's wearing bloomers."

He nodded knowingly. Hobbling toward a bench, he invited me to rest there with him. The terraced grounds were alive with his passion: The old professor, mostly bald now and gray, had spent many youthful years organizing expeditions to collect specimens from afar. Here in the garden of the villa Sampolo, between hedges of boxwood and laurel, amid statuary of draped angels and naked gods, some of his rarities had sprouted for the new season.

And it was not only here, in a stream valley at the foothills of the Apennines, that he nurtured them. He was a scholar eager to share. Besides the botanical garden in Bologna that he established for the edification of his students and the public, he had also assembled his "theater of nature" with more than eighteen thousand specimens of flora, fauna, and minerals that showcased the world's diversity, including seven thousand preserved plants. He developed a way to dry plants on paper so that the impression appeared painted. These he called his "dry gardens." Spending large sums to procure seeds and specimens and to hire artists to draw them and assistants to help him record all that he observed, he amassed eighteen volumes of color plates with three thousand drawings.

"*Nihil dulcius quam omnia scire,*" an ancient Latin proverb, was the philosophy that had driven him since youth—"Nothing is sweeter than to know all things." His interests were comprehensive indeed, leaning to the bizarre. Among the volumes he wrote was *Monstrorum Historia,* a history of monsters and monstrosities, of freaks and abnormalities—all part of nature. Shortly after his death, his cabinet of curiosities was expanded and opened for tours, with a dwarf serving both as guide and as an exhibit.

And Aldrovandi didn't always have a grasp on reality, as we understand it: His displays included what he purported to be the remains of a miniature dragon that might have perched upon his hand. After his cousin was appointed pontiff, a fearsome dragon appeared in the Bologna countryside, according to reports. Aldrovandi wrote that he had personally inspected its carcass and determined that all would be well for the new pope.

"See over there," Aldrovandi said, nudging my arm. He pointed to his thriving *pomo d'oro*. That marvelous vine, he told me, came from seeds he obtained from the New World. We could not imagine, he said, what further wonders awaited us there. The seeds sprouted, now, in gardens throughout Romagna and beyond.

"The plant has stalks and leaves similar to the eggplant," he pointed out, "with fruit like the golden apple." The Spaniards had found it growing in the tropical highlands of the lands they had claimed, and there were those, he had heard, who were now partaking of it, who had overcome the fear of poisons within.

The Italians will be making the most of this one, I thought.

We sat awhile in the vernal light, and he asked if I'd like to see his library. I helped him to his feet and he took my arm, with his hen still roosting on his wrist. He led me slowly into the house and through the oaken door.

He had catalogued and described it all, so that no one might ever forget, he said. He pointed to the volumes surrounding him: It was his life's work, everything he had been able to learn. Pulling down a well-worn volume, he hunched over it. I could make out Aristotle's name on the spine. He opened the tome at random and peered at the page, his finger trailing down it.

"So many have tried to tell us," he said. "Great beauty lies around us, waiting for us, but so do dangers ready to pounce in the night. We must explore, and learn all we can of the world we inhabit." He stroked his moustache, which draped over his ample sideburns and fringe of beard.

"And respect it," he added, gazing at me. "There are dragons all about." He straightened himself as best he could, closed the book with a thud, and led me back outside.

I heard water gurgling, somewhere, and I thought of my own little garden. I wondered how Ulisse would tolerate the weeds. I imagined him relaxing in our garden. Suzanne would slice him some heirloom tomatoes, though he might not dare eat them, and I'd tell him about the new brood of baby peeps we were raising, under a heat lamp in the farmhouse, near the woodstove and the pile of old blankets where our potbelly pig, Sophie, sleeps next to my easy chair, where I rub her bulging belly with my toe as I sit writing at two o'clock in the morning.

Aldrovandi, I think, would think this fitting, and he'd find me to be accepting of his eccentric and secretive hen, which sleeps only amid his books, late at night, in his library. I think my little Blue might feel just as comfortable roosting on his foot.

I don't think my world would bewilder him, so much as fascinate him. I'm sure he'd ask to borrow my ballpoint, study it a moment, and start scribbling furiously. Everything seems to have enthralled this man who knew so much.

And I'd be proud to fill him in on what he might not know.

Joy in the Morning

I awoke to twitterings, soft scratchings, and, somewhere, a voice. "We need a coop."

Squinting at the silhouette by my bedside, I became conscious of curves and angles, then corduroy and cardboard, and a cascade of red coalescing into the tresses of my new wife, a beauty in a work shirt holding a box over me. A box brimming with life.

We'd dreamed of raising chickens—someday, someday. Up since dawn that March morning, Suzanne had visited a Quakertown farm supply store where hatchlings by the tubful skittered under heat lamps. Overcome by spring, she decided that someday was here: She brought home fifteen newly hatched peeps.

I arose early each day in that delicately lovely spring of 2004, priming myself on caffeine and waiting for the sun to rise to a decent height. I didn't want the neighbors down the way to awaken to the *whacketa-whack* racket of my hammer. I know what it's like to suffer construction noise. The woods and meadows that surround Lilyfield create an idyllic illusion that is too often shattered by the growl of dozers trying to make better use of Worcester Township's open space.

Peeps need the warmth of their mother's body and the protection of her wing, and since the boxful of them that Suzanne had brought home had never seen the grown version of their species, together we became the surrogate hen. In our farmhouse kitchen, we attached a heat lamp to the edge of a large plastic tub, lined it with a few inches of wood shavings, and set up a feed tray and water dish inside. In went the peeps, which made themselves at home in an instant—no shy moments of trepidation, just a dash for the feed tray, filled with a special mix for hatchlings.

That first spring, we raised several breeds, including some old-time barnyard classics: Buff Orpingtons, an affectionate bird with golden plumage; Silver-Laced Wyandottes, whose silvery white feathers are laced with black edging; and Barred Plymouth Rocks, a zebra of the chicken family, painted in wavery lines of charcoal and white.

We also raised a few Americanas, which matured to be thick-necked and wild-eyed. They are derived from the Araucana, a rare Chilean breed. Both breeds lay eggs of blue or green; hatcheries sometimes sell Americanas as "Easter eggers." Our Americanas look nothing alike. One turned out calico, a crazy quilt of coppery white and iridescent black-green. One is golden with black fringing, and another white with charcoal fringing.

That's how it is with chickens. Within each breed are several types of feather patterns and colors: laced or barred, penciled or cuckoo; black, blue, red, or buff, to name a few. Our Wyandottes are silver-laced, for example, but they also come in such varieties as golden-laced and lemon-blue. And many breeds of chicken have a smaller, "bantam" version.

One of our peeps was unlike any of the others, though we think she came from the Americana bin at the farm store. We named her Tim. Four years later, we still don't know what she is. I don't really want to know. She's golden brown with red highlights. Her bright red comb flops over her right eye; it hangs there like a latex glove attached to her head as if she were about to do a Howie Mandel routine. Believing that Tim was an Americana, we expected that she would produce bluish green eggs when she and her sisters began laying in September. Tim gives us white ones.

We worried and fussed over Tim and her sisters. Suzanne scrubbed their water bottle daily and added medication that promised to keep them thriving. We played with them until they lost all fear of us and hopped readily into our hands to be fed. I found myself getting up at 3 A.M. to check on the heat lamp, and learned that peeps do a good job of regulating themselves: Too hot, and they move to the shadows at the edge of the tub; too cold, and they move closer to the light, or huddle in a heap. They do tend to clog up their water dish with wood shavings, though, since even in peephood their instinct is to kick and dig, as if looking for grubs.

I soon noticed another instinct: They disliked shadows gliding over them. The peeps in our kitchen knew nothing about hawks and such. No mother hen had taught them the ways of the wild. Peeps don't know what makes a shadow, but they cower from it nonetheless. If you tease them with a sharp *braawk*, they scurry for cover, then freeze in a tableau, each with one eye staring upward. Softly say *buck, buck,* and they resume pecking. You could do this repeatedly, if so inclined. Their instincts guide them when their brains otherwise fail. It's their wiring for survival.

Suzanne warned me from the start: Those fifteen chicks would likely end up as a brood of seven or eight. She expected to lose about half of them to sickness and predators. She figured a half dozen hens would make a good starter brood, so she'd purchased twice that many.

We lost none. In that first spring, not one of the peeps succumbed to the dread maladies that one reads about in how-to-raise-poultry books. We never had to inspect their anuses to make sure they weren't pasted shut—which I imagine could lead to dire consequences, explosion perhaps. None of our peeps failed to thrive or grew lame. They did grow larger and hungrier; some turned bossy and others passive, depending upon temperament, as they jousted for dominance. The hellions among them took running leaps across the tub and jumped atop the feeder and even made it to the tub rim, playing king of the hill.

After a couple of weeks, we carried the brooder tub out to the yard and let the peeps venture out to explore in the grass, keeping the tub nearby in case they needed to retreat. As they became acclimated to the outdoors, and as the weather warmed, we ceased to worry much about them. No predators came with honed teeth and claws to claim their heads. When their bag of starter mash ran out, we bought them some grower pellets, but what they really wanted was the assortment of creeping things they sifted from the soil. As the weeks progressed, they foraged and fed themselves with little help from us.

Our brood included thirteen pullets and two cockerels—that's what hens and roosters are called early in their first year, after they've grown feathers but before they've matured. As peeps, the males and females can be next to impossible to tell apart, which leads to cross-sexual name selections, such as "Tim." Each bird soon distinguished itself as a unique being. Suzanne became partial to a buff that she named Buffy who jumped up to greet her, in a bustle of wings, and would even try to join Suzanne inside her car. Buffy trotted after her, but this was not love, exactly. If you feed a chicken out of your hand, such are the consequences. Four years later, long consigned to the ordinary ranks of coop life, Buffy is still an unusually cordial hen—a sign, I think, of her early favored status.

Fending for themselves as they grew, the chickens instinctively searched for safety at dusk. Since they had no house of their own, they took up nightly residence high in the branches of the weeping cherry tree next to the house. This wouldn't do. I imagined them huddled there still, come winter, as the wind howled and ice glazed their wattles. I turned my attention to completing the coop.

"Now just look at that," I told Suzanne, tossing down my hammer and wiping my brow with my cap. I shook my head and pointed toward the faithful old Ford rusting behind the barn.

"What?"

"Chickens. On the tractor."

She acknowledged my accuracy, then unclipped a tape measure from her belt, measured the windows I'd framed, and frowned. She jotted something on a notepad. Suzanne is never without a tape measure and notepad.

Down by the barn, I was assembling the skeleton of the coop to come, having scavenged old doors and siding and roofing to finish the job. My new bride wanted a coop, and eager to please her I'd set right to work, as the young chickens watched dubiously. I'd sketched a basic design, which Suzanne resketched, and we'd revised each other's revisions until we had the concept of a coop that any chicken should covet. Meanwhile, the chickens took to hanging out on the seat of our ancient tractor.

A tractor is no place for chickens to be roosting. They need shelter, a house of their own, a place where they can find some semblance of security, where they can get up off the ground and away from things that snuffle in the night, where the whistling winds cannot reach them, where they can softly cluck and poop the evening away in peace.

They're not particularly choosy. They'll make do, if need be, with a horse stall in the barn, occupied or not. They'll take to the rafters. They'll even resort to a tractor seat, but a caring farmer wants better for his chickens, not to mention for his tractor.

This project was a balance between Suzanne's standards and mine, with the chickens' preferences unspoken. We worked out the fundamentals. We would build a separate compartment within the coop for feed and equipment storage; the coop would face south to take advantage of the winter sun; the nesting boxes would have a hinged lid that could be raised from outside the coop to collect eggs; the roosts would be installed over plastic tubs that could be pulled out through a hinged flap for easy cleaning.

I've seen coops too foul for any fowl and others nicer than the housing that much of the world's population endures. Suzanne's design skills helped us to avoid the former; my practical bent steered her away from the latter.

"No fowl-house is what it ought to be, unless it is in such a state as to afford a lady, without offending her sense of decent propriety, a respectable shelter on a showery day." Such was the recommendation of the Rev. Edmund Saul Dixon, who in 1849 published *A Treatise on the History and Management of Ornamental and Domestic Poultry*, which helped to propel the Victorian chicken craze.

A respectable shelter for a lady? I imagined Suzanne on such a showery day, kicking off her galoshes as she entered the coop to admire my work. There, against the west wall, three full rows of roosts over a spacious waste pit. The roosts would be spaced just right, with the proper sloping so that the biddies sitting higher in the pecking order wouldn't soil their sisters of lower status. Each chicken would have at least two square feet of floor space to call its very own. Milady would not only take shelter in such a coop but would seek it out.

"You build your coop so nice, friend," Justino observed, peering up at me as I straddled the rafters, hammer in hand. "Those will be some really happy chickens." Justino, a project manager, had stopped by to talk business with Suzanne, who uses his contracting services on the houses she renovates. Real houses. She had long since advanced beyond just coops.

Suzanne and her tape measure reappeared around the side of the barn. "In Mexico," Justino told us, "some people nail together crates and pallets to build a coop." He smiled at me. "Mexican chickens are happy, too."

No doubt he's right. A chicken would judge you respectable if all you gave it was basic wood and wire. If you have an outbuilding, call it a coop. A storage shed will do, with a few accoutrements. Some folks fashion a coop out of one of those big wooden spools that the electric company uses; they just tack some wire mesh around the outside, and presto. It works well for a few hens, aesthetics notwithstanding.

A family to the west of us in Pennsylvania, near the town of York, turned a coupe into a coop: A derelict Volkswagen Beetle, on blocks in the backyard, became their "poults' wagon." It just needed a few roosting poles laid across the seats, some boxes for nesting, and a cleated ramp for access. For chickens, that's traveling in style, as limited as their horizons might be. Just roll up the windows at night, and they're safe from the perils of the road.

Downright respectable, I'd say, and I did have an old VW that seemed to be puttering on its last fumes. But I suspected somehow that such an arrangement wouldn't meet Suzanne's standards, and I was determined to please her. Our wedding had been scarcely a year earlier, and this was a woman who had turned an old farmhouse into a showplace through sheer willpower. She deserved a decent coop.

From their perches on the seat of the old tractor, and upon the steering wheel, the chickens followed my movements. It was well into June, on the cusp of summer, and I was sweating each morning as I worked on the coop for a few hours before heading into the city. I had nailed on the siding and trim and was trying to figure out how to string the mesh for the chicken run.

"I wonder where I can get me some authentic Ford blue paint," I told Suzanne, motioning to the tractor.

I imagined myself high on that seat, the chickens banished to their new coop, as I rode proudly in a parade along with others showing off their treasures new and restored. The tractor would glow as it had in 1941, fresh off the assembly line.

"Why?" she asked. I commenced hammering, unsure how to answer.

Two years earlier, soon after we'd met, Suzanne had taken me on a tour of her farm. Behind the barn sat the old 9N, one tire flat and another sagging. I climbed into the seat, turned the key, and pressed the starter button. Nothing. A week later, I drove down the lane to visit her and found the tractor sitting in front of the barn with a bright new muffler, black tires, and fresh hitching pins.

"Try it now," Suzanne said. A few whirs, a shudder, and the tractor clattered into action.

"Not many old-timers around anymore who know how to work on these things," she told me, but she had found one who puttered and tinkered till he managed to crank it up once more. "Now it's up to you."

I looked at her and let the implications sink in. Either I, too, qualified as an old-timer endowed with rare low-tech mechanical acumen, still able to crank it up, or I was a whippersnapper whom she already trusted enough to want to keep around. Either way, I saw something in Suzanne's eyes.

"Got to make sure you give 'er fuel and fire," the true old-timer told me when I called the next week to ask him why the tractor wouldn't start. "Give 'er both, and there's no stopping her." He told me a gallon of gas should do the trick, or I could just open the auxiliary tank.

On the Internet I soon found a trove of advice on repairing vintage Ford tractors, as well as mail-order sites for parts that not so long ago would have taken hours to find in salvage yards. I bought the original shop manual and stocked up on plugs and points and such that a man should have around.

I knew that the tractor and I would come to understand each other. It would appreciate that I liked to get caked in its grease and plunge into its innards, feeling more manly that way, somehow, than behind a typewriter. And I would be sensitive to how very old it had been feeling, though it wouldn't want me to say so—it wanted to do the work of a young tractor. "All you need is fuel and fire," I told it. "You'll go on forever."

"Why?" Suzanne repeated.

"Why go on forever?"

She tilted her head. "Why paint it?"

I looked at the rusty fenders streaked with chicken manure, the dangling headlight, the dented grille. "I could make it look like new again."

Suzanne ran her shapely hand over the fender, then gave it a slap. Two chickens jumped aside. "It deserves to be rusty," she said, as a feather settled onto the seat. "It has a—you know, a patina."

I smiled and put down the hammer. Taking off my shirt so I could feel the sun and breeze, I climbed into the seat, sending the rest of the chickens squawking. I choked the carb, fired the ignition, eased the throttle.

Not knowing why I'd started the tractor, I drove it around the barn, then back around again, looking for something, anything, to pull or push or lift, then parked it on the hill and cut the spark. Suzanne wouldn't understand. Most any man would know, without our even having to talk about it.

My dear friend Brian, for example. He had stopped by on his Harley late in the afternoon of an early spring day—what I call the "scruffy spring" season when wild onions sprout amid the grass tufts. He'd been a farm boy, too, tending cows in Wisconsin. I met him by the pasture fence, next to the old Ford, and each of us rested a foot upon its hitch as we talked. I pointed to the grease-caked engine. "You know," I said, "she's spurting oil pretty bad, and half the time the starter won't take hold unless I tap it with a wrench, but once she's going there's no stopping her."

He nodded, then pulled out a cigar and offered me one. We bit off the ends and fired them up. As the mellow smoke wafted around us, he motioned with his cigar toward the barnyard, where piles of junk spilled through the gate and into the pasture, ready for the Dumpster. "Spring cleaning?"

I groaned. "Years of spring cleanings."

I had been clearing out the clutter in the barn and workshop for weeks, ever since I strolled down from the house one evening and found Suzanne there, measuring. Her clipboard was loaded with graph paper. "We'll need to build new stables," she announced. A chicken coop was not enough. She had bigger ideas. We would upgrade the barn and take care of horses.

Suzanne's willpower could harness the wind. She has long survived that way. She spent part of her childhood in tough neighborhoods of North Philadelphia, where she had only her Belgian shepherd, bigger than her, to protect her. She started a business—buying, renovating, and renting lovely old houses—from nothing but guts and charm, because she was determined to do more than just endure. She would thrive, now, out here in the country.

As I cleared the barn to make way for the stables, I found the detritus of her life in boxes and battered suitcases and the clutter of things overflowing not from abundance, or from neglect, but from so very much to do. The contents of an upset carton lay scattered on the floor: old letters and photographs and court papers.

In a broken frame in a dusty corner lay a cartoonist's original sketch from *The Philadelphia Bulletin* of Suzanne's great-grandfather, Kid Gleason, a long-ago pitcher for the Phillies. He went on to manage the Chicago White Sox, the scandalous "Black Sox" of 1919 who conspired behind his back to lose the World Series.

A wood and leather box sat moldering on a shelf, and inside were the tools and calipers of a diemaker, each inscribed J.S.M., instruments of exactitude now badly tarnished and pushed aside. These had been the tools of her grandfather. In her troubled girlhood, she had run to him. She brightened his final years here, at the farm, holding his arm as he hobbled on knees wrecked from youthful baseball. He was an Irishman with eyes the color of the blue urn in which she buried his ashes, at the edge of the porch, under the weeping cherry she'd planted just for him: John Samuel Maher, so long the only man who had shown her love.

I saved what seemed sentimental or useful and chucked the rest. Soon I was shoveling horse manure daily. As a boy I'd spent years shoveling cow manure into wheelbarrows, and this was déjà vu. The difference: This time, I enjoyed my labor. I had left the farm, done my time in town and city, and come home. I'd prayed that God would give me the wonderful woman I'd met. He gave us much more.

"This is how someday we'll say it was," my sister, Joanne, once told me, wistfully, as we recognized that our parents were old and ailing and we'd have to sell the farm they'd long nurtured. My sister's words return to me so often in the night.

Brian and I shared words far simpler as we smoked by the tractor. We chatted about stables, and coops, and cranky engines—"but once she's going there's no stopping her." It's what I like about talking with men. The matters of the heart only seem to go unspoken.

"I was thinking I could make this tractor look like new again," I told him. "But then again, what's the point. It's old." He neither agreed nor disagreed but hoisted himself into the old Ford's seat, started it by instinct, and took it for a spin around the barn. He'd gotten her going, all right, and I prayed he could stop her: I'd been working on the brakes.

And now it was me on the seat of the tractor, parked on the barn hill. I looked at my wife as she began to busy herself with chicken wire, attaching it to the run as if this were the hundredth coop she'd built. I'd been around the barn twice, and that was parade enough for me. I swung down from the tractor, took Suzanne's hand, and as we walked to the house for lunch I stopped to kiss her. Fuel. And fire.

Trumpet to the Morn

I t's a fabulous tale, as fables tend to be: A certain woman had a hen.

Where and when she acquired this hen, we don't know. But she was a woman of certitude, and things seldom end well for those so vested. Her parents had often warned her: "A certain young lady's in *big* trouble."

Of this the woman was sure: If her hen laid one egg a day, she could lay two, if only the woman fed her more. Plying the hen with grain, she dreamed of a bounty from her biddy. Instead, the hen grew so frightfully fat that even one egg was more than she could manage.

Such is the fate that befalls the greedy, according to this apologue that Aldrovandi mentions in his *Ornithology*. The moral: Avarice lays waste.

A certain major corporation had some hens. . . .

Since chickens were first domesticated, they have abounded in fables and lore, in rituals and religions. They have come to symbolize the best and the worst of human nature. Chickens are either devoted and doting caretakers, or they are craven nitwits.

In endless sayings and tales, the hen is a dope or coward or alarmist (as in "dumb cluck" and "chicken-hearted" and "the sky is falling!"), or she is the essence of estrogen, of maternal nurturing. The rooster is courageous and vigilant and an earnest provider, as in several of Aesop's fables, or a lustful libertine, as in more than several jokes. (I'll tell you a decent one later.)

We humans have had a long love of chickens, though few of us know how difficult they can be, day to day, as they peck and squawk and carry on so—and who really wants to put up with that? We'd rather see them all dressed up for dinner.

Our affinity for the chicken, when we first met, was more than just a desire for the flesh. Most people didn't even think much about that, then. We admired chickens for their beauty, and particularly for their character—their fighting spirit, their virility. Nobleman and commoner alike hoped to show off the biggest and best cocks in all the land, to demonstrate their prowess in the pit.

Our more spiritual connections came later. We entered into solemn counsel with chickens on matters of love and war; we sacrificed them in a flurry of feathers to appease the gods. We plucked them to ornament our own bodies with their plumage, and we picked them apart to find cures for our maladies. With time, we discovered that many of these pursuits did not benefit us all that much, nor the chickens. But by then we'd tasted of something special.

Down by the coop, the chicken chores that should take me mere minutes each day often stretch to half an hour or more. One moment, the chickens may be pecking placidly; the next, one among them imagines it sees something shiny and races off, the others following inanely until they forget what they're doing and begin exploring a new pasture.

Drama surrounds me: Hens maneuver to establish their place in the harem, and cluck incessantly—brawk-brawk-BRAAWK—to announce the arrival of an egg. Some sulk in their nest, days on end. Roosters duel each other out of principle, and do their wing dance to bid their hens to squat. They can be rough, these Casanovas of the coop, but they're fiercely protective, too; they keep an eye to the sky as they forage, and when they find a treat, they call their hens to partake of the best.

As I watch the chickens chasing the glint of the sun, defying fences, roosting and brooding, laying eggs, and making a mess of the garden, I can understand why *Homo sapiens* and *Gallus gallus* bonded so readily. Too many times I've followed shiny things and lost my bearings. Peckish and skittish and confused, we earned our reputations together, these chickens and I.

Eduard Vogel wiped the last of his poached egg from his chin and broke the wax seal of the morning's post. He had been chosen, the letter said, for an expedition into central Africa to deliver supplies to the great German explorer Heinrich Barth. The young astronomer was delighted at the opportunity to do some exploring of his own.

A year later, in 1853, he delivered the goods to Nigeria and set out to explore the regions surrounding Lake Chad. On December 1, 1855, he headed eastward toward the Nile in Sudan. Nobody ever heard from him again.

Vogel, whose name means "Ed the Bird" in English, ate virtually nothing but hens' eggs—an avid Atkins diet man a century and a half ahead of his time. It isn't clear where he procured a supply of his coveted cackleberries, but it seems he would have had two choices: either barter with the local tribes or skulk off into the Sudanese night to secretly feel around under their hens.

Several expeditions failed to find him. Nearly twenty years later, another German explorer in the Darfur region heard stories of his fate there: The Bird had been murdered. Historians conjecture that he was either suspected of spying or killed by local tribesmen in disgust after they caught him slurping down excrement—which is what some cultures in the region considered eggs to be. His diet could have raised questions about European sensibilities.[2]

Though Vogel's egg addiction may have been more fetish than reverence, the egg has long captivated numerous cultures as an emblem of rebirth. Eostre, the Anglo-Saxon goddess of spring, cradles an egg in some depictions—a symbol of fertility and new life. She was central to festivals of the vernal equinox, that moment when daylight ceases to dwindle and begins to come back to us once again. Death and rebirth abound in nature; they are the pulse of the seasons, the way of the seeds.

Christian hearts, as well, embrace the promise of new beginnings that Eostre's egg represents. Most scholars agree that the word *Easter* derives from her name, and from the same roots arose other words related to illumination and dawn and the direction from which it breaks: *east, aurora, Australia.*

The egg, like the evergreen tree—like the cross itself—serves as a symbol for Christian tenets: The egg's shell represents Jesus' tomb, and from inside that tomb arose life anew. Decorating eggs celebrates things dawning—a tradition hardly limited to one creed. The Persians gilded and painted eggs thousands of years ago and bestowed them as gifts.

"Christ is risen!" Mary Magdalene told the Roman emperor Tiberius after the Resurrection, according to tradition. She held out an egg as a symbol of the miracle. Tiberius laughed. He no more believed that a man could rise from the dead, he told her, than that the egg could turn scarlet, right in front of him—which it promptly did. In another version, Mary Magdalene and the Virgin Mary place a basket of eggs at the foot of the cross. After Christ's blood dyes them red, Mary Magdalene presents them to Tiberius.

The art of the decorative egg reached its zenith in tsarist Russia with the fabulous creations of French jeweler Peter Carl Fabergé, who had immigrated to St. Petersburg. The classic Fabergé eggs, produced from the 1880s until the Bolshevik Revolution, were highly favored by Nicholas and Alexandra.

The House of Fabergé produced fifty eggs for the imperials. After the 1917 revolution and the murder of the royal family, the Bolsheviks stored the eggs in crates in the Kremlin, but most were sold off to Western collectors during the Stalin years. Only ten remain in Russia. Eight are missing—stolen during the revolution or destroyed in the looting.[3]

Inside each egg's bejeweled crust was a surprise treasure, such as an intricate carriage of gold, platinum, and diamonds, as in the Coronation Egg; or a golden hen with a rubied crown, as in the first Fabergé egg commissioned by the imperials. In a 2004 auction at Sotheby's, a Russian industrialist purchased the Coronation Egg from the Malcolm Forbes family; the price was undisclosed, but the auction house had estimated it could sell for $24 million.[4] That same year, the egg was stolen—in the movie *Ocean's Twelve,* that is, a tale of a grand heist in Rome with a plot as intricate as the egg itself.

The Christmas tree also represents life that cannot fade, and that tradition, too, has pagan roots. Decorated at the winter solstice in late December, the tree was a sign that summer was not dead—its spirit was alive, forever green. Summer promised to return. Decorating trees with eggs at Easter is a popular German tradition that immigrants brought to the New World. It is common in Allentown, Pennsylvania, and environs, a nexus of the Pennsylvania German culture where I lived and worked for many years. There, folks hang bright plastic eggs from bare trees—saplings, mostly, just breaking into bud. The dollar-store version of the tradition endures in America.

The egg has symbolized not only renewal and rebirth, but also birth itself—the beginnings of all we know. A cosmic egg, floating upon the primeval waters, begat all creation, according to ancient Hindu belief, which emphasizes the cyclical nature of existence—creation and destruction, rebirth and reincarnation, without beginning or end—much as scientists have theorized a universe eternally expanding and contracting, born, too, in the explosion of a primal "egg."

After a year's incubation, the Hindu egg split asunder into halves of silver and gold: earth and sky. The shell became the mountains and valleys. The liquids gushed out into oceans, and the veins of life inchoate rippled into great rivers. The delicate films of the membranes became clouds and mist and snow.

Within this egg was Brahma, who rose with the sun, bright and brilliant. He is the creator in the Hindu trilogy, reigning along with Vishnu the preserver and Shiva the destroyer. As the egg opened, all beings arose with shouts of hurrah.

Eggs have been revered in some tribal cultures, forbidden in others. Cultural attitudes that arose throughout the world followed similar patterns. People often kept chickens for magical reasons but restricted the eating of eggs. Their symbolism was too sacred, or sexual. Or they were filth: In Tibet, eating eggs was forbidden altogether; they were considered as unclean as the sinful, worm-eating creatures that produced them.

In many lands, such as Cambodia and Thailand, people kept chickens not for eating but for divining the future. Shamans broke eggs to study the patterns and colors and predict what would be. Such a powerful oracle merits respect. Naga tribesmen of northeast India believed that women should eat only eggs laid by a proper chicken. If the hen is indiscriminate in where she lays her eggs—if she lifts her tail whenever and wherever she feels the urge—a woman who tastes of such eggs might follow suit.[5]

The Azande people of the southern Sudan and Congo had a particularly astute way of flushing out witches from their midst. They simply asked a chicken whether so-and-so was the witch who had caused such-and-such misfortune. Chickens do best with the direct approach.

To do so, the Azande chose a ritual leader, who avoided sex for several days to prepare for the great task. He positioned himself before the chicken and asked the question, at the same time forcing poison down its gullet. If the chicken lived, the accused was innocent. If it died, the Azande were not quick to judgment: They consulted a second chicken, poisoned it, and evaluated its death throes.[6]

Lest we think such rites were an anomaly confined to societies we might now consider primitive, the Greek and Roman versions show that even revered thinkers and engineers entrusted their futures to the chicken. Eviscerating a chicken to read the innards is quicker and surer than poison.

The Romans, those dear hearts, came to embrace a gentler method: They merely let the flock out in the morning and observed its behavior. If the chickens burst forth from the coop hungry and pecking, their feed flying, it was a good omen. Woe unto the keeper whose birds flew the coop without breakfast. If a general could rally his troops, or a husband his wife, with the news that he'd fed the chickens, the battle was won. (Pliny endorsed this method, though he also valued the truth of the entrails.)

Every day, at our Lilyfield Farm, the chickens burst forth hungry and pecking, their feed flying, by which I take it that great victories lie ahead. Or that we need to get down to the Agway for some more sacks of feed.

The Roman naval commander Publius Claudius Pulcher mocked the chickens aboard his ship when they suggested he would be unwise in attacking the fleet of Carthage at Sicily. *"Ut biberent, quoniam esse nollent,"* he said—"If they won't eat, let them drink!"—and threw them overboard, according to accounts by the historian Suetonius. Most of the Roman ships joined the chickens at the bottom of Drepana Bay.[7]

Hauled back to Rome, the general found himself charged with sacrilege for ignoring what the chickens had to say. He died in exile. It pays to heed popular opinion, whether from chicken or Senate—and though Cicero mocked the auguries as "true delusions of the devil," they nonetheless mattered to many.

It's many a wishbone I've broken with my family as we sat back after disassembling a chicken. Make a wish, snap the collarbone, hope for the larger piece of fortune. Near the holidays, my mother would dry out the wishbones and wrap them in tinfoil to hang on the tree. This was a harbinger of good fortune that may have explained how I managed to evade lumps of coal most Christmas mornings.

I don't know about the tinfoil trick, but breaking a wishbone is a custom older than the ancient Romans. The Etruscans, who lived in what is now Italy before the Romans swept through in the sixth century B.C., kept chickens in temples to divine the future via the art of alectryomancy.

Dead or alive, the chicken was magical. The alectryomancers knew how to tap the power of the living chicken. A temple priest would scribe a circle on the ground, mark the letters of the alphabet around it, and place a kernel of corn on each letter. Inside the circle he would position a sacred chicken. "Who will be the next emperor?" the priest would ask, or some such urgent question. As the chicken, wise and hungry, began eating, the priest paid rapt attention. And a remarkable thing happened: The chicken produced *a sequence of letters,* which the spellbound Etruscans found profound, in Ouija-like wonderment.[8]

In an apocryphal account of alectryomancy gone awry, the fourth-century philosopher and magician Iamblicus did indeed ask a rooster who would be the next emperor. The bird pecked out a *T,* then an *H,* an *E,* and an *O,* and stopped. When the Roman emperor Valens heard of this, he executed prospective rivals named Theodorus, Theodotus, and Theodectes and, in the true spirit of stoning the messenger, began giving a hard time to astrologers and soothsayers as well. Iamblicus quaffed a draft of poison rather than face the vindictive Valens, who was succeeded by Theodosius.[9]

You can't just fling such a sacred bird into the Dumpster when it dies: The Etruscans dried and saved the bones, particularly the collarbone, which they took to rubbing to curry divine favor. By the time of the Roman Empire, the rubbing became breaking: Whoever was left holding the larger half would be granted a wish.

Though chickens in many cultures have been admired and revered, they also have often been treated indelicately, put to death, and chopped up for supper.

In ultra-orthodox Jewish societies of Israel as well as New York and other major cities, chickens sometimes pay the ultimate price during the approach to Yom Kippur, the Day of Atonement. In a ritual known as Kapparot, the man of the house procures a rooster for himself and a hen for his wife. As the couple recite verses, each shuffles their chicken from right hand to left, then waves it thrice around the head. "This is my atonement," they say, bidding the chickens, a symbol of their sins, to die so their caretakers might live long and prosper. The chickens are forthwith slaughtered.

Rabbis and animal rights activists alike have taken issue with the long-standing practice, pointing out that it is a medieval custom not officially sanctioned by Jewish law. They perceive the ritual as cruelty, incompatible with the spirit of Judaism. The Kapparot chicken swinging continues, as evidenced by markets stocking up on live poultry in the approach to Yom Kippur—though many Jews now substitute a piece of pottery to smash, or money to be donated to charity.

Chickens that don't get invited to Kapparot, or that get loose from a backyard coop, sometimes end up scratching in Brooklyn flower beds. Some of these city chickens are escapees from another fate: In neighborhoods with sizable populations of Haitians, voodoo practitioners commonly slaughter chickens in rituals at home altars and in basement temples.

With tens of thousands of Haitians in New York City, many chickens succumb while in the presence of various spirits: the Rada, the sweet one from West Africa; the angry Petro from slavery days; the rum-swilling Gede, spirits of death, humor, and sex. In eighteenth-century Haiti, slaves from Africa combined the ancient beliefs of the

Yoruba and the Fon with the new religion of their masters, and the spirits began to share identities with the saints of French colonial Catholicism.[10]

Such traditions as Vodou, Santeria, Obeah, and Candomblé focus on healing and the natural forces of earth and water, fire and air, according to practitioners. They wish to dissociate their beliefs from the media-induced imagery of zombie spells, bloody feathers, and hideous pin-pricked dolls, but animal sacrifice indeed plays a role in their rites. It's a role all too familiar to chickens: The ancient Egyptians sacrificed them to Osiris, the Greeks to Jove, the Romans to Asclepius. Many cultures have perceived in chickens the power of atonement.

Chickens also have come to represent resurrection and power over death. Like their eggs, they are a symbol of Easter. Along with the eggs and sweets in the Easter basket are often cute little peeps— the marshmallow kind, that is. And you can still buy real Easter peeps in a spectrum of garish colors—orange, red, pink, blue, purple, green. You can find them in tubs at many feed stores as the season nears. Only thirteen states and the District of Columbia forbid the sale of dyed chicks.

The chemical is injected into the eggs before they hatch.[11] It's a nontoxic dye that eventually goes away, according to the sellers. The chicks inevitably end up in the eager paws of children dressed in similarly bright finery, who I suspect just love them to death. Though thousands of dyed chicks are sold each year, few of those customers' families have a coop or build one. Perhaps the chicks are lucky that way. Imagine yourself, a purple newcomer, entering the gantlet between the roosts as rows of black eyes glare over sharp beaks. Dead peep walking.

Catering to the Eastertime urge, some farms offer "rent-a-chick" services in which the paying customer takes several home in a brooder to feed and nurture for a few weeks. Pretty good deal—for the farmer, certainly, but also for the families, who get their fondling fix, and for the chicks, who eventually return to a relatively sane life.

The Christian spirit and the Jewish spirit and any spirit of decency should cry out against cruelty, even against lowly forms of life. My tradition teaches that what we do for the least among us, we do for our Lord; if we ignore those who are hungry and hurting and lonely and in need, we are turning our backs on him. "How often I have longed to gather your children together, as a hen gathers her chicks under her wings, but you were not willing," Jesus said in his lament for Jerusalem.[12]

A chicken would no doubt agree that our sins are grievous, though it would prefer not to be our means of atonement. Diverse cultures have deemed the chicken magical, empowered to obviate our transgressions, divine our future, determine truth. So it was with the Sudanese tribesmen and the Roman generals and the Etruscans with their ancient Wheel of Fortune. Even among the more edified among us, traditions and folkways continue, with the chicken as a symbol in a ritual of forgotten roots. So it is with those who dye the Easter peeps for the holiest of Christian holidays. So it is with the Jewish chicken slingers, and those who wish upon a bone.

I can testify that the chicken is a lowly form of life, friends. But it does understand something about the sun. And it is that kinship with the sun—the giver of life that drowns nightly in the sea and rises anew each morn—that has made the chicken an emblem of rebirth and resurrection.

The rooster was the symbol of Mithra, the Egyptian god of the sun and light. And the rooster crows, the Greeks maintained, to announce the arrival of their sun god, Helios. They had figured it all out, so long ago. It was Alectryon's doing. He was a comrade of Mars, the god of war, who had a little thing going with Venus. During one of their trysts, Alectryon stood guard at the chamber door, but he soon fell asleep—it can be boring when you're just listening—and Helios caught the lovers doing the deed. A furious Mars turned Alectryon into a rooster, who has never since forgotten to announce the sun.

I remember lying under a tree at the edge of the woods when I was a lad, reading *The Immense Journey* by the poetic naturalist Loren Eiseley. He recalls playing behind a farmhouse and lifting the cover to a pasture well. Peering down where a shaft of light struck a rusty pipe, he saw something hairy scurry into the dark:

> Something that did not love the sun was down there, something that could walk through total darkness upon slender footholds over evil waters, something that had come down there by preference from above.

On a visit home to my childhood farm when I was perhaps twenty-five, I watched a spider closing in on a trapped fly dancing in a web on the milkhouse windowsill. I had come down there from the house at midnight to see why my father was so late returning from the barn, and I found him, old man, kneeling in prayer on the concrete floor in the only light that one bare, specked bulb could cast against an August night.

His day was nearly done. He had opened the barn door, the cows had gone bawling into the black pasture, and now he finished his final chore. "You pray, too?" he asked, and I knelt with him, embarrassed, because I didn't really believe, then. Life had yet to buffet me as it had him, and I was not frightened of the night. I could only hear the frantic buzz from the window, and I arose, thinking I could wipe away the web.

Light, resurrection, life: Give me a chicken over a spider any day.

"Now the winged herald of light has sung," wrote Ovid, praising the rooster that "wakes wretched men to their work." It's a solar animal, wrote Aldrovandi: "This fact has been daily observed both by children, old men, and, as one is accustomed to say, by bleary-eyed people and barbers, that roosters have a fellow-feeling with the sun."

The rooster drives away the night. "No spirit dare stir abroad," Shakespeare wrote in *Hamlet,* "nor witch hath power to charm, so hallowed and so gracious is the time." The Bard is referring to cock-crow time, when spirits vanish—even the ghost of the King of Denmark:

BERNARDO: It was about to speak, when the cock crew.
HORATIO: And then it started, like a guilty thing
Upon a fearful summons. I have heard
The cock, that is the trumpet to the morn,
Doth with his lofty and shrill-sounding throat
Awake the god of day; and at his warning,
Whether in sea or fire, in earth or air,
The extravagant and erring spirit hies
To his confine . . .

We have bestowed upon the rooster many a noble quality. It is a model of family devotion. Don't kill the rooster, Pythagoras warned, it's a friend to man. Aldrovandi praised the rooster's liberality and kindness: He doesn't keep for himself what he has scratched together, nor should any man. He forages for food, announces his find, and stands guard as the hens have their fill. The rooster keeps one eye on the provisions and makes sure his coopmates have a share; with the other eye he looks heavenward, wary of the devilish hawk. We should be like that, said Aldrovandi, attentive to both human and heavenly affairs.

And, like the rooster, we should mind our business. The ancients associated the rooster with Mercury, the fleet-footed god of trade and profit—the very word *commerce* derives from the god's name, as does *merchandise,* from the Latin *merx.* In the Royal Palace of Amsterdam, Mercury takes his place among the other classical deities, most sculpted by Artus Quellinus in the seventeenth century. Mercury stands chiseled and nearly naked in his winged sandals, proudly clutching his caduceus. At his heel a rooster crows.

Aldrovandi had seen other such depictions; he explained that Mercury kept a watchful rooster "because at cockcrow, merchants rise to carry on their business." And if, in their daily scratchings, these good men of business should strike a fortune, they should trade it all for a barleycorn. That's what the cock wishes he could do in an ancient fable often attributed to Aesop: Upon digging up precious jasper in the manure heap, the cock esteems it of less value than a kernel of grain and resumes sifting through dung. What does it profit a bird to gain the world and lose a meal? The chicken's business model is not a traditional one.

Devoted, yes, and industrious: These things we believe about the chicken. We know that the Little Red Hen, upon finding a grain of wheat as she scratched, nurtured it into a harvest and enjoyed her bread as the lazy Duck, Cat, and Dog starved. Such is our fabled work ethic. We believe that a hen desires to protect and guide her children, as our Savior watches out for us. We believe that the chicken is rise-and-shine punctual and quick to the task. But it's not otherwise particularly swift, in our estimation. In the "Cock and the Jasp" story, for example, the rooster is less than cunning. This is our perception of the chicken as birdbrain, as if it can help it.

The evidence in support of the stereotype, however, is compelling. The chicken lives but a few seasons, "stands looking with stupid eyes at the sun, becomes sick and dies," Sherwood Anderson, author of *Winesburg, Ohio*, wrote in a 1921 essay, "The Egg," in which he tells of life growing up on his parents' chicken farm:

> A few hens and now and then a rooster, intended to serve God's mysterious ends, struggle through to maturity. The hens lay eggs out of which come other chickens and the dreadful cycle is thus made complete. It is all unbelievably complex. Most philosophers must have been raised on chicken farms.
>
> One hopes for so much from a chicken and is so dreadfully disillusioned. Small chickens, just setting out on the journey of life, look so bright and alert and they are in fact so dreadfully stupid.

They are so much like people they mix one up in one's judgments of life. If disease does not kill them they wait until your expectations are thoroughly aroused and then walk under the wheels of a wagon—to go squashed and dead back to their maker.

Generations of children hear how an acorn bonks Chicken Little, sending her flitting off in a tizzy to tell the king that the sky is falling. As she stirs up mass hysteria, she and her entourage meet Foxy-woxy, who tries to lure them into his den for dinner. In a modern retelling, the king's hounds rescue them, but in older versions, in which her name is Chicken-licken, the fox finds her finger-lickin' good. Foxes are like that. I once sat upon the lap of my dear old Uncle Bill, who was an inveterate teller of tales, as he concocted a horror story in which the fox lured Br'er Rabbit's audacious offspring, Bobby Rubbernose, into an Iron Maiden. I still have fox nightmares.

In *English Fairy Tales,* an 1890 collection by folklorist Joseph Jacobs, the high-strung heroine is named Henny Penny, and the fox operates a charnel chamber. It's a tale beloved by many a soul, forever warped. The fox shows Henny and her pals a shortcut to the king, via a narrow and dark hole. Turkey-lurkey is the first to enter:

He hadn't got far when "Hrumph," Foxy-woxy snapped off Turkey-lurkey's head and threw his body over his left shoulder. Then Goosey-poosey went in, and "Hrumph," off went her head and Goosey-poosey was thrown beside Turkey-lurkey. Then Ducky-daddles waddled down, and "Hrumph," snapped Foxy-woxy, and Ducky-daddles' head was off and Ducky-daddles was thrown alongside Turkey-lurkey and Goosey-poosey. Then Cocky-locky strutted down into the cave and he hadn't gone far when "Snap, Hrumph!" went Foxy-woxy and Cocky-locky was thrown alongside of Turkey-lurkey, Goosey-poosey and Ducky-daddles. But Foxy-woxy had made two bites at Cocky-locky, and when the first snap only hurt Cocky-locky, but didn't kill him, he called out to Henny-penny. But she turned tail and ran back home, so she never told the king the sky was a-falling.

Imagine those generations of English schoolchildren sitting on nanny's lap: "Tell us again how that ole fox snapped off those heads, *hrumph,* and piled 'em up high!" Ah yes, my dearies—beware those dark and narrow holes.

There is even a Chicken Little Award for people who whip up a media frenzy. "The good news is . . . the bad news is wrong!" is the motto of the National Anxiety Center (the name alone sends me under the covers), founded in 1990 by conservative journalist Alan Caruba. Somebody tell the king.

And so the chicken bumbles along, managing to survive in our lore and our literature. The lesson is clear: Danger lurks all about. It might be a fox. It might be a spider. But it waits to trap the unwary. Stupidity can be deadly. The animal we have elected to play the role of the dumb cluck and the fluttering twit is the chicken. It is a creature of light, indeed, but we don't consider its bulb to be the brightest.

That the chicken is a peckerhead is indeed a fundamental and ancient assessment; if there is any doubt, a bronze bust in the collection of the Vatican Museums lays it to rest. Inscribed with the Greek words *Soter Kosmou,* "The Savior of the World," it attests to yet another symbolic significance we have assigned to this creature.

Upon the shoulders of a man, the sculptor has placed the head of a rooster, held high and erect. Its prominent beak is a turgid penis, under which testicles descend like wattles. Scholars, secretly smirking, theorize about the early Gnostic influences that could have produced a work such as this, as ancient magical beliefs melded with the new concept of salvation. Gnostics, members of an ethical movement in conflict with early Christianity, professed to having attained profound intellectual depth. Some scholars question the authenticity of the statue, but somebody somewhere made the thing. Whether it was created by Gnostics or a garden-variety numbskull, the question remains: "What were they *thinking?*"[13]

Examples of penile-headed roosters can also be found in Greek relief sculptures. The intent, it seems, was not to defame the rooster but to celebrate his sexual prowess and to vest in him the virility we value so highly. A rooster testicle, wrapped in lambskin, serves as a strong aphrodisiac, Pliny wrote, not explaining how he knew. And if a Grecian lady could be persuaded to dine on such an hors d'oeuvre, she would be more likely to get pregnant—provided, that is, that she ate it immediately after sexual intercourse. Meanwhile, as she basked in her afterglow, if anything remained of it, her husband might have bundled up the rest of the rooster as a present for his other true love: Greek men were known to bestow roosters upon boys to seduce them.[14]

The rooster's sexual reputation runs deep, even to the roots of our language. The word *cock* originated, innocently enough, as an imitation of the rooster's crow, its *cock-a-doodle-do*. The word is similar in other languages: In Sanskrit, it's *kukkuta*. In the Senga dialect of Zambia, it's *kuku*. The old Teutonic word is *kok*. In German, it's *Küken;* in Dutch, *kuiken;* in French, *coq.* Observant beings that we are, we also noticed the rooster's propensities for procreation, and the word *cock* has long been slang for *penis.* In the nineteenth century, more reserved Americans began to call their barnyard buddy the *rooster* (they had noticed that it roosted), and the word has stuck—except in reference to those fine, upstanding cocks bred for fighting, for whom the earthier word still seems fitting.

Phallic wordplay was common in English by the time of Shakespeare, who made gallant use of *cock* in double entendres. The earliest recorded slang use, according to the *Oxford English Dictionary,* was in 1618: "Oh man what art thou? When thy cock is up?" The reference is in *Amends for Ladies* by Nathan Field. (His father was a Puritan preacher who railed against public entertainments, if you'd like to imagine the atmosphere at family gatherings.) The sexual association has not been lost on other cultures: The Balinese word for *cock* means *penis,* as well—and also *hero, warrior, bachelor, dandy,* and *political candidate.*[15]

Because of the rooster's indiscriminate erotic appetite, he also represents impiety itself, Aldrovandi contended. "He leaps upon his mother in copulation . . . and he likewise cruelly treads upon his father." Whether the object of his desire is his mother or daughter or sister, or even ole dad, the rooster doesn't take time to consider. Even though he concedes the rooster is a mother-diddler, Aldrovandi is ready to forgive because of the good family example that the rooster sets. "The so-fervent love of the rooster toward his family also admonishes us to love our wives and to reject all prostitutes, who are nothing more than a pestilence and destruction to husbands."

I cannot say that my own observations around and about the coop bolster this perception of roosters as models of conjugal devotion. I can say I've noticed they do seem to keep close tabs on the ladies, for whatever reason. The rooster awakens to hop down upon his first wife—meaning the first one he sees—and proceeds to make the rounds throughout the day.

Which brings me to the rooster joke I promised earlier, which I shall relate here in the guise of literary enlightenment:

Farmer Jake wants to perk up his hens, so he buys a rooster named Randy to give them some loving attention. "Go to it, boy," he tells Randy, setting him loose in the coop. When the feathers settle, a dozen hens lie dazed and panting. Pleased with his attentive rooster, Farmer Jake is heading up to the farmhouse when he hears a ruckus in the barnyard. He returns to find the ducks looking disheveled—and then he hears the geese honking hysterically down by the pond. Farmer Jake doesn't sleep well that night, worried that his rooster will diddle himself to death. In the morning, it's as he feared: He finds Randy lying still and stiff in the barnyard, claws in the air, eyes rolled back, as a buzzard circles overhead. "Oh my poor rooster, look what you've gone and done; why, why didn't you slow down?" Farmer Jake laments. Randy opens one eye, points the tip of a wing upward, and whispers, "Shhh!"

Courage: a quality of spirit that embodies fearlessness, determination, and ingenuity. The rooster's intrepid side has long earned him man's respect. "His crest stands for the soldier's helmet," Aldrovandi observed. "He wears his spurs as a sword. He testifies the reveille with his crowing," and crows again in his victory. His erect tail, fluttering in the fury of the fight, is his battle standard. "He often dies rather than yield to an adversary."

Plutarch wrote that the rooster represented the conquest itself, "a hieroglyph of victory." Greek soldiers carried roosters into battle and paused to sacrifice them during the heat of a charge.

Even the lion cowered before the rooster, according to Aldrovandi, so fearsome is that visage of hooked beak and wrinkled wattle and beady eye. Everyone says so: "If we believe Pliny, Aelian, Solinus, Lucretius, Proclus and others," he wrote, oddly defensive, "it will be established that any rooster whatever is feared by the lion."

The Greek philosopher Proclus thought the rooster and lion detested each other because they're both "solar." Lucretius believed the rooster sent out seeds that jabbed the lion's eyes. Whatever the reason, Pliny the Elder wrote, just mix some garlic with rooster broth, smear it on your body, and no lion will touch you.

"At least not for twenty minutes, till you're good and marinated," Suzanne offered when I shared this ancient recipe with her.

As an authority on dragons, Aldrovandi knew the rooster's power over the most nefarious of beasts. Even a basilisk—the king of serpents, a cockerel with a snake's tail—will tremble unto death when it hears the rooster's crow, he wrote. He attributed this knowledge to the Roman natural historian Aelian.

If a snake is allowed to brood a cock's egg, according to legend, a basilisk hatches. It lies hissing in its lair—"always infected with a pestilential breath," according to Aldrovandi—and can kill with a look, or the dance of its tongue. In 1474, a rooster was hauled into court in Basel, Switzerland, and convicted of laying an egg, thereby establishing itself as being in league with Satan. The rooster and the egg were burned at the stake.[16]

Aldrovandi himself had heard an account from faraway Zirizaea— a name as fanciful as his tale—that a doddering old rooster had taken to laying and hatching eggs. The alarmed citizens had crushed the eggs with clubs and throttled the rooster, lest the cock's eggs hatch into basilisks.

Not one to be taken in by nonsense, Aldrovandi pointed out that a rooster egg cannot produce a basilisk because, as any fool should know, *a rooster can't lay an egg*. What a rooster may lay, he conceded, was "a rolled-together concretion of the decayed matter within himself." He rolls it into little balls. Aldrovandi did not speculate upon whether such a rooster writes on bathroom walls.

Mostly it's a habit of crotchety old roosters, when the Dog Star is rising, he wrote. And because cocks' eggs aren't really eggs at all, he emphasized, nothing can hatch from them, certainly not a basilisk— ergo, he said, such a ghastly beast must arise from other realms. And, by zounds, it fears the crow of the stout-hearted rooster. The master was resolute in standing up for the truth.

Courageous as he thinks he is, "the rooster is most powerful on his own dung heap," or so says an adage meant as a reproach to those who are big and brave at home but ineffectual and bumbling in the outside world. This is the rooster as blowhard, in the true spirit of Foghorn Leghorn—and I say, I say, there's something kind of *yeesh* about a boy like that. When preparing to fight, he crows loudly as if he has already won. The rooster's reputation as swaggering braggart with little real power is an old one.

Better, though, to be a dunghill dweller than a falcon, wrote Robert Burton, the British scholar who published *The Anatomy of*

Melancholy in 1621. The humble barnyard chicken, he wrote, pecks at offal all its life, yet when it dies it feeds a lord at a fine table. The falcon consorts with lords and perches on his master's fist, "but when he dies is flung to the muck-hill, and there lies." Burton's message: To the humble go the rewards; to the haughty, disgrace.

A courageous man gives not a thought to his own danger, and so, too, does the rooster exemplify this trait—at least the part about lacking a thought. Of their own danger, however, chickens are more than dimly aware. Let a broom come swooping down upon them in the garden, for example, and off they run squawking, being creatures of adequate intelligence. My dear Suzanne will attest to this. This defensive behavior is particularly striking among the hens: They manage to conclude, with what little endowment they have, that it's best to depart; the rooster, by contrast, who thinks like a cock, is more likely to try to show the broom who's who.

It's the hen's doing, then, that the species also has a reputation for cowardice—for being, alas, chicken. Etymologists trace the usage to the fourteenth century. By the time of Shakespeare it seems to have been common vernacular, as in this reference from his 1609 play *Cymbeline*, set at the time of the Roman conquest of Britain:

> *A rout, confusion thick; forthwith they fly*
> *Chickens, the way which they stoop'd eagles; slaves,*
> *The strides they victors made: and now our cowards,*
> *Like fragments in hard voyages, became*
> *The life o' the need. . . .*

"To play chicken," or risk death in a contest of nerve, is newer slang. It dates to the America of 1953, when teenagers revved up their hot rods as their steely willpowers clashed head-on. They were roosters, flapping their wings and charging, on high-test testosterone, as their hens clucked for cover. Any rooster who shows himself unwilling to die has rendered himself a hen.

Craven though chickens may be, there are those among us who fear them. The ailment is called alektorophobia, one of the more pathetic of human afflictions. Such souls rearrange their lives to avoid the prospect of encountering a chicken. Psychologists have been known to treat the condition with boisterous laughter.

As he was attending to a dying child in 1923, William Carlos Williams, a family doctor and poet from Rutherford, New Jersey, looked out the girl's bedroom window, which was streaked with rain, and saw a red wheelbarrow and a couple of white chickens. He turned to write down his not-so-long thoughts, "The Red Wheelbarrow," in which he declared that everything depended upon that tableau.[17]

These things I know: A wheelbarrow is dependable for mucking out a coop. The chickens don't care if it's red unless it hauls feed, in which case chartreuse would do. And if it's really raining, white chickens can turn brown.

It's not that I don't understand the poet's heart. Williams believed that if we are to glimpse the profound, we must look for it amid the simple props of our world. "No ideas but in things," he wrote. Chickens aren't big on ideas. They are the apotheosis of the clueless. They are indeed simple things. The chickens in Williams's poetic still life, however, seem laden with symbolism. They represent our agrarian roots, surviving in a wheelbarrow world. Or perhaps, as some have interpreted the poem, they are socialists amid the capitalists. "A poem should not mean, but be," wrote his colleague Archibald MacLeish, a wise man.

As a physician, Williams may have appreciated the chicken's contribution to our medical wisdom and pharmaceutical cabinet. As a writer and poet, he may have appreciated its role in literature, folklore, and mythology. In more ways than one, the chicken has stood for so much.

Who's to say that the potions and lotions that the ancients concocted from the hen and rooster didn't have a good measure of common sense about them? The chicken was dissected and prescribed for everything from sore throat to psychosis, and chicken cures were commonly recommended up through the nineteenth century. We should respect the medical knowledge of antiquity because primitive insights and folk cures have often proved valuable. Even our modern remedies sometimes rely on chemicals from the rain forest, where cures still wait to be discovered before vanishing forever.

If you should wake up with an inflamed penis (and what man doesn't, now and then), the quick cure is to mix some eggshells with plenty of cumin and rub it in briskly. It has a "remarkable effect," the Greek physician Galen advised. Not only was he official physician to the Roman emperor, he had also been a physician to the gladiators and, as such, learned much about treating trauma and accrued an early mastery of anatomy, if not of pharmacology.

Rooster blood is reputedly the best thing for a brain hemorrhage, when you're having one, said Galen. And if you find yourself vomiting blood through your mouth and nose—your own blood, that is—roast up some eggs and enjoy the cure. Doctors everywhere recommend it, according to a similar remedy reported by Giovanni Battista della Porta, an Italian scientist and naturalist of the Italian Renaissance.

Pliny knew how to cure a headache: Starve a rooster for several days, pluck off all its neck feathers and its comb, and apply them as a poultice to the head. (He doesn't address what to do about the rooster's headache.) If a physician presses the still-throbbing heart of a rooster against a woman's pelvis, he can speed up labor and induce childbirth, Aldrovandi reported in his medical citations.

Chicken dung in water induces vomiting, according to an ancient prescription that Pliny related; no doubt it was commonly accepted as true, and indeed, I accept it even without verification. Dung rubbed into the scalp reverses baldness, he also maintained, which is sure to please the ladies.

Such was the knowledge of medicine at the time, and it made full use of one of the most common of creatures—its flesh and its organs, its feathers and its various fluids. On faith people accepted the wise men's ministrations, and on faith came much of their cure.

The best testament to the long bond, healthy or otherwise, between chicken and human is the sheer volume of words that classical writers devoted to the subject. Pliny and Columella. Aristotle and Varro. These were men who grappled with the weighty issues of the day. Far from dismissing the chicken, they seemed to take it almost absurdly seriously.

Aristotle, for one, wrote extensively on the subject. He made astute observations, including a day-by-day report on what happens inside an egg during incubation, but he also let his imagination soar. A hen, you know, routinely sprinkles herself with water after she lays an egg. Aristotle said so. His student and successor, Theophrastus, dutifully agreed. Pliny, too, professed the truth of the matter, and who, by god, was going to doubt the likes of Aristotle? I humbly raise my hand and offer that I've never seen a hen do such a thing.

Aristotle was full of hooey on this one. But sixteen centuries later, Aldrovandi defended him valiantly on point after point. In a rare instance in which he challenges Aristotle (concerning why chickens have spurs), he does so "with deference toward so great a man." He was likewise apologetic for dissing Hippocrates—"so great a man, whom everyone admires"—by siding with Aristotle's assertion that a chick developed from the egg white, not the yolk. There's a lesson here for historians and researchers.

The chicken has been the subject of the scratchings of writers through history. "Do chickens have hands? It looks to me like a hen wrote this letter," a slave teases his master in *Pseudolus,* by the Roman playwright Plautus. Likewise, Aldrovandi reports, an old Dutch word for bad handwriting is *hennescrapsel,* or chicken scratchings, an expression we use to this day.

A common creature is bound to inspire common sayings. "Don't keep your eggs in one basket," my coworkers advise me daily, as I schlep my morning's haul of eggs into the newsroom. In my fantasies, I turn, grab the offender by the lapel, and shout: "Did you know, did you have *any idea*, that the earliest English usage of that expression, *the very first time* it was recorded, was by Giovanni Torriano in his collection called *Italian Proverbial Phrases*, published in London in 1662, and therefore obviously used in Italy long before that—were you *aware* of this? You are *NOT* the first."

But instead, I pull out a smile. Traditions endure, and I, as a keeper of old ways, must accept these well-worn phrases—or even newer ones like: "So . . . where's the walrus, egg man, *goo goo g'joob*?" And so, here are a few more chicken and egg expressions, in no particular order, along with the date of an early, if not the earliest, reference:

Coming home to roost, Geoffrey Chaucer, "The Parson's Tale" (1380): "And ofte tyme swich cursynge wrongfully retorneth agayn to hym that curseth, as a bryd that retorneth agayn to his owene nest."

Don't count your chickens before they hatch, Thomas Howell, *New Sonnets* (1570): "Counte not thy chickens that unhatched be."

Cock-and-bull story, Robert Burton, *The Anatomy of Melancholy* (1621): "Some men's whole delight is, to take tobacco, and drink all day long in a tavern or alehouse, to discourse, sing, jest, roar, talk of a cock and bull over a pot, &c."

Henpecked, John Crouch, *Mercurius Fumigosus* newsbook (1654): "They henpeck all their men, making them gravel-carriers, insomuch that night and morning they crow over them whilst the poor henpecked wretches lie sprawling in the hole."

Mad as a wet hen, Joseph Doddridge, *The Dialogue of the Backwoodsman and the Dandy* (1823): "A weddin made a great rumpuss in a neighborhood every body that was not ax'd was mad as a wet hen, so that there was often a great deal of fun, and a great deal of mischief at a weddin."

A bad egg, Desiderius Erasmus, *Adagia* (1500): *"Mali corvi malum ovum."*

Nest egg, 1606; originally meant a decoy egg to induce a hen to lay; used since 1700 to mean a primary source of wealth.

Empty nesters, c. 1970; the term was later popularized by the NBC television sitcom *Empty Nest,* which premiered in 1988 and ran seven seasons; the previous year, an episode of *The Golden Girls,* which spun off the series, also was called "Empty Nest."

Egghead, 1907 as bald, 1918 as intellectual; *spring chicken,* 1780 as a small broiler, 1906 as a youthful woman; *to egg a person on,* c. 1200; to *raise your hackles,* 1881; *hen party,* 1887; *go suck eggs,* 1906; *egg on your face,* 1964.

And so many more: *scarce as hens' teeth, dumb cluck, mother hen, flew the coop,* and one of my favorites, *like a chicken on a Junebug.* A few of these could enliven virtually any conversation, whether between lovers or diplomats.

Apples, eggs, and nuts one may eat after sluts. Since 1586, its earliest known utterance (probably in an English pub at some profoundly advanced hour), this charmer has waited to be analyzed for all its nuances. I don't want to sully its beauty by venturing a guess about the meaning, for now. I just want to keep saying it.

And I'll lift a glass to another British profundity, collected by the bibliographer William Carew Hazlitt, from his *English Proverbs and Proverbial Phrases,* published in 1907:

> *He that buys land, buys many stones;*
> *he that buys flesh, buys many bones;*
> *he that buys eggs, buys many shells;*
> *but he that buys good ale, buys nothing else.*

Chicken stories often imparted a moral, à la Aesop. In a tale related in *Ornithology,* two good friends from Bologna sit down to a chicken platter. One of them minces the meat and pours a peppery sauce on it.

"You cut that so well that St. Peter himself couldn't put it back together," his friend says. "St. Peter?" he responds, resuming his slicing. "Listen, man, Christ himself couldn't do it." At that, the rooster springs up from the plate, scattering the pepper over the men and turning them into, oh no, lepers.

The men are condemned to a life of servitude, with all their progeny doomed to leprosy as well. The poor wretches are often heard gibbering about the lesson they learned. Once, the rooster had ratted Peter out, signaling to the world that the disciple had lied about his dear Jesus. But now, by punishing these boys from Bologna for their loose lips, the rooster "testified his approval of Peter reigning in heaven with him whom he denied."

The rooster likewise jumps from the plate in a story from "a certain noble city of Spain," Aldrovandi says. This one, too, typifies the morality tale. The reassembled rooster rights a wrong, though the moral is decidedly less certain:

A handsome young man is traveling with his parents to the shrine of Compostella to see the body of St. James. They stop at an inn, where the innkeeper's daughter (an early version of the farmer's daughter) spies the hunk. He excites her fantasies, and, as sometimes happens with young women who believe they are in love, she displays for him her wares and offers them to him.

He puts his hand on her bare shoulder and bows his head, then quickly looks to the ceiling: "I dwell on higher things," he explains. He points out that his loyalty lies with mom and dad and almighty God and their holy pilgrimage. "I do not wish to surrender myself to illicit lust," he says.

Standing there feeling exposed and awkward, she decides this guy's got to go. She hides a silver plate in his knapsack, then kicks up a fuss after the young man and his parents leave. The guards fetch

him back, and he's convicted of theft. The punishment: He's cruci-
fied on a two-pronged fork.

His grieving parents, who never really liked the girl anyway,
return to the shrine and tell St. James all about her treachery, then
begin plodding home. As they approach the crucifixion hill, they see
their son there—and he's alive, and he's happy, and he's presumably
down off the two-pronged fork.

They tell the tale of their adventure to one and all, but the mayor
back in town doesn't believe them. "Sure, sure, he's alive all right, as
alive as . . ." He points to the platter that a servant is carrying to the
table. ". . . as that roast rooster!" They hear a lusty crow, and the
rooster jumps from the plate, sporting a full coat of new feathers.
The mayor is impressed, calls for the innkeeper's daughter, and
straightaway issues her a fine.

Chaucer's comedic morality poem "The Nun's Priest's Tale" in-
troduces us to the barnyard hero Chauntecleer. Written in the fourteenth century, it falls within the tradition of beast fable—a long line
of storytelling from Aesop to Uncle Remus to Looney Tunes. The
Chauntecleer account is a highlight of *The Canterbury Tales,* considered one of the greatest works of verse in English (iffe you coude
colle it thate).

I declare this the pinnacle of the chicken's literary heights:

A poor widow and her two daughters live a bleak life. Down in
the barnyard, though, the chivalrous rooster Chauntecleer and his
seven sister chickens make merry. It's seven brides for the brother,
and among them is fair Pertelote, the number-one wife, the only hen
who truly has his heart.

One night Chauntecleer dreams a fox is after him, and he awakens
his lady love, who berates him and tells him it's just a dream. He
protests that prophets often dream their own deaths, but she'll hear
none of it. Must have been something he ate, she says. He belittles her,
and they debate the matter vigorously, citing scholarly authorities.

Chauntecleer prevails, and, his ego pumped and libido aroused, he hops down from his safe roost, treads his damsel twenty times, and basks in the sunshine of a new day.

One would think he'd lie low under such circumstances, but his descent into danger might not have been his decision alone—perhaps his prophetic leap was God's doing, or maybe it was the hen's fault for trying to encourage him. Chauntecleer "tok his conseil of his wyf, with sorwe," and, as we have known since Eden, "wommenes conseils brought us first to wo / And made Adam fro Paradys to go."

Enter the fox, who has been lurking in the cabbage patch. He prevails upon his prey to perform his best crow, and the charmed Chauntecleer stretches his neck long and high, closes his eyes, and begins to sing. The fox snatches him and runs, chased by the poor widow and all the denizens of the barnyard.

Dangling from the fox's jaws, Chauntecleer humbly suggests that the fox boast to his pursuers that they'll never catch him. The haughty fox actually thinks that's a good idea, and as he opens his yap, Chauntecleer breaks free and flies into a treetop. The fox tries in vain to lure him down. He apologizes for scaring him and tells him he meant no harm—just come out of the tree, he says, and he'll explain.

And there you have it. Talking animals, dumb and vain—our literature at its best.

As the narrator spins his story, he draws parallels to ancient accounts of chicanery and chivalry. He has seen, through experience, that people speak volumes without thinking things through or finding a practical application (scholars and academes being high on that list). And keeping your mouth shut and eyes open is one moral of this complex piece—among several, depending on whether you take the perspective of a pilgrim, rooster, hen, or fox.

Chaucer uses the simplest form of storytelling to examine the nature of guile and gullibility, of bragging and blame. He parodies the literary traditions of romance, with a henhouse version of knights and courtly love; and of debate, with elaborate chicken perspectives on the significance of dreams and free will and original sin. Above all, he advises, avoid reckless decisions—put not your "truste on flaterye."

"Mordre woll out," the rooster tells his dulcinea as they analyze their dreams. Those who snatch up a chicken to gobble on the go will get their comeuppance. Far more than just a quick meal, Chaucer's rooster, and chickens everywhere, have plenty to tell us about our world and ourselves.

Crossing the Road

Eight thousand years ago, the chicken primeval foraged in Southeast Asia and India. As the Red Jungle Fowl pecked through the underbrush, our forefathers watched this quarrelsome creature. They soon set a snare—not because it looked tasty, but because it seemed nasty. *Homo sapiens* and *Gallus gallus* were kindred spirits, and we captured it and took it home to play.

It wasn't a poached egg, or a roast leg, that first buoyed our enthusiasm for our new companion. Cockfighting came first, archaeologists have concluded. We convinced ourselves that the rooster's peevishness was, in fact, courage. By letting it prove its mettle, we proved something about ourselves. We were no flighty hens.

Early on, however, we did discover that the chicken and its eggs were delicious, too. In the forests, the jungle fowl lay only an occasional egg, no more than needed to produce a fertilized clutch for hatching. Among most birds, egg laying is a seasonal thing, a spring fling. But hens that are robbed daily of the fruit of their labor tend to work overtime to make up for the loss—such is the importance that species place on reproduction.

Biologists have theorized that the hen's egg habit developed in concert with our own love of eggs and our penchant for cockfighting. We bred both the rooster and the hen for performance—he in the ring, she in the nest box. We identified the very best layers, made sure they canoodled with the finest of roosters, and allowed only those hens to keep and hatch eggs. All the lesser eggs and listless chickens we ate. Different breeds, different focus: The gaming sorts never became good layers; the laying sorts have a gentler bent.

Whether its specialty is eggs, meat, or fighting, the modern chicken can trace its bloodline to the Red Jungle Fowl. The early breeds on the Indian subcontinent developed from it, such as the Malay and the fighting Aseel, broad-chested and muscular, the pride of kings and noblemen. These ancient breeds spread from the ancestral homelands over the trade routes and via military conquest, throughout the Far East. Archaeologists have discovered evidence of chickens as early as 6,000 B.C. in China, where no native breeds existed—suggesting that they were domesticated elsewhere even earlier. They spread eastward to the Pacific Islands and west to the Mediterranean lands, then north to Europe and Scandinavia and south to Egypt and Africa.[18]

Cockfighters exported their avocation around the world, and many cultures embraced it, except for those that came to regard the chicken as sacred. In ancient Greece, young Olympians escorted their charges onward to glory, and for centuries thereafter cockfighting continued to flourish as a respectable sport. In England, the church frowned upon cockfights, but Henry VIII encouraged them nonetheless. The king, who had a few other issues with the church, built an elaborate indoor pit and made the sport a popular pastime. In France and Belgium, too, it took root. Cockfighting was a passion among many of the crowned heads, including the kings of Sweden and Denmark.

In the United States, cockfighting was entrenched in colonial culture, and though it had enthusiasts among the founding fathers, including George Washington and Benjamin Franklin, it became largely a pastime of the poor—as opposed to its status in England, where men of wealth and title dominated the sport. It flourished in the slave and Irish immigrant cultures, and later in the Southwest, where the hardscrabble locals of Spanish descent tended not to worry about the welfare of a chicken.

In much of the world, cockfighting still thrives—openly in many cultures, and surreptitiously just about everywhere else. It's popular in the Red Jungle Fowl's homelands of Southeast Asia, and in India, where chickens rank somewhat lower than cows in the Hindu hierarchy. (The Hindus developed the "naked heel" standard; the spurs were given no razor assists, allowing the cocks to endure for hours, with quick moves and maneuvers.) Spain doesn't flinch at cockfighting, nor does most of Latin America.

Increasingly, however, the sport has become regarded as barbaric, or the gambling as immoral. The British showed that they were among the first to develop qualms when they discouraged the "battle royal," in which several roosters were set loose in the pit at the same time and allowed to stab and hack until only one remained standing. Once a common amusement, the battle royal was disappearing by the late 1700s as British sensibilities came to regard it as somehow uncivil.[19]

In 1835, cockfighting was formally banned in much of the British Isles, though the Scots held out for another sixty years. Today, cockfighting is verboten in numerous nations. Others permit it with restrictions: France allows it only in limited regions where it has long been a tradition.

A century after the British banned it, cockfighting still flourished in the United States. When the bans did begin early in the 1900s, they came only in states where cockfighting wasn't popular anyway, and as the momentum built, some states outlawed the fights but not the birds or their accoutrements. Laws progressively became stricter through the century, culminating in the federal Animal Fighting Prohibition Enforcement Act of 2007, which made it a felony to transport gamebirds or cockfighting implements across state and federal boundaries.

The last holdouts steadily fell in the new millennium. In Oklahoma, the ban came in 2002; in New Mexico, in 2007. The last state to officially give up on cockfighting was Louisiana, where the legislature voted to ban it as of August 2008. Louisiana political leaders had been speaking out against cockfighting, fearing it tarnished the image of a state needing federal aid for Hurricane Katrina victims. Today in the United States, cockfighting is legal only in the territories of Puerto Rico, the Virgin Islands, and Guam.

In most states, even watching a cockfight is illegal, but enthusiasts still connect through networks and magazines. Cockfighting is the oldest spectator sport, its fans say, and it seems no law can stamp it out. Fighting is what roosters do, according to their handlers; it's their nature, and they are letting the birds be true to their bloodlines.

To help their birds be truer, cockfighters through the ages have attached weaponry to the roosters' natural spurs—either razor-sharp blades or curved spikes, depending on tradition. The handlers introduce two roosters in the pit, help them get to know each other with a few jabbing thrusts, and the excitement begins.

The fans cheer and slosh their brews as the cocks go at it, hackles raised, each truly believing that the real enemy is this other bird. (A Roman gladiator, as he dispatched the immediate threat, at least understood that the pageantry itself was contemptible.) The fight ends when one of the birds is sliced to death or skewered or finally cowers, which can take minutes or hours. Wagers are settled, feathers are swept, and the next fight begins as the defeated warriors pile up in the trash, just as nature intended.

Cockfighters are fond of citing Abraham Lincoln's take on the matter: "As long as the Almighty permitted intelligent men, created in his image and likeness, to fight in public and kill each other while the world looks on approvingly, it's not for me to deprive the chickens of the same privilege." They claim the young Lincoln earned his

"Honest Abe" reputation because he was a fair referee at cockfights: He liked to watch those roosters wrassle.

The quote is included, for example, in the winning defense arguments from a 1963 legal case in Oklahoma, *Lock v. Falkenstine*. A cockfighter had been hauled into court, accused of violating a statute targeting anyone who "instigates or encourages any animal to attack, bite, wound or worry another." The chicken isn't an animal, the court decided. Among his reasons for dumping the statute, the judge cited the biblical book of Genesis, which distinguishes between "every beast of the field and every fowl of the air." Besides, if taken literally, he said, the statute made it illegal for a boy to send his beagle after a rabbit, which would likely worry it.[20]

It was Aldrovandi's contention that cockfighting was a solemn rite by which humans had observed, since antiquity, how a real man should behave. Their love of battle is why roosters have those fighting spurs, he said, daring to contradict Aristotle, who claimed they only have spurs because they're too heavy to fly away quickly and need something to protect themselves. Some roosters, indeed, were created to fight, Pliny maintained.

"They prepare a kingdom for themselves by means of war," the Florentine poet Poliziano wrote in *Rusticus*, a 1483 celebration of the country life. "They burn in spirit." The victor crows to an adoring flock as he stamps upon the vanquished, who struggles pathetically trying to find cover—but the loser has lost his will, Aelian wrote. "His spirit is broken."

As the chicken went off to see exotic lands, we soon learned these birds were good for a lot more than cockfighting—they were, in fact, *good*. Roasted or fried, chicken pleased our palates. Poached or scrambled, eggs made our day. We didn't need to know where the chicken came from.

And for thousands of years, we didn't. When Captain Cook

arrived in Tahiti, he found chickens strutting among the greeting party. They had been on the island since time began, the Polynesians told him, but to the explorers these birds looked very much like the old Asian breeds.[21]

It was Charles Darwin, the father of evolutionary theory, who in 1887 identified the Red Jungle Fowl as the ancestor of today's barnyard chicken. Later researchers confirmed his conclusion,[22] though some have argued in favor of multiple origins from three other jungle fowl—the Grey, the Ceylon, and the Java, all from Southeast Asia and the Indian subcontinent.

By about 3,000 B.C. the Egyptians were managing large flocks. They had built incubators of clay bricks that could brood up to ten thousand chicks, according to Greek accounts. Fires burning within these huge brooders, carefully tended and regulated, kept the temperature precisely right for incubation.

The Egyptians produced great quantities of eggs "in an astonishing way," Aldrovandi related: They hatched within a few days. The best Italian incubators hadn't managed to handle more than a thousand eggs at once, and I can say with confidence that they took twenty-one days to hatch.

Mass production no doubt proved valuable for the Egyptians responsible for feeding the slaves who were building the pyramids. The economy depended on a reliable source of food, and a shadow market thrived as well to serve the needs of those who raised, collected, distributed, and prepared the poultry and eggs. The Egyptians' scale of production was not matched until the twentieth century.[23]

The early Greeks bred chickens at first mainly for cockfighting and medicinal uses, but later they focused on the production of eggs and meat. Meanwhile, the chicken's foreign travels would spread wider after the Persians invaded its Indian homelands in 520 B.C. and, two centuries later, Alexander the Great's armies defeated the Persians and conquered most of the world known to the Greeks.

Pythagoras was one such Greek with a thing for chickens. He was the mathematician and philosopher who, while playing with triangles, figured out that $a^2 + b^2 = c^2$, taking eternal credit for discovering a fundamental principle that the Babylonians had understood a millennium earlier and that allowed us to do such tricks as measure the size of the earth and the distance to the moon.

But he did love roosters, particularly white ones, according to an account by Aldrovandi, and denounced those who ate them "because they wake us from sleep, search around for scorpions, and by their fighting engender in us both zeal and a certain emulation of bravery." If Pythagoras saw a white rooster, he would sometimes greet the bird as if he were a blood brother and beckon him to come near.

What he would do then we may never quite know. Some maintained that Pythagoras, despite his peaceable expostulations, would sometimes pounce upon the rooster and eat him, or sacrifice him to Jove. And which account is correct? This mattered to Aldrovandi, the old soul, and he pondered the contradiction. Maybe, he conjectured, the Greeks misunderstood their brother: When he spoke of the chicken's nourishing qualities, he meant for the spirit, not the body. Aldrovandi seemed inclined to think the best of anyone who kept a chicken near.

While the Greeks concerned themselves with such matters, their civilization began to give way to the Romans, who eventually prevailed, picking up the chicken habit in the process. Being Romans, they trained cocks to fight like gladiators, conducting the matches with ceremony and solemnity. And they began to accord the chicken great respect, treating it as a sacred bird with a spirit worthy of philosophical discussion, a prescience worthy of military consultation, and a taste worthy of spices and sauce.

All those roads that led to Rome also led out of it: The empire advanced the spread of chickendom as it pushed into new territories—though often the chicken had gotten there first, by other means, as in Britain. Chickens find a way. The vintage breeds pecked and fought their way across Europe and Asia and were a barnyard staple throughout the Old World by the time the early explorers crossed the Atlantic. The conquistadores sought glory and fortune, the Seven Cities of Cibola, in a lush new world gleaming with gold.

And there they found chickens.

Certainly the explorers brought their own chickens, a galley staple, with them aboard their ships, and these breeds later proliferated in the Americas, but something chickenlike had already staked a claim.

Within thirty years of Columbus's first voyage, the Portuguese explorer Ferdinand Magellan, in his trip around the world via the tip of South America, reported stocking his ships with fowl provided by a tribe living in what is now Paraguay. A few years later, in 1526, Sebastian Cabot, an Italian who was exploring for Spain in what is now Argentina, Chile, and Paraguay, reported poultry that laid blue eggs.[24]

The bird that Magellan described resembles the Araucana, which survives to this day in show clubs around the world. Common features are feather tufts around the ears and the lack of a rump. The breed takes its name from a tribe in the Andes that the Spaniards called the Araucanos. These are the proud Mapuche people (the Spanish term is now considered derogatory), who had resisted Incan subjugation and remained unconquered by the Spanish for three hundred years.

Their chickens joined in the resistance: The bloodline remained pure in the unconquered pockets of the high plains even as the Spanish chickens relentlessly advanced. Today, in outdoor markets near Temuco, Chile, farmers peddle eggs of many colors, the most remarkable of which is blue. This is the classic Araucana egg, for which Temuco is renowned.[25]

What was this creature—so familiar yet so unlike the breeds the Europeans knew—doing so far across the sea? The early explorers, encountering all manner of strange flora and fauna, may not have wondered much, but the question remained: Did this New World chicken arise spontaneously in America, from a genetic pool separate from the ancient breeding grounds of Southeast Asia?

It was long debated whether any chickens at all existed in the Americas before the Spanish introduced them from the same old Asian lines that had consorted with Cleopatra and sailed with Alexander. Some biologists reasoned that these American chickens were indeed from those lines, but had arrived far earlier than the Spanish, possibly by way of early Chinese or Polynesian expeditions that brought them eastward across the Pacific rather than westward over the Atlantic.

So what's with the blue eggs? None of the Asian chickens do the blue. One theory is that the indigenous people, interested like manly men everywhere in producing fighting cocks, crossed a nasty native pheasant with their domestic hens. These hybrid hens laid blue eggs just as the pheasants did, and though most, of course, were infertile, a few did hatch—and a new breed was born.[26]

In a 2006 genetic study of forty-two Araucanas and other native breeds, researchers found DNA sequences for some that could be traced to East Asia and others to West Asia. The western sequences could have come from Spanish introduction in the Americas; however, the presence of the eastern sequences suggested that those lines might have been introduced before Columbus.[27]

To know for sure whether the chicken or Columbus came first, the authors of the study said, archaeologists would have to dig up some ancient Chilean chicken bones and let them tell their DNA tales. It sounds rather like the divining of the entrails.

The next year, such bones showed up—they were excavated on Chile's Arauco Peninsula, the homeland of the Araucana. Through DNA analysis of the bones and the carbon dating of pottery found with them, the researchers learned that the chicken lived between 1304 and 1424, or about a century before Europeans showed up in the New World. What's more, the bones were genetically similar to chicken bones that had been excavated at prehistoric sites in Tonga and American Samoa. The conclusion: Polynesians had reached the Americas by canoe, well before Columbus and the Spaniards, and brought a few of their island chickens with them.[28]

Chickens do get around. The Isle of Mull, off Scotland's west coast, is a bonny retreat of wild beaches and braes, of sea caves and forest waterfalls, where chickens are known to wear earmuffs and lay blue eggs. The Sea Chickens of Mull came long ago, some Scots say, by way of traders from Chile whose ships had foundered in a storm off the Hebrides.[29]

Let the DNA trail wander where it will, but I would like to believe this story is true even though it's far from verified. I imagine Latino chickens splashing ashore in a brave new world of tartans and haggis. Their ancestors were Asian chickens that crossed the Pacific long before the *Santa Maria* sailed, and fooled with pheasants till their eggs turned blue.

Chickens have had their moments in the sun and darkness, their glory and ignominy, for millennia, but for the most part they were taken for granted until the Victorians took notice of them in the 1800s. The chicken, or at least the idealized version of it, fit well into this world, in which the male was the ruler, defender, and provider, and his female gave him a large family to which she devoted herself. Coop life reflected the family. Victorian ladies, observing the hen, understood what she endured from the rooster so that she might have her brood, and it wasn't so bad, really.

These were good days for chickens, at least from outward appearances. It was an age of fine feathers and fashion and the promise of technology. The eighteenth-century agriculturalist Robert Bakewell had revolutionized the breeding of cattle, turning the scrawny into the brawny, and it was high time to do the same for chickens. Gentleman breeders gave Darwin a helping hand, crafting wondrous new varieties. Chickens became the realm of fanciers, not mere farmers.

Opium addiction had a lot to do with the new craze. For generations, the British had smuggled the stuff from India into China and found that, remarkably, demand grew. Opium became a trade substitute for silver: The British satisfied their craving for the wonders of the Orient by capitalizing on the cravings of an addled population.

The Chinese government tried to stop the smuggling. Two waves of hostilities broke out in what became known as the Opium Wars. The first (1839–1842) was between China and Britain; in the second (1856–1860), the French joined the British in the fight. The Chinese succumbed each time and agreed to concessions, and the resulting treaties greatly widened trade with the West.

Aboard the ships arriving from the East were curious new breeds of chickens, including some with a few feathers on their legs. The Cochin, a big bird and gentle, a generous giver of eggs, was particularly popular and caught the imagination of poultry breeders, who called it (as well as the other Chinese breeds) the Shanghai. They began to build a better chicken, crossing breeds in search of the best traits. The fluffy Cochin soon sported fully feathered leggings.

These Asian imports—the Cochins and Brahmas, the Sumatras and Malays—became the breeder's palette. A major poultry exhibition at the London Zoo in 1845, the first of its kind, saw an explosion of interest in show birds. Among the fanciers was Queen Victoria, who built a poultry hall at Windsor. Countesses and courtiers and subjects followed her lead, of course, as did the Americans: At the first major poultry show in the States—in 1849 at the Boston Public Gardens—about 10,000 visitors came to see 219 exhibitors.

Breeds flowed into major ports from the corners of the world: the Hamburgs from Holland, the Faverolles from France, the peculiar Polish varieties. No longer did chickens migrate willy-nilly around the globe; now, they arrived by special order to be kept in fancy coops by virtue of their brilliant or unusual plumage.

An 1890 article in the journal *The Century,* "Chickens for Use and Beauty" by H. S. Babcock, reported the trend in words as florid as the birds. Barnyard mongrels, he wrote, had "given place to well-defined breeds, carefully differentiated into varieties, with colors as rich in hue and regularly disposed as if laid on by the hand of an artist, working not in lifeless clay and dead pigments, but in inanimate objects and living colors."[30]

In *The History of the Hen Fever: A Humorous Record*, written in 1855, George P. Burnham described what he called the "epidemic" that had gripped Victorian society for a decade:

> Never did any mania exceed in ridiculousness or ludicrousness, or in the number of its victims surpass this inexplicable humbug, the "hen fever." Kings and queens and nobility, senators and governors, mayors and councilmen, ministers, doctors and lawyers, merchants and tradesmen, the aristocrat and the humble, farmers and mechanics, gentlemen and commoners, old men and young men, women and children, rich and poor, white, black and gray—everybody was more or less seriously affected by this curious epidemic. The press of the country, far and near, was alive with accounts of "extraordinary pullets," "enormous eggs" (laid on the tables of the editors), "astounding prices" obtained for individual specimens of rare poultry; and all sorts of people, of every trade and profession and calling in life, were on the qui vive, and joined in the hue-and-cry, regarding the suddenly and newly ascertained fact that hens laid eggs—sometimes; or, that somebody's crower was heavier, larger, or higher on the legs (and consequently higher in value), than somebody else's crower.[31]

As the fever began to break late in the nineteenth century, another was taking its place: Many people began to think they could strike it rich in chicken farming. The march of progress had not left the chicken behind. Technology was raising the prospect that farmers could squeeze a profit out of the bird, rather than just the paltry few eggs or pocket change it supplied for the family.

Our farm forebears proudly made their own way. Through the seasons, they grew and raised much of what they consumed. They foraged all the day, and rested well come roosting time.

Chickens, like many people, still lived on farms. And they had many urban cousins. Townsfolk kept them in backyards, and they were common in cities—a 1906 census found one chicken for every two people.[32]

Families kept chickens for their eggs, mostly, and enjoyed their flesh as a bonus. Poultry had yet to take its place at the dinner table, except on special Sundays. Regular folks could scarce afford to buy it in markets, where it could cost more than steak or lobster. It was a fledgling poultry industry, by today's measure.[33]

In the Roaring Twenties, before America tasted privation, the grand old Republicans lifted a three-hundred-year-old line from the French king Henry IV—*une poule dans son pot!*—and called for "a chicken in every pot" in their quest to put a Hoover in the White House. Today we'd usher away to the cuckoo's nest any candidate who pledged us our fill of chicken. But in 1928, it was a dream—as was "a car in every backyard." Right next to the coop.

Serving the family had long been the chicken's role. In 1852, Caleb N. Bement advised homesteaders in his *American Poulterer's Companion* that they needed to keep only a few chickens, enough to pick up waste and "what might escape the pigs." Having relegated them to scavenger, he pointed out that "much of the refuse of the kitchen can again appear on the table in a new and better form."

But whatever the form, breakfast or dinner, chickens were a fixture of our homes. Chickens roved barnyards, and women and children tended them. Such work was not considered manly.

Those farm women, looking for a little pin money, helped to change the world of the chicken forever—and the chicken, likewise, changed women. It taught them they could survive on their own.

In her book *Mama Learned Us to Work,* Lu Ann Jones tells of the relentless toil of the American farm woman in the South, who worked the fields from dawn until she made dinner, then returned to her labors till sunset. When she needed supplies, she asked her man to pick them up at the general store—which was a masculine world of commerce and conversation where women felt awkward.

But they had an alternative: the "rolling store." Peddlers drove wagons, and later trucks, loaded with foodstuffs, merchandise, and medicinals, even perfumes, into the remotest regions. Farm women felt far more comfortable dealing with them—particularly since they gladly swapped goods for farm produce. The peddlers found that most of their customers were women, who bartered and sold milk and butter, berries they'd picked—and, primarily, chickens and eggs.

Since women tended to the coop, chickens became a form of currency, with change paid in cool cash. The peddler's wagon became a market where women could, in effect, sell the proceeds of their own labor. They found the money freed them from their husbands' control; they could obtain things for their children that their men would not provide, such as school tuition. Often, women earned enough to keep their families afloat.

Family dynamics changed now that women were learning to manage their own money. They gained a sense of their own abilities and power, and government programs and social workers helped to bring the wider world to the back roads. In Jones's book, a public health nurse tells of one woman's discovery of the condom through a program touting birth control. When the free distribution ended, the woman told her husband she'd just have to sell a hen to keep them in Trojan money.

During the Depression, women built increasingly bigger flocks, and bigger incomes, while men still eschewed the work as beneath them. A decade later, that was changing. Soldiers returning from World War II, impressed by tales of profits to be made, increasingly tried their hand at poultry farming.[34]

All along, the experts had been trumpeting the rise of technology.

"More than ninety-eight percent of the poultry and eggs of the country are produced on the general farm," Milo M. Hastings wrote in *The Dollar Hen,* a 1911 primer that warned professional poultrymen, the source of the other 2 percent, to heed the new ways.

"A farmer can disregard all knowledge and all progress and still keep chickens," Hastings wrote, "but the man who has no other means of a livelihood must produce chicken products efficiently, or fail altogether."

It was a growing sentiment. Efficiency. Knowledge. Progress.

Inventors had rediscovered the incubator and produced models heated by gas that could hatch, praise be, nearly a dozen eggs at a time—soon to get better. Then, at about the turn of the century, commercial hatcheries began to open as they realized that a baby chick needed no food or water for two days after hatching and therefore could be shipped by rail for hundreds of miles. Nature makes the hatchling that way, so it can survive while its mother stays on the nest finishing work on its brothers and sisters. The hatcheries provided the farmer with cheap peeps, saving him, and the hen, a lot of time and trouble.

The hen was on the same path she had taken in ancient Egypt and China: With the development of the incubator, she no longer had to waste time on motherhood and could pursue other interests, such as getting fat and laying ever more eggs. To allow a hen to romp with a rooster, lay a clutch of eggs, worry over them, and raise her brood could squander two or three months of her productive time.

Farmers began to focus on breeds such as the Leghorn that laid plenty of eggs but seemed indifferent as mothers. Many hens "go broody," hunkering down and refusing to leave the nest, trying to hatch eggs that aren't there because they are taken away each day. Not so the Leghorn. Its big white eggs were another reason it became a popular production chicken. An ancient Mediterranean breed, the Leghorn had been valued by the Romans for its ability to foretell their future. I wonder what wonders it saw for itself: a favored position in a promised land?

Along came a handy innovation called the trapnest. It gave the hen a one-way entrance into her nesting box through a hinged door that fell closed behind her so that she couldn't leave until the farmer freed her. Using the trapnest, the breeder could identify his best performers more easily, and he let only those birds reproduce. He bred the broodiness away. Good-bye, mother hen.[35]

During the Depression, the egg industry began to see the light: Research had shown that production was directly related to cycles of daytime and darkness. Light stimulates hormones that make the ovaries work overtime. The concept had long been recognized but never, it seems, taken seriously. In 1600, Aldrovandi pointed out in his *Ornithology* that lantern light confounded hens into laying when they otherwise would not. This technique seemed to work particularly well when a little salt was rubbed under their tail feathers.

In the dawning technological age, the light manipulation disturbed some farmers on moral grounds—isn't rising with the rooster what farmers do?—but one must compete, one must eat, and the county agents kept harping about the better ways.

Since 1922, it had been possible to administer the daylight in a dose: Scientists learned to synthesize Vitamin D, the "sunshine vitamin" that prevents rickets. During the 1930s, researchers developed antibiotics, the magic bullets that would save countless human lives. Antibiotics would also allow poultry to be kept in cramped quarters without succumbing to a host of diseases.

Equipped with such technological advances, poultrymen began to move the chicken inside, under banks of bulbs. To keep egg production even through every season, the standard became twelve hours a day of controlled lighting, and farmers gradually kept the bulbs on even longer. The artificial light took away the hen's slow season, rendering her manic.[36]

And so the chicken fancier's aesthetic interest gave way to the farmer's business interest. Pamphleteers promised prosperity. Poultry journals proliferated, brimming with advice on how to get started, the modern way. With the rapid industrialization at the dawn of the twentieth century, chickens turned from a hobby into a commodity, and it seemed everyone wanted a piece of the action.

Sherwood Anderson knew those times. Here's another glimpse of the American short story writer's childhood in Bidwell, Ohio, where his parents, like so many other starstruck souls, made a foray into chicken farming:

They rented ten acres of poor stony land on Griggs's Road, eight miles from Bidwell, and launched into chicken raising. I grew into boyhood on the place and got my first impressions of life there. From the beginning they were impressions of disaster and if, in my turn, I am a gloomy man inclined to see the darker side of life, I attribute it to the fact that what should have been for me the happy joyous days of childhood were spent on a chicken farm. In later life I have seen how a literature has been built up on the subject of fortunes to be made out of the raising of chickens. It is intended to be read by the gods who have just eaten of the tree of the knowledge of good and evil. It is a hopeful literature and declares that much may be done by simple ambitious people who own a few hens. Do not be led astray by it. It was not written for you. Go hunt for gold on the frozen hills of Alaska, put your faith in the honesty of a politician, believe if you will that the world is daily growing better and that good will triumph over evil, but do not read and believe the literature that is written concerning the hen. It was not written for you.

So much else was happening. Cold storage made it possible for the producer to save eggs for months and put them on the market when the prices rose, allowing a steady income year round. Specialists called "sexers" learned to peer closely at a peep after it hatched and tell, right away, whether it was a boy or girl—not an easy trick. The egg farmer no longer wasted time raising roosters;

the hatchery dispatched those before they could touch a speck of grain.

Despite such advances, the vast majority of inexperienced home-steaders who tried out chicken farming failed, losing everything, while the poultry industry flourished. Small operators couldn't keep up with the demands and expenses of technology. It was the dawn of an age of mass production and the economy of scale.

The old heirloom breeds survived only in memory and in the coops of fanciers, whose numbers were dwindling. People began to think of chickens not as Wyandottes and Orpingtons but as dark meat and white—and then as legs and thighs and breasts, and, still later, as patties and nuggets.[37]

Laboratories promised to be the making of the poultry industry, creating ever more prolific layers, fast-fattening broilers, and fabulous new feeds. And get this: If you took away that feed—just for a week or two—you could force the hen into molt, thereafter improving her production dramatically. The learned ones also concocted chemicals and compounds that could bulk up a chicken like an athlete on steroids.

In 1925, before the new age, a peep didn't mature into a 2.5-pound broiler for sixteen weeks. It needed nearly twelve pounds of feed. In 1950, it needed only about nine pounds of feed, on which it grew a bit bigger, averaging 3 pounds. And market time came six weeks sooner.

Since the 1950s, large corporations have taken over the industry. They strive to be "vertically integrated," meaning they keep their fingers in the business top to bottom: how chickens and eggs are produced, processed, packaged, marketed, sold.[38]

And their chicken delivers. By 2006, the typical broiler was getting to market in seven weeks or sooner. It was 5.5 pounds, well over twice the size of a '25 model, yet the producer could get this fatso to market on a pound less feed than it took in the Roaring Twenties.[39]

Chicken is cheap today. Most anyone can afford it. The 9 pounds of chicken we each ate in 1928 became nearly 60 pounds in 2008, much of it pop-in-your-mouth convenience food—nuggets and tenders and strips galore. We're chowing down twice as much chicken as we did even in 1980.[40]

We've come so far. Today's techie is smarter than the Hooterville homeboy of old. We've rallied our brainpower to produce prodigiously for a hungry world. Had we not subdued nature, had we not tamed the night, had we not taught the hen to disregard her rooster's crow, chicken farming would have remained the realm of rubes. Had we not trusted Big Chicken, the roosters and hens would never have advanced beyond the barnyard, and steak might be our meal of choice. Or lobster.

The chicken had entertained such high hopes in those heady days of hen fever, when we finally took notice of this remarkable bird that long ago gave up flight for a life of serving us. We finally valued it, admired it—and the chicken even found itself consorting with the queen. Rubbing our hands, we sized it up and considered the possibilities. We beckoned it to come inside, to stay.

And then it was over. The history of the chicken, as we knew it, ended there.

Homegrown

Many people still imagine their breakfasts and barbecues come from a barnyard like ours at Lilyfield. They picture a regal rooster husbanding his industrious hens as they forage in bliss. Such is the scene sketched on many an egg carton. I've yet to see one portraying tiers of cages and boasting "Factory Farm Fresh!" or "Battery Cage Best!"

It takes an industrial chicken to stand up to modern appetites. Poultry is a commodity, supplied to meet our demand. Those cartons and packages in the supermarket come from production systems geared for mass consumption, peep to plate in as little as six weeks.

Consumers created Big Chicken. Striving to prosper, as do we all, the industry cultivated and marketed its products. Not only has poultry become the centerpiece of family meals, surpassing beef in 1990,[41] but it is also a fast-food staple worldwide. "Eat chicken, it's good for you" was the mantra, and we swallowed it.

Though these are creatures of seasons and sunshine, we brought them inside to serve us in dimness. But we still treasured our storybook rooster and hen, so the poultrymen gave us the retro chicken.

"Free-range" farms and the like provide the illusion, at least, of our barnyard bygones.

A groundswell of consumers want more than illusions. They want to know what Green Meadows was like before it became a subdivision. In suburban backyards and on city rooftops, they are keeping a few chickens of their own—or they are getting their eggs and poultry from those who do. They want to buy local produce from real farmers who sustain the land, giving back what was taken.

"The shifting man, who hurriedly robs the soil of its accumulated wealth, will never develop the industries," warned a 1907 circular titled "The Hen's Place on the Farm" from the Kansas State Agricultural College. Most of the state's chickens and eggs came from responsible farmers who owned their spreads, the college said. The smart consumer, it said, would seek out these wholesome foods and give up "coarser articles of diet."

Many people have never eaten of the fruit from birds that peck about the fields. Once they have, there's no going back: The eggs sit high on the griddle, the color of a desert sunset. Their taste is intense. The bird's flavor is ethereal; the dark meat deeper and richer, the fat golden. Some folks say it's far better for the body. It's certainly better for the soul.

The very thought of it is enough to put a farmer in the spirit again. Farmers' markets and cooperatives are booming across America. Feeling far afield, consumers are trying to get home, and they have some dollars to spend on the simple life. Farmers of all stripes see the new demand, and they aim to please. They're grabbing their gum boots and their calculators and heading back out to the fields.

I'm one of them. My chickens are free to range, though they do get into all manner of nonorganic mischief. Though I give them plenty of cracked corn and feed mix, which I buy from a local mill, they spend their days foraging for whatever they can find. Styrofoam packing peanuts are a chicken's delight, if it gets the chance. I'd prefer not to explain how I know this.

And one day as I scraped an old window frame on sawhorses out on the lane, I turned in dismay to find a few of my flock trying to peck the paint flecks. Lead can make the brain grow dim, a particularly troubling consequence for a chicken.

Such elemental dangers lurk all about in the environment, and the chemicals of industry permeate the land. Though I keep a close watch on my brood, I know it's acid rain that nurtures these lush fields, and so a diet of earthworms might be less than wholesome.

Yet this is what comes naturally to chickens in the great outdoors. It's what they do. Through their beaks goes just about whatever they encounter. I don't think I could call my chickens organic. They have too much discretion over their diet. They're far too free.

If you toss a plateful of table scraps to a chicken along with a scoop of fortified feed, it will dash aflutter to the first morsel it encounters and peck away greedily, scratching for more. It wastes little time in choosing its cuisine.

Modern shoppers, though, stop to scratch their chins as they peer into the supermarket cooler or freezer. They face a perplexing array of labels in their quest for quality, and they'll pay dearly for food that they deem wholesome, produced by a farmer who respects the good earth and his animals.

The chickens from one farm are "free-range," from another "cage-free" or "free-walking" or "free-roaming." The consumer may exult to find out the package is "organic." Or that the farmer has eschewed hormones, or antibiotics. If it's "all natural," who could go wrong? Shoppers want to do the right thing. Fearful of things unseen lurking in their food, they scan the labels and make their choice—trusting marketers and dietitians more than their own gut feeling.

Despite good intentions, we don't necessarily choose wisely and well. As demand for friendly foods grows, the suppliers rise to the occasion, and marketers have much to gain by persuading consumers to keep doing the right thing—namely, buying the product. Health, nutrition, safety, animal welfare, and the environment are not necessarily top concerns. In our zeal to do good, we can do harm.

It's hard to knock corn, for example. It's a staple of our diet—in fact, it permeates our diet. Those who ballyhoo biofuels sound like they have a smart idea: Imagine, fuel from the sunny American midlands rather than slimy foreign oil. We could even harness the raw power of chicken dung and other animal wastes.

And then imagine feed and meat prices rising as the corn is diverted to ethanol. With higher prices, corn production surges, then farm profits tumble. Subsidies and tariffs rise as Brazil and other nations market better biofuels from sugarcane. Meanwhile, speculators slash and burn rain forests for biofuel plantations. And we could use more fossil fuel to truck around the corn and the poop than we've saved. Unintended consequences.

So, too, can we be fooled in our choices at the supermarket. The government strictly regulates some labels, but pays no heed to others. The labels do offer valuable guidance, when used legitimately, but the designations also spell dollars, and the sellers are often a step ahead of the buyers.

Eggs with special labels can cost a dollar or two extra a dozen. Surely a farmer who cares for a hen's freedom must also care for her pursuit of happiness. If a chicken is organic, the farmer, too, must be an organic kind of soul. And even if a shopper suspects these birds endure the same indignities as their factory-farm sisters, the extra buck or two at least buys hope.

"Free" is fundamental to our hearts. We find it on the "range," where the buffalo roam, under not-cloudy skies. Seldom are heard two less-discouraging words. Free-range poultry must live under the stars like prairie chickens—or at least they're at liberty to hop the barnyard fence to explore the great pasture.

But "free-range" means only that the bird can go outdoors—that's how the label is defined by the United States Department of

Agriculture for broiler production. The agency's Food Safety and Inspection Service allots the term a single sentence: "Producers must demonstrate to the Agency that the poultry has been allowed access to the outside."[42]

From those applying for the "free-range" label, the USDA wants to see photographs or drawings of the housing structures that show the way through the door. In the past, arrows have sufficed.[43] And only meat producers need show such evidence of their sincerity. Egg farmers can flaunt "free-range" freely.

"You have access to the outside," I often told my teenagers, or words to that effect, pointing the way through the door as they pecked at their keyboards and cell phones. They looked at me blankly, much as my other brood does.

On pleasant days, I sometimes come down from the big house to find the chickens lolling about their pen, its door wide open. They should be out playing. A chicken's concept of freedom, however, arises not from the heart but the gut. The communion with nature ends when the chickens hear me rattling inside at their feed bin, at which time they charge back through the hatch, into the dimness, and struggle to burst through the wire mesh into the feed room. And when they see me heading around to their run with a scoop of scratch, out they'll charge again. And so forth.

A chicken is like that.

Danish researchers reported in 2005 that their studies of commercial free-range flocks had found that only about a tenth of the chickens went outside, and most stayed near the coops. Their willingness to wander depended partly on the weather: When it's nasty out, why not stay in? More chickens ventured farther out when they could loiter in a roofed shelter—in other words, they went out but ran for cover.[44]

A study from Britain reported similar results: The birds in free-range operations are often reluctant to leave their coop unless they have a place to take cover, such as shelters.[45] Numerous other observers have noted that it seems the chickens don't appreciate something beyond the door. Open spaces, apparently. The elements. Nature.

They can never know what they might encounter out there. So many predicaments can trip up even the most cautious among chickens. In Dubai, a farmer reported that his mother saw one of his sheep eat nine of the flock—meaning that something was seriously amiss with either the farmer, the mother, or the sheep. Several years ago in Colombia, a mud slide buried sixty thousand chickens alive. Thirty-five survived. It's a challenging world for a chicken. One minute it's pecking peaceably on the free range, and then along comes an avalanche or a killer sheep.

No wonder so many would simply rather stay inside. They stand near the door of the only home they've known and behold the wider world, decide they would rather not know it, and turn back to their bulb-bathed building, where the weather is predictable because there is no weather.

And for the more free-spirited among them, what's the point of going out? Oftentimes only a crowded pen awaits them. It's hardly big enough for thousands of chickens to rove, whether it satisfies the USDA or not. It's little more than a large cage, segregated from the world, sometimes barren.

"When we visited one free-range chicken farm," *Consumer Reports* noted in November 2002, "we found a penned, 10-by-30-foot patch of dirt topped with chicken manure and grass. A second 'range' consisted of a larger pen, but the birds chose to stay in a small area filled with weeds and an old drum."

A free-range chicken could haul itself out to such a paradise, if it were so inclined and had directions to the door. But inside, joy of chicken joys, is food in abundance—power pellets that pump the birds up for market, containing everything they need and so much more. It's easy peckings. Ponderously plump, bred for bulk, they don't move all that much, and why would they leave the food line?

It's not as if they know any better. The only range such birds will ever encounter is the one in the kitchen. They are no more free to be real roosters and hens than the birds living in battery cages, the tiers of tight quarters in stacked rows that many people find appalling. They've never bathed in the dust, never copulated with wild abandon in the tall grasses—never copulated at all—never sacked a garden or fled a farmer's foot. They would not know what to do outside; it seems almost cruel to bid them go there.

To strike closer to honesty, some producers use the label "cage-free," which has no legal meaning. The USDA does not regulate or certify the label, but at least it's probably true: Their chickens aren't kept in cages. That's where most eggs originate, so the label tells the consumer something worthwhile: The birds that made their breakfast aren't wired into place, though they're hardly out drilling for grubs.

Chickens raised for meat, though, aren't usually kept in cages anyway—they're free to move as much as they can manage as they grow to gargantuan proportions—so the "cage-free" label on a package of meat hardly enlightens consumers. Some farms call their chickens "free-walking," making no pretense to any outdoor excursions. Still, it sounds as if they're out for a stroll down a country lane.

My brood, although enamored of the feed scoop, finds plenty to appreciate out beyond the hatch. Down that little slatted ramp, out through the screen door in their enclosed run, the chickens take on a world of worms to pluck, daylilies to decimate, compost to conquer. They rendezvous for sensuous dust baths in our horseshoe pits, fluttering and rolling and kicking. They're into dirt: The baths work the powder under their feathers to smother any mites and lice, and they swallow grit to grind their food.

Manure is their manna. Digging deliriously, they spread it and shred it as they look for undigested bits of fodder. In the good old outhouse days, farmers sometimes put up their privies in the chicken yard and let the birds do the cleanup work. A stablemate once told me that chickens helped him muck his horse's stall. "Cuts down on my work," he said.

I give them a good life, far as I can tell. I let them spread their feathers over five full acres. They have a cozy coop, bedded with sawdust, where they can retreat from the shadows of buzzards or the cold west wind and roost all night over Tupperware tubs.

All this is theirs. I just want their eggs.

So do the other egg producers—and for all the USDA is concerned, they could keep their chickens in shackles and still call them "free-range." They're given carte blanche to use the term. And though the agency says free-range broilers, raised for meat, must be able to get outside, it doesn't consider what "outside" is like, or what they eat, or how much space they get. The chickens are packed in to pack it on, then packed up for slaughter. The USDA only requires a way out.

If I were such a chicken, getting my neck stretched might be the best way out. On my way to the slaughterhouse, I might even glimpse the sky or a patch of pasture, a little place of my own. Free at last.

Poultrymen who proclaim their broods "free-range" or use similar labels are not necessarily charlatans. Many small farms that sell eggs and meat at stands and markets give their chickens a decent chance to show whatever dignity they possess.

Organic farmers, too, are often dedicated to principle, as they humanely raise small flocks of a few hundred to a few thousand birds. The farmers may keep organic vegetable gardens as well. They fertilize with manure. To control weeds, they rotate crops or spread mulch—or actually pull them out. They are attuned to the environment and conservation.

They process their food on-site and sell it locally or regionally, directly to consumers, restaurants and stores, and farmers' markets. A sullied reputation is the death of a local businessman, so they guard their integrity. And these farmers find a strong demand for what they produce, a trend that managers of farmers' markets around the country have reported. This is genuine organic.

And then there is the other kind of organic. It's a highly regulated niche, and for good reason: The term can easily be abused. All poultry, after all, is organic. The word bespeaks living things, or what once lived. The poultry I buy for the table once lived, I presume, though at times I've wondered.

The USDA has breathed its own meaning into the word. Since 1999, it has allowed the use of an "organic" label for meat and poultry, prohibiting the word on any food packaging that doesn't satisfy its rules. Producers who sell over $5,000 worth a year must be certified. The agency calls for annual inspections of organic operations and periodically examines the foods for nonorganic residues, pesticides, or toxins.

Organic chickens cannot be nurtured on antibiotics, which farmers have long used to stimulate their growth and to keep them from keeling over from a host of diseases. A genetically engineered chicken cannot be called organic. The meat and eggs cannot be irradiated with lasers to kill germs.

An organic chicken's feed must be made from grains that were grown without chemical fertilizers, sewage sludge, or pesticides. The agency keeps a list of other controlled substances and can slap a $10,000 penalty on violators for each offense.[46]

You will not necessarily be eating a tastier chicken, though, or a safer one, or a more nutritious one. The label promises none of those things, although many people imagine their organic meal tastes more like nature intended. But what you eat can taste like library paste and still qualify. It's what the chicken eats that matters.

Nonetheless, the organic label provides some assurances against obnoxious additives. What it doesn't do is guarantee that the chicken goes outside. It doesn't mean the farmer is particularly friendly. Large-scale organic poultry production in some ways can resemble the conventional methods that animal lovers abhor.

Meanwhile, major chains are stocking their shelves with organic food. Wal-Mart, for one, has gone organic in a big way, trucking in the offerings of corporate producers from miles away. You can get an organic TV dinner from General Mills, replete with such suspicious-sounding substances as "natural chicken flavor."[47] The food can meet all government requirements and still be far from farm-fresh. This type of organic is certified nonsense.

Small farmers fear that the retail behemoths will drive down prices and plow them under: It's not as if it hasn't happened before. The quaint little spreads just can't satisfy such a huge organic appetite. It takes a farmer in a business suit to fill these troughs, and we're not talking about Oliver Wendell Douglas.

Organic sells. The market in general has seen 20 percent annual sales gains since the mid-1990s. For organic eggs and poultry, retail sales almost quadrupled between 2003 and 2007, the USDA reported. It expects organic egg sales to rise 40 percent and organic poultry sales to more than triple by the end of the decade. It's easy to find organic eggs and poultry in stores these days.

They cost a lot more, too, sometimes two or three times as much. The agency expects that trend to continue, as well, pointing out that organic feed can cost twice as much and that the smaller flocks are more expensive to keep.[48]

And, of course, the producers will get what people are willing to pay: The agency projects that consumers will keep bearing these prices as they increasingly fret about their health, the environment, and how animals are treated. With every food scare, particularly the spread of "mad cow" disease, organic sales have peaked. As this alt-market has grown, reaching 1 or 2 percent of total food sales, agribusiness has moved in. It knows a sustainable market when it sees one.

Sales would be even higher, the USDA says, were it not for competition from "natural" products—a market that the meat industry developed before the organic label was allowed. The larger producers, the agency says, still focus on the "natural" market, though they've introduced organic lines. Such foods should not carry synthetic colors or be overly processed. The ingredients, and anything injected, should not be artificial. The label must do its best to explain just what "natural" means.

However, the USDA requires no certification for "natural" foods, and puts no particular restrictions on what goes into the animal feed. Naturally, cost-conscious producers will use less expensive feed than organic grains, and they might not stint on antibiotics and other economic enhancements.

The agency lets producers mark "no antibiotics" on their meats if they send in documentation, but nobody certifies them for that, either. And if you read a package label declaring "no hormones added," look closer: You should find a note explaining that "federal regulations prohibit the use of hormones." It's forbidden—poultry producers cannot fatten their profits using hormones. So what the label says is akin to: "No hormones because they won't let us." They can use drugs, however, and some of the same antibiotics that producers contend are needed to control disease work nicely as a growth stimulant as well.

It's good to know that your food is fresh, though I've been perplexed a time or two to pull a broiler from the supermarket cooler that appeared to have just arrived from the Arctic ice shelf. In the world of USDA labeling, "fresh" can be as low as 26 degrees—and if the meat temperature ever dips below 26 degrees, the label must be removed. (Or the word can just be crossed out, though consumers might find that disconcerting.)

But only if the meat gets below zero is it called frozen. The nether region between zero and 26 degrees was once labeled "hard-chilled" but today carries no designation. The government dropped it a decade ago, along with "previously hard-chilled" for meat that had thawed some.[49]

As for eggs, the "fresh" ones you buy may be days old by the time they get to the supermarket cooler, weeks old by the time you use them. A properly refrigerated egg in a sound shell will last a month or more. Unrefrigerated, it spoils four times faster.

"An egg forty-eight hours old that has lain in a wheat shock during a warm July rain would probably be swarming with bacteria and be absolutely unfit for food," Hastings wrote in *The Dollar Hen*. "Another egg stored eight months in a first-class cold storage room would be perfectly wholesome."

He counted better storage as a chief reason for the rise of the nascent poultry industry. "Any old-timer in the business will tell you stories of things as they used to be that will easily explain why our fathers ate more ham and less eggs."

Fresh or free-range, organic or natural—such labels offer more or less useful information, but most don't address what some consumers care most about: How is the animal treated? How is the land treated? The label game can turn a sincere effort to inform consumers into a seduction for their dollars.

"Organic" doesn't mean the Earth Mother plowed the furrows or bestowed gratitude upon the animal's spirit for its sacrifice. "Natural" doesn't require that the chicken or turkey frolicked au naturel through verdant pastures. It doesn't necessarily mean the farmer gave a hoot for nature, for his land, for sustaining the blessings of all creation.

What the farmer wishes to sustain is a profit. That's hardly a dirty word: A profit sustains a livelihood, a way of life. Corporate profit margins captivate many an investor in the stock markets. A profit allows a small farmer to survive, to endure by his own hand, to compete against the big boys. Isn't that the spirit we sowed in all those rags-to-riches tales, the lore of the entrepreneur, independent and self-reliant?

Some producers do try to get away with whatever they can under the regulations, hoodwinking their well-meaning customers. If you thought that was a happy chicken you were eating, it's possible you bought into a lie. It's possible your granny lies, too. Let's be fair: Most producers are trying to make an honest living while giving the buyers what they want.

The food labels appeal to a niche market—people who want wholesome food, of all things. And though the labels are often abused, they give small farmers a fighting chance to sustain a way of life that faces extinction.

For all the talk of "sustainable agriculture," you'd think it was a new discovery. The term arose a generation ago, finding its way into the 1990 Farm Bill among methods of alternative farming. Farming responsibly, it seems, has become so rare as to be designated an alternative lifestyle.

For thousands of years, though, farmers have sustained themselves, and their efficiency in recent decades has sustained much of the world. They support populations that could not survive without modern agriculture. Today's know-how, exported around the globe, fills the bellies of those who otherwise would starve.

At the same time, our tormented environment might seem beyond sustaining. Agriculture has stripped rain forests, sullied streams and bays, threatened the world it helps.

Here, if you can bear it, is how "sustainable agriculture" is defined under U.S. Public Law 101–624, Title XVI, Subtitle A, Section 1683, 1990:

> The term sustainable agriculture means an integrated system of plant and animal production practices having a site-specific application that will, over the long term, satisfy human food and fiber needs; enhance environmental quality and the natural resource base upon which the agricultural economy depends; make the most efficient use of nonrenewable resources and on-farm resources and integrate, where appropriate, natural biological

cycles and controls; sustain the economic viability of farm operations; and enhance the quality of life for farmers and society as a whole.

Far as I can tell, here's what that means:

Sustainable agriculture is what farmers do as they raise good food, season by season, using the land wisely and respectfully so it profits all of us now and always.

It's a philosophy, not a system of rules and regulations, and therefore is open to anyone's interpretation. The emphasis is often on food that's locally farmed. Food concessions in major national parks such as Yosemite and Yellowstone offer meat and produce from the region, with entrees that are organic, free-range, all-natural, grass-fed. These qualify as sustainable, according to the Park Service.

Maybe so. The term isn't regulated, so the words might mean little or nothing. But they mean much to those who honestly practice farming that respects the land.

"Pasturing poultry" is one such method that seeks to keep a balance between man and nature. The birds live out in the fields inside portable wooden pens enclosed with chicken wire on the top and sides, with a covered section for protection against rain and sun. The farmer moves these floorless pens most days to a fresh patch of grass, by either hand or tractor. The chickens learn to walk along. Typically, each pen is about ten by twelve feet, a few feet high, with an occupancy of about seventy-five.[50]

Inside these field cages, the birds enjoy the pasture and fresh air, if not exactly spacious freedom. They no doubt appreciate, though, that they're safe from predators, except for the occasional crafty raccoon that reaches through the wire and nabs a witless victim resting against the side of the pen. (Some farmers set up electric barriers.)

The chickens feed on the greenery, insects, and worms, as well as grain supplements the farmer provides. As they scratch about, they work their manure into the soil, fertilizing it, until the farmer moves their pen to where the grass is greener and they begin afresh. It's a fair-weather system, good for the growing season. As the birds fatten into profit, they do double duty as mower and manure spreader.

The bureaucrats call it a management concept. A thoroughly modern chicken might indeed think it revolutionary, or reactionary. Through the early 1900s, though, most broilers and layers were raised outdoors. It made sense, somehow, to let chickens out to peck in the pasture. They needed the sun, in those days.

The USDA doesn't regulate or certify this pastoral practice, but it does recognize and define the label. Instead of merely providing outdoor access, this "modified free-range system" makes the birds get out and stay out. In this way, the agency says, chickens can get a fifth of their feed from pasture forage. Sunshine feeds the grass, which feeds chickens, which feed people. The light becomes us.

You won't find an "organic" label, generally, on this poultry, since the methods and feed may not conform to all the technicalities. It's "beyond organic," says Joel Salatin, author of *Pastured Poultry Profits* and other books on back-to-basics farming. He has lectured widely on the trend he's often credited with popularizing in the 1990s on his Shenandoah Valley spread in Swoope, Virginia.

Farming, he says, is his ministry, and it's not "organic" that he's preaching. It's "local." Salatin, for sure, did not start the buy-local trend, which began when the first farmers harvested their crops on the banks of the Tigris and Euphrates. But he has trumpeted the cause of good food produced close to home.

He doesn't sell his meat and eggs to supermarkets, nor ship them to faraway buyers. Consumers within his local "foodshed" purchase the produce of the 550-acre farm he calls Polyface, where he raises chickens and turkeys, cattle and pigs, lambs and rabbits. At most, people drive a few hours over country roads to pick up their orders at his farm.[51]

Passionate in his beliefs, Salatin extols what he calls "relationship marketing," in which consumers know their farmer and look him in the eye. He has about a thousand regular customers, who he says yearn for authentic food from land they've visited and walked. They'll pay a premium for a taste they once knew. It's worth it, to them, to see animals treated well. They want quality, and decency.

And they want something more: They want to reconnect to the land, and to those who work it, live on it, believe in it.

I was transported. On my laptop screen, I could see two hens dozing on their roost. They were stars of a live-action webcast, straight from a faraway coop.

The ever-alluring Internet lets the serious surfer observe, first-hand, such marvels as corn growing minute by minute in an Iowa field. On an impulse I searched for "hencam"—a logical name for a chicken's digital domain.

In Bradford, England, where it was 5:54 A.M., I visited Tilly and Milly, sleeping in. Near Boston, Aunt Marge engaged in a similar pursuit in her coop. Then it was back across the pond to Cornwall, where I beheld a free-range flock. I checked in on chickens in a citrus orchard in Bonsall, California. Another camera took me to the Massachusetts coast.

One site offered to help people like me set up our own cameras, since so many had inquired. It touted itself as "the best and friendliest hencam in the U.K." Another laid claim to being the original.

What's going on here?

A 1920 poultry primer praised the "thousands of small flocks of fowls on town and village lots and in city backyards." The trend was growing, Harry M. Lamon wrote in *Practical Poultry Production,* and together these flocks were becoming an economic force in food production.

Those were the days before most farmers began to keep their

chickens indoors. Now, out they go again. I read about this phenomenon in *The New York Times*. Urbanites and suburbanites are keeping their own coops. Hatcheries that sell chicks are talking about the trend, as are poultry supply shops.[52]

It could be part of the organic movement, the article said. Or maybe it's Martha Stewart's doing—the grand dame of things domestic has featured fancy fowl in her magazine and on her show.

Another reason for the outdoor exodus, some have conjectured, is the desire of parents to get their video-entranced kids out of the house and interested in something real. I saw one video game in which, if so inclined, you can kick a chicken, sending its feathers flying; in another, you get to load it onto a catapult to assault the ramparts. I had pounded past the portcullis before Ross, my affable son, reclaimed the controls.

More people are longing for things genuine. They want wholesome food, and they want to get outside and closer to nature. As this becomes a trend, others join in because it's fashionable: It's cool to have a coop, even if you live in a town or city.

In Seattle, you can take a tour of urban coops, courtesy of the Seattle Tilth, a nonprofit that promotes community gardens and organic, sustainable growing. On your stroll, you might see henhouses fashioned after a Wild West saloon, a modern condo, or a cedar chalet.[53]

In a brick row house in Brooklyn, a family raises Araucanas and Marans. They bought their starter chickens on impulse a few years ago from a Mennonite farmer while staying at a bed-and-breakfast in Lancaster County, not far from my own backyard.

They're hardly alone among New York City chicken fanciers. A group called City Chickens has been promoting urban henkeeping. It's an initiative of Just Food, another nonprofit dedicated to sustainable agriculture. City Chickens has assisted schoolchildren, retirees, and Puerto Rican families who say their hens remind them of home.[54]

A similar group, Mad City Chickens, encourages urban fowl in

Madison, Wisconsin. Started in 2004 by "the poultry underground"—citizens who fought for their right to keep backyard coops within city limits—the group focuses on teaching people about the benefits of raising their own food.[55]

So they're out there, in the east and west and heartland, too, clucking and growing, right in our own neighborhoods. In New York and Seattle and Madison and points between, chicken support groups encourage regular folks to get back into farming in the most basic way. Could the backyard contingent become the economic force in the poultry industry that Lamon envisioned in 1920, before we got so smart?

We are starting to fill our baskets again with eggs and apples grown nearby. The "eat local" trend is unmistakable. Take a look at the government's figures: Of the nearly 4,500 farmers' markets in the United States as of 2006, about half hadn't existed a decade earlier.[56]

At the same time, townsfolk have been getting to know the farmers and contracting with them directly in CSAs. The letters stand for "community supported agriculture," in which farms sell shares of their harvest to urban and suburban subscribers: You pay the farmer up front and get regular deliveries of produce. About 1,200 of these enterprises are operating around the country, up from just a few hundred in 1990.[57] The concept originated in the 1960s in Switzerland and Japan, where farmers and consumers formed partnerships to promote safer food and stable markets; the CSAs first took root in the United States in the mid-1980s.[58]

The markets and CSAs are giving consumers more insight into where their food comes from. Shoppers actually talk to the farmer, commiserate about the weather and feed prices, haggle and shake hands—the kind of relationship that's gone by the wayside over the generations. We are getting a little closer to home again, though we've miles to go. Only 1 or 2 percent of the food that Americans eat is locally produced, according to estimates from the environmental research group Worldwatch Institute.[59]

That's down from about 100 percent a few centuries ago. Villages prospered, or failed, on the strength of the local harvest. They took care of themselves, without railroads or interstates. They developed local favorites based on the crop or livestock that suited the region's soil and climate and terrain—peaches, cranberries, sheep, salmon. Homemakers in both country and city canned the produce from local farms—and most were still doing so through the early 1900s.

A century later, home canning is for hobbyists. The meat and vegetables on the American dinner plate are trucked, on the average, about 1,500 miles to get there, researchers found in a 2001 study at Iowa State University's Leopold Center for Sustainable Agriculture. A typical prepared meal in America, it reported, contains ingredients from at least five foreign countries.[60] We can't find locally what we demand, so we ship our food products in, spewing yet more diesel fumes into the global hothouse. To most people, the farmer remains a complete stranger. We've lost our connection to what we eat.

All those farmers' markets, and no connection?

If we have thousands of hencam voyeurs on the Internet, we could have thousands of farmers' market aficionados. If you yearn for a special honey or ham or barbecue, you could "meet" the producers on the Internet, see the land, get a close look at what they offer, ask other folks how they like it. You'd go shopping for the food you wanted; they'd send it to you in bulk, when practicable; and you'd be supporting local agriculture—within the larger neighborhood.

Small farmers could reach out and sell directly to those who appreciated them, as in a simpler time. They'd manage to work out the logistics, with the help of legislation and food-policy councils encouraging their enterprises. Our economy and society have much to gain by keeping small farmers productive.

In a connected community, people of good taste can find one another. If enough people solicit businesses that work with local farmers—markets, restaurants, Internet peddlers—the world will continue to enjoy a tasteful bounty rather than subsidized pseudo-foods produced cheaply and recklessly.

By buying locally while thinking globally, we can preserve recipes infinitely more interesting than the new one-world cuisine served at drive-through windows. If international trade and mass communications have taken us to this sad place, these same tools can help us find our way home.

Nearly nine thousand people longing for such connections came together in Turin, Italy, for a conference in 2006 called Terra Madre—"Mother Earth." Representing 150 nations, they were small farmers, fishermen, breeders, cooks, restaurateurs, and professors.

It was the second such conference sponsored by Slow Food International, a nonprofit whose mission is "to counteract fast food and fast life, the disappearance of local food traditions and people's dwindling interest in the food they eat, where it comes from, how it tastes, and how our food choices affect the rest of the world." No bureaucratic blather there—if those words need translation, it's only because Slow Food members speak many of the world's languages.

At Terra Madre, a Canadian could confer with an Ethiopian about wheat, a Peruvian and Californian could compare notes on orchards. What common struggles might a Scandinavian reindeer farmer and a Tanzanian dairyman face? When an organic farmer from Chiapas, Mexico, lifts a glass with a dried-grasshopper producer from Oaxaca, what secrets do they share?[61]

It was an opportunity to work together to find ways to promote and preserve the flavors of old and diverse cultures. Participants hope to find new markets. The farmers and producers are working with professors and chefs, getting to know one another and keeping in touch. In the universities, they find knowledge, and a forum for their concerns about what it has wrought. In the restaurants, they find those who interpret and enjoy the knowledge that the farmers themselves bring to the table.

The Slow Food organization was founded in Italy in 1986 by a man who had long been interested in local flavor. Carlo Petrini had worked toward the revival of his country's folk music, starting a festival that included a new level of intimacy: Musicians went into people's homes to sing them the songs of their ancestors.

As an activist student in the 1970s, he had launched an independent radio station, and he began tackling issues of wine, food, and other traditional tastes. He helped to open a restaurant featuring Italy's regional cuisines. Arcigola, the group he founded to advance the cause of food fundamentals, went international as Slow Food in 1989; it now has more than eighty thousand members worldwide, eighteen thousand in the United States.

Throughout the world, it identifies 1,583 "food communities" worthy of preserving. Spice producers in Gabon and Madagascar. Cheesemakers in Turkey and Niger. Farmers' market operators in Mali and Lebanon. Shepherds in Azerbaijan. Snail farmers in Finland.

Among the Mapuche people of Chile, chicken farmers produce the coveted Araucanas, which lay blue eggs. In Cameroon, the Guiziga tribe of the Diamaré plains are keepers of bizarre bare-necked chickens. They cook them with okra and sesame paste and serve them with couscous.

"You see, when one loses a flavor, one loses a recipe," Petrini told the British magazine *The Ecologist*. "When one loses a recipe, one loses the knowledge of the use of a natural product. And when one loses this knowledge, one loses the ability to cultivate that product.

"As a result, we are slowly losing animal breeds and varieties of vegetables, and this means communities lose the capacity to maintain themselves—the whole fabric of society disintegrates, and the scene is set for dependence upon multinational products."[62]

The nature of a region's soil and climate—its rains and its breezes, the cycle of its seasons—flavors its food. The concept is inherent in the French expression *goût de terroir*—taste of the terrain, the soil, the land. The earth itself becomes the chef, blending its ingredients into its special recipe.

The word has long been applied to vineyards from a common region, where the weather and soil combine with grape variety and tradition to lend a distinct personality to the wines. If it was "a very good year," the weather favored the flavors of the vintage: The rains came, or stopped, with exquisite timing. The subtleties of bouquet arise, too, from the soil—sandy or loamy or clay, acidic or alkaline, or well-drained on a gentle slope. It's a chemistry divine.

In France, where the Gallic rooster is the proud national symbol, farmers have also applied the *gout de terroir* concept to the Label Rouge brands of poultry from small, family operations—a movement that the government encouraged forty years ago as consumers began to reject the production-line pabulum that was replacing their rich traditions.

The regional brands, about two dozen of them, associate the taste of chicken with the French countryside where it was produced. Farmers within a region use a common label, widely recognized among consumers. One trades on romantic images of rolling, unfenced countryside. Another conjures a portrait of the pine forests of the Atlantic coast.

The chickens are raised similarly to those in the American pasturing system that developed much later: They are kept in touch with the land in movable, floorless pens. The producers often market their poultry directly to consumers, helping to preserve the lifestyle of the small farmer.

Though consumers can pay twice as much as they do for conventional offerings, the Label Rouge brands generally have claimed a growing share of the French poultry market each year—up to a third or more of total sales, according to various reports.[63] As avian influenza threatened the nation in 2006, the farmers were hit hard by restrictions on outdoor production, despite their strict standards of quality, and by other nations' import bans. Poultry sales plummeted—yet another example of farmers at nature's mercy. Sales have since recovered.

The birds are bred from traditional farm breeds that are hardy and grow slowly. They aren't expected to reach market size for twelve weeks—twice as long as it takes some production broilers to fatten for sale. Their feed contains no growth stimulants and few other additives. The farmers must be nationally certified, and strict compliance inspections come regularly.

Taste tests are frequent, too: The meat must be "vividly distinguishable" from regular supermarket fare. In what other system do inspectors dig in to see for themselves whether the stuff is even edible? By doing so, they also vividly distinguish the Label Rouge system as one in which farmers can once more feel pride in what their own hands have done—as neighbors cooperate to make their local brand a standout among standouts.

In the pine forests of Aquitaine, near Landes, poultry producers embraced the movement in the 1960s. There, forty years later, one of those who pioneered the better way, George Berbille, was still raising birds in his portable shelters. No longer a young farmer, he had lost a leg to a harvester. But he still worked his land, growing corn that he mixed into feed in a mill on his own farm, with his own hands.[64]

In the Pennsylvania that I knew as a child, four thousand miles away, we, too, ground our own corn, mixing it on the barn floor with the oats we'd threshed. My brother, Jeff, and I shoveled it into a leaky old gristmill, mended with burlap and binder twine, which belched out just enough grain through its cracks to keep the guinea hens content.

Our father worked the hopper, while Uncle Bill filled the sacks with grain. I disliked that job, then, but now sometimes at night, when I cannot sleep and scenes from the past appear and disappear, I can hear the hum of the mill's hammers slowing to a clatter when everything is done.

We mixed our grist and baled our hay and put the cows out to pasture and lived through the mud-times and the droughts and blizzards and come-what-may—while in the southwest of France a young man walked his fields and looked for better ways.

That's the spirit that sustains us, the one that looks to the land, and finds a way to endure. It's in the hearts of the George Berbilles and the Joel Salatins and the Burt Sheasleys that the world has known. If we keep working, we can keep this good thing going.

SUMMER

A Season to Grow

You know, Ulisse, you *are* a bit heavy on the Aristotle," I ventured, dropping any pretense of formality. I was face to face, after all, with an old gentleman stroking a bird. "It seems like every other page you write . . ."

I had stepped through the gate to find his garden brimming and lush. I strolled to a stand of cypress in the center of the grounds. The smell of growth hung thick and fragrant in the air, as tendrils reached for me. Not a soul in sight. Neither Aldrovandi nor his hen waited for me there.

I followed the path past lilies and orchids, brought here from the woodlands to be tamed and ordered, and entered the house through a vined bower sweet with yellow jasmine. I found them in his library. Standing at his oaken table, Aldrovandi was leaning close to a sheet of parchment, an open inkpot nearby. I startled him, and he peered at me, then grasped my hands with both of his and pumped joyously.

I glanced at the parchment. Atop the page he had scrawled *"De Animalibus Insectis Libri Septem"* (On Insects, Book Seven). Here was Ulisse Aldrovandi, at age eighty, at it again.

Born in Bologna on September 11, 1522, he had pursued many

interests during his life. He had studied law and logic. He was a philosopher and physician, botanist and zoologist, pharmacologist and geologist, and a notary, too—and was eminently qualified for what he saw as his life's mission.

Aldrovandi considered the teeming diversity of the natural world as part of the cosmic order, integral to the universe. As a young man, he hung around the docks of Rome as the fishermen came in, asking to examine their catch. His observations on species of fish later became a central part of the museum he would establish. Because all things interact, he believed, it was therefore prudent to catalogue in encyclopedic detail the world's knowledge—including chickenalia.

And it was chickens I had come to talk about. I wished to commune with a man who might understand. I had questions, such as this: Why should I care anymore?

It was the summer of our fourth year of raising chickens. In the second and third years, we had increased the size of our flock to thirty. Instead of picking them out at the feed supply store, we'd ordered them through the mail from a hatchery in Iowa. We lost very few to accidents and predators, and the whole affair seemed impossibly easy. We took reasonable precautions but didn't truly appreciate what could happen.

Then, in the spring of 2007, our confidence blooming, we ordered seventy-five hatchlings. We had ambitions of tripling the size of our flock. This time we went to the local Agway, which placed an order for us and several other customers with a hatchery in Arizona. I'd begun gathering materials for a second coop, by the fencerow near the house.

By early summer, we had twenty-five chicks left. We lost fifty to a combination of raccoon, skunk, a feral tabby cat that prowled the thickets, and our pig Sophie—who decided as she rooted for food one morning to hurl their cage into the air. Several chicks tumbled through the bottom of the cage, which crushed them like mice in a trap.

It was the cat that got Blue, I'm sure, little Blue, who had chosen me as her companion and guardian, who had waited for me each morning to lift her from the brooder tub because she couldn't hop out as the others could. She was a Blue Cochin, an old Chinese variety that looks like a feathery puffball. Hers were gray feathers, though, not blue, and they covered her legs and feet. We had ordered two of her kind, but I was partial to Blue. She seemed to need me. The other chicks dismissed her as a weakling, and they made her keep her distance from the feed tray until they'd had their fill. In the afternoon, Blue liked to forage and dig near the thicket at the edge of the meadow fence, where the cat lurked.

"Ulisse," I said. "These are just chickens, right?"

Aldrovandi settled into his chair. "Chickens are like people," he offered. His hen jumped into his lap and nested there as he ruffled her neck feathers. She blinked once, slowly, and cooed. "They reflect who we are."

I might have expected that Aldrovandi would hold chickens in such esteem. His writings bestow human qualities on the chicken, as do those of his trusted sources such as Pliny and Aelian and others—and Aristotle, in particular. Aristotle, who knew it all, who could do no wrong. I wanted to know what was up with that.

Aldrovandi began a valiant defense of his ancient Grecian guru. Aristotle, he said slowly, mattered. His was the philosophy of the sciences as pure and practical—nature in its glory has a design, and a purpose for existing. We are beings who must see, and therefore we have eyes. We do not merely see because we have eyes. This could be a religious view, or a secular view, he said, and that's the point: Nature should be studied on its own, without conditions.

He rousted his hen from his lap, and she flopped to the floor under the table laden with books. The table fronted several long rows of library stacks. His extensive collections were impressive, and many a page on the natural sciences had been penned by Aldrovandi himself: His writings filled 363 volumes, with thousands of drawings of fruits, animals, and flowers, though he had managed to publish only a few, including his *Ornithology* and a work on ancient statuary. He wrote not only of birds but of snakes, and dragons. And now, of insects.

Aldrovandi's knowledge of chickens was unparalleled, though he had trouble separating facts from the fabulous—and sometimes, as with his treatises on unicorns and dragons and basilisks, he seemed to accept it all.

He had seldom wanted for money. His ties to the Vatican helped somewhat, and he was paid handsomely in his posts at the University of Bologna and worked in various civic appointments. But he knew troubles. He had been accused of heresy for his religious views, and of incompetence in his role as inspector of drugs. He was vindicated for both, though he served time under house arrest.

In 1560, he fathered an illegitimate son, and his family urged him to find a wife. He was careful to choose a virgin, as Scripture required—a lovely girl of eighteen, half his age. She died within two years. Aldrovandi remarried, selecting another beautiful and talented young woman, who helped him with his correspondence and his work. They had two children. Both died in infancy. The boy whom Aldrovandi had fathered—and to whom he had provided a good education—died at age eighteen, in a fall from the balcony of his home. Such are the scars of a lifetime. These are what can slow a man down, dissipate his dreams.

One must endure, he said, and accept the grief, the disappointments. Death is a part of life, and we must move ever onward, like the seasons. "All things work together," he told me. "I think we should count it all for good."

This was a man who had known a few disappointments and his share of grief. And I'd had my share, too. As I thought of troubles overcome, the lost peeps paled into insignificance. There would be more springs and more Blues and more joy in the morning.

I owe Aldrovandi. In his *Ornithology*, his warmth for chickens is obvious, as it is in the words of so many of the great thinkers he cites. Time and again, I want to thank him for his ideas, right or wrong (and they were so often wrong). But whether he turned to Aristotle out of intellectual respect, or out of affection, or kinship, I'm proud to have turned for all those reasons to Ulisse Aldrovandi.

The Killing Fields

I bolted upright in bed at 3:12 A.M., certain that the cats were still there, surrounding me, their mouths open, red. I felt Suzanne's hand grip my shoulder.

Somewhere far down where the brain stem connects to surreal realms, I have stored startling images. I wonder whether I put them there as a five-year-old blinking in awe as he watched his father and uncle slit open a cow that they'd slung with a block and tackle from the limb of a maple tree in the orchard. The cow's womb had come out with her calf as she gave birth at midnight, and I'd awakened to the hasty preparations for butchering. Hiding in the shadows, I was frightened of the floodlight's glare, of the gunshot that pierced the skull, of the tumbling bowels, of the horned Holstein head watching from the edge of the light. But I came to understand, as we all come to understand, sadly, so many things.

"What's wrong, honey?"

"The cats came."

"The cats?"

I blinked and looked for the clock. "One of those dreams. You know the kind—awful things, don't know where they come from. Gruesome things . . ."

"Uh-huh."

"You know what I mean, right?"

"No."

Suzanne clicked on the bedside lamp and peered at the specimen she had married.

"They were all through the house, scrawny ones. You and I had been sitting in the garden, and we came up to the house, but it wasn't this house anymore, it had strange passages and plywood ramps. And the cats were all over, and the chicks were everywhere, too. Pieces of them."

"Oh my word!" Suzanne said. She searched for something reassuring to say. "And I was dreaming the chickens came down to the garden and ripped out the hollyhocks, right there in front of us."

"They'd gotten to all the chicks," I continued, oblivious to her, "except for one, and I had this thought, like, at least they spared some of our favorites. And several were still alive but they were hurt."

"Did you have liverwurst and onions again last night?"

I pretended not to hear her. "Some of the cats were hurt bad, too," I said. "Something else had got to them—they were trying to drag one another out of there, out of that slaughterhouse."

"Killer peeps?"

I told Suzanne that I was going downstairs for a glass of water, but really I wanted to check on our new brood, which I found sleeping under the heat light that I'd attached to a tub in the kitchen. We'd been raising them there as we waited for warmer days when they could face the world, motherless. At my approach, they began flitting around the tub, peeping full force.

This was in the late spring of 2006. Those peeps grew to give us many an egg for our breakfasts.

As summer began on a sparkling morning a year later, I awoke to the billows of our bedroom curtains in a freshening breeze. Suzanne entered the room carrying two cups of coffee and praising God for such a day.

Still sleepy, I sipped the coffee. We went downstairs to the kitchen.

"Let's sit on the deck and look out over the pond," Suzanne said.

"How about the back porch," I said. I thought we could let the new season's peeps out of their cages under the magnolia tree and watch them foraging around the ruins of the stone springhouse, playing in the periwinkle, dodging through daylilies, digging and sparring and practicing the art of being a chicken.

"No, the deck—the light's nicer there," and she was already opening the screen. Her conversation was as breezy as the day itself. She primed herself on the java, and after ten minutes of banter, she looked at me.

"I have to tell you something."

"How many did it get?"

"Bob, it's awful. It got most of them. I didn't want to talk about it right away. I didn't want you to have to wake up to that."

"Did it get the Blue Cochins?"

"One of them. I think the other's still there. I don't know if it'll live. They're scattered all around, pieces of them."

I trudged to the killing field. We kept the chicks in two large cages in a patch of lawn beyond the farmhouse's covered stone porch. In the daytime we let them out to explore, and each night we corralled them and latched the cages. For two years this had worked well, and eventually we introduced each new brood to the older chickens in the coop.

One of the cages housed about twenty of our newest hatchlings (we call them peeps when they're tiny, and anyone who has heard a wee bird's incessant chirruping understands why). These were Marans, a French breed, and Welsumers, from Holland, which grow up to lay eggs with shells the color of dark chocolate. They were so small that we kept them in a tub inside the cage so they couldn't escape through the wire. These peeps, secure in the tub, survived the night unscathed.

In the other cage, we were raising older chicks, a medley of about ten breeds, some exotic, that we'd chosen from a chart at the Agway feed mill: Egyptian Fayoumis and Gold-Spangled Hamburgs and a few Cochins from China, both blue and partridge. Some of our old favorites, too: Wyandottes and Barred Rocks, and a couple of Leghorns whose pearly white eggs would contrast starkly with the nearly black ones we expected from the Marans and Welsumers. This cage contained about twenty-two lovelies.

Not anymore. It was nearly empty, since many of the victims lay scattered out by the meadow fence, yards away. Only seven chicks remained in the cage, all unhurt, and one of them was my Blue. More than anything, they seemed distressed by the fact that their feed tray was empty. They were hopping over pieces of wings and thighs, eager for their ration. I didn't know whether to be annoyed or grateful for their unfeeling ignorance. Birds and beasts live mostly in the moment, but these seven survivors had experienced the primal dread of the thing in the woods and by all rights should feel frightened, not famished.

I could have prevented the carnage. We'd been forewarned. The previous morning, we had found one chick dead in the cage, its head protruding pathetically through the wires. This chick was more or less intact, though, except for an awful wound to its backside, which lay well inside the cage. I showed Suzanne.

Peeps will do this, we told ourselves, and we recalled what had happened to Rosie, a beautiful white Brahma, in our second year of raising chickens. One morning, when she was just a week old, we found her struggling in the brooding tub as the other peeps ripped at her rear. They had seen a speck of red there—she had bled a bit, for whatever reason. Chickens of any age will turn on one another when they perceive weakness or injury or distress. They become cannibals in a twinkling. There's nothing cute about avian instinct, even in a peep.

We put Rosie in her own box and nursed her back to health, but she never grew tail feathers, so severe was the trauma. For months she had a reddish rear, and thus her name. Rosie is one of our best layers to this day, darling hen. She has found her place midway in the pecking order. After healing, she was no longer a target.

Surely, I thought, as I flung the dead peep far back into the thickets, a morsel for the feral cats, this, too, was a case of cannibalism. It was not. The peep was the prey of a night stalker, out for a practice run before unleashing havoc. The killer had snuck up to the cage, thrust its narrow, toothy muzzle through the wires, and munched a deep bite from the butt of a hapless bird sleeping against the side. Having tasted of the blood, it withdrew, for the moment, to ponder the prospects. The next night, it would not be startled by the frenzy it caused but rather would revel in it.

I surveyed the scene. Next to the cage, a little Wyandotte lay dead but untorn. It was a work of perfection, of smooth feather and folded wing. Who can know what turned the killer away just then to let these other seven live? The sunrise? I picked up the Wyandotte and ran a finger over the silvery, black-tipped lacing of its wings and felt something unmanly tightening in my chest, and so instead I hurled the bird deep into the blackberry bushes and shouted an unmanly profanity that, yes, I'm sure the neighbors could have heard.

"Goddamn you, skunk!"

That which wells up from within is sometimes what one once knew. Two men raised me: my father, warm and poetic yet volatile, who knew God but at times invoked him in curses; and my gentle uncle, nostalgic and pacific, who once, while we shoveled corn from a frozen crib, uncovered a dead cardinal that had fallen amid the cobs and, removing his gloves, knelt to brush the snow from its wings. "I'm sorry," he told it. "You're beautiful."

What had happened in our farmyard, I believed at the time, was classic skunk. I pictured the scene: Upon its return on the second night, the skunk terrified the chicks into a corner. A few of them stretched their necks in terror through the wires, offering their heads and jugulars as convenient fast food; as for the others, the skunk reached in with tiny sharp-tipped paws to yank them out, disassembling the larger ones as necessary. One at a time it dragged them off, tore at their heads and hearts, and when the struggling stopped went back for a fresh challenge. It drank the blood but ate little. The slaughter must have taken most of the night.

I saw part of a Fayoumi by the water dish. Out by the meadow fence, a Leghorn's leg. I counted fourteen bodies, as best as I could reckon. I considered whether the predator might be a raccoon, which also will bite off a chicken's head and drink the blood, but I wanted to blame the skunks that I knew had been skulking in the yard.

A month earlier, something had gotten into the coop on a night we forgot to secure the door, and it had spirited three of our grown hens away. Come morning, the barnyard was awash in feathers, white and brown and sheening green, and I could see, out in the pasture, the three bodies, mauled but uneaten. One hen was still trying feebly to drag herself, so I rushed for a hatchet, and as I raised it to end her misery she looked at me with the last fire in her eye, and slowly opened her bleeding beak as if to peck me, and I alone was her enemy then—he who had stolen her eggs, and let the beast get in, and now this. "I'm sorry," I told her. "You're beautiful."

I blamed a skunk for that slaughter, too. Suzanne rigged a box trap behind the coop, and the next morning there it was, crouching miserably: a skunk, so small for what had seemed such a big crime—though I knew it was guilty of nothing. It had done what skunks do. It had killed—and apparently for sport, for the joy of the kill. It squandered far more than it consumed.

When I was a boy, I liked to go rabbit hunting—mostly for the camaraderie of my buddies. We roamed pasture and woods and talked about things we maybe shouldn't have talked about, and now and then we'd flush a rabbit and shotguns would blast. I didn't particularly like the taste of rabbit, but after shooting one I'd cut it up into pieces and leave it in the freezer and not think of it again. I suppose my mother eventually fried it up, and I no doubt had a piece or two, but eating it wasn't the point. I had done what people do. Nobody, so far as I knew, had wished God's condemnation on me for bagging a bunny, unless it was one of my buddies who thought he'd had a better shot.

But kindred spirit or not, I still detested the skunk that glowered at me from the trap. It had to go. I was efficient, and the skunk's defenses served it naught—but the whole thing stunk anyway. I dispatched it to the pest cemetery: a hedgerow far beyond the barn where skunks and groundhogs and all incorrigible critters go.

The countryside seems overrun with skunks. Stinking skunks—they're all about us. I'd only gotten one. The rest were still out there, and one of them had developed a taste for chicken tenders, all packaged up conveniently. No-good, rotten skunks.

It's hard to respect creatures that kill because they can. You'd want to destroy a man who would do such a thing. You'd want to destroy a man who destroyed a man for doing such a thing. We take revenge, God's province, into our own bloody hands, because we know we're right, and hatred flourishes. It's hard to respect a creature that kills because another has killed, and I confess that I am such a one.

But then again, it was a stinking, no-good, rotten skunk. I lobbed it into a tangle of wild multiflora roses, yet another contemptible invader that I have been known to curse (quietly, under my breath, since a man standing in a field shouting "I hate you, vile rose!" might leave bystanders concerned). I left the carcass to rot, deep, deep in the briar patch, for whatever scavenger might stoop to claim it.

You can tell a predator by how it kills, what it kills, and what it leaves behind—the forensic evidence left at the scene.[1] I was, frankly, surprised it was a skunk that the box trap had yielded. Because the victims were mature hens, I'd expected to find a raccoon, that thief in the night, one of a chicken's worst enemies. Raccoons are braver than skunks, but both are wont to decapitate their prey and drink the spouting blood. There was evidence of this in both the henhouse and cage raids: heads plucked from several peeps, and all three hens in the field missing theirs, as well (though in one case I had finished the beheading, out of mercy).

Raccoons will avail themselves of full-grown chickens, but skunks are somewhat timid and shy ("skulking" is a better word) and so for their chicken dinner they tend to keep to the peeps, when available. Hens can intimidate a skunk, though the skunk will attack them if it can't find easier pickings. Skunks are also notorious egg-suckers; they'll go through a clutch, break each egg by crushing it in at one end, and slurp down a treat even less threatening than a peep. This case involved no eggs (I'd collected them all at nightfall), or peeps, just three headless hens, with the suspect in lockup, in a striped suit, waiting for its death sentence. I must tell you: There's a chance I executed the wrong perpetrator. Evidence was circumstantial, without witnesses, and all that had happened could have been a raccoon's doing. I'd noticed no skunk odor after the killings. But it was a skunk that I captured, and no farmer can tolerate one around his coop.

Coop keepers who own a dog would do well to study that frolicking friend's face for any sign of guilt if there has been trouble in the coop. Dogs, too, kill for sport. Such was the fate a few years ago of Big Red, a rooster beloved of the town of Scio, Oregon, population 700. Big Red daily made his rounds from feed mill to deli to neighborhood porches and back, collecting his handouts. For eight years, he was a town fixture and was even the star of a few national television news features—until one July day in 2006, when a dog inside a parked car saw him strutting past. Only one thing to do: It leaped out the open window and delivered the rooster a mortal mauling. The dog soon noticed that nobody seemed proud of the deed. Townsfolk say the rooster staggered until he collapsed at the front door of a nearby veterinarian's office. There was talk of having Big Red mounted for display at a local store. I don't know whether this was actually done. I don't want to know.

I had three pullets succumb in the summer of '06 under circumstances that pointed to a dog: daytime attack, bodies mauled but uneaten. I found them in an empty horse stall, as if they'd been cornered there. We owned no dog at the time, though, and I'm still scratching my head over what happened.

Coyotes? Not in Pennsylvania. I hear them gibbering and caterwauling in the woods of New Hampshire, where we've often visited dear friends at their sheep farm, and the sound of it alone would strike my chickens dead. A coyote, of more meager means than a dog, would be likely to trot off with its catch firmly in its jaws. The family dog leaves its kill to be found where it lies, like some macabre offering to its master.

A year earlier we'd found our peacock, Groucho, similarly slain in a stall—roughed up, but little blood. I was at a loss there as well. Cats aren't that brave; even a chicken is generally more than they're willing to tackle, though they might snatch a chick. Groucho, who for years had the run of the farm, seemed to have been dogged to death like the pullets. Most predators are wary (or contemptuous) of the gaudy peacock, but Groucho had been safe for years roosting in the rafters.

It was the dead of winter when I found Groucho, luxuriant amid manure, and since he was a longtime pet I deemed him deserving of a proper burial. The ground was frozen, so I wrapped him in layers of plastic bags and put him on a high shelf behind my workshop. One balmy April day, as I was bagging lawn debris, I remembered him. I wrapped a bandanna around my face, opened the door to the seldom-used storage area, and reached up to the shelf. Nothing there: The bags and clusters of brilliant feathers were scattered at my feet, and there I saw what remained of Groucho, half under a cabinet: a skeleton, intact, glistening white and bare of flesh. Barn cats. Their tiny teeth, like scalpels, had picked him delicately clean.

A weasel, close relative of a skunk, also has tiny teeth, and if it gets into a coop it will make ample use of them, though its method isn't what you'd call surgical. A farmer who finds dead chickens routed out from the rear might have had a weasel visit. If the weasel turned tail before the job was done, as weasels do, the chicken might have gotten away with severe lacerations to its cloaca, or vent, where its eggs and, yes, its droppings come out. The tissue of this all-purpose chute is soft and vulnerable, with easy access to the gut. The weasel can chew its way in, given a chance. Feed the chickens a diet of little rolled-up balls of ashes, Pliny the Elder suggested, and you'll no longer have to put up with weasels—presumably because the anal offering won't taste as good. You'll no longer have to put up with chickens, either, with such a remedy, and some farmers will conclude that's just as well.

There's another attacker that goes for the hen's vent, as well as her head, feathers, eyes, whatever it can reach. This culprit is harder to eradicate: It's another hen, or a rooster gone bad. Chickens sometimes peck their coopmates viciously, particularly when confined in less than optimal conditions. If chickens have no room to run, the pecking order can become the pecking mandate.

I've known weasels, on the farm and off, and I tell you they'll do whatever they can get away with, whether in the coop or in court, at home or in the office. They'll bite from the back, chewing greedily but running away when challenged. If you've ever had to deal with one, you'll understand how hard it is to tolerate its weasely ways. Butt-biting, sniveling, sneaky—it's enough to make a man turn predator himself. Not that the world isn't full of human predators who make a weasel look honorable: Pick up a newspaper, click on the radio, and cry. *Homo sapiens,* unlike a weasel or skunk, is known to prey on the young, immature members of its own species, taking what it can from them, using them, leaving them for dead.

Let me give tribute to a predator that I truly can respect: the fox. True, it's no friend of the chicken farmer, and folklorists have hardly

held the fox in high esteem (you'll recall Foxy-woxy, who *hrumph!* beheaded all those barnyard beasts, as well as the fox who was the bane
of Br'er Rabbit). Still, a fox, when it kills, does so with dignity.

On a June afternoon, Suzanne reported seeing two red foxes gam-
boling in the field beyond our pond, and that night I double-checked
the coop latch. The evidence of a fox raid is little evidence at all.
There may be feathers about, the sign of a brief struggle. A fox will
lay claim to one chicken, take it whole, and abscond with it to its lair
for the feast. What's left it will bury to eat later. It may decide to return to the coop to cull another chicken from the flock.

Devastating as this can be to the poultry population, I find something there to admire. The fox has no concept of thievery; it sees the
coop as a cornucopia filled with bounty. It claims only what it needs,
killing quickly and privately. What distinguishes a fox raid from one
by a messier predator is that a bird or two will have simply vanished.

How to foil a fox? Pliny recommended that its flesh be fed to the
hens, mixed with its regular feed, because no fox will eat of its own
essence. Dried fox liver works best, he wrote. Aldrovandi pointed
out, astutely, that the fox must first taste the chicken to detect its
own essence, and therefore the chicken is unlikely to ever fare well in
the encounter—though he conceded a deterrent effect. But try this
instead, he said: Rub the chicken down with wild rue, then hang the
rue under its wings. Predators will avoid the rue (as well as, I'm sure,
the maniacal flapping). Pliny also offered an alternative to fox essence:
Require the chicken to wear a fox skin around its neck, and the attacks will cease—at least until the fox stops guffawing. We may laugh
at all these absurd suggestions, but I, for one, have hardly been
successful in thwarting predators and would try anything once.

A fox's modus operandi is similar to that of *Homo sapiens*. If a human gets into your coop, you'll likewise find little evidence other than
missing birds. Like the fox, the human will take a chicken away to eat
alone, or with his kin, but the human knows full well the wrong that
he has done. And that's what makes his raid, unlike those of the

other beasts, a crime—the knowledge of good and evil, a hallmark of humanity since Eden.

No matter what a human does to an animal, it is currently illegal in every state and most of the world to trap and skin *H. sapiens*. Some in our species need such protection. In New York City, authorities responding to a complaint of a dead rooster on a Manhattan fire escape saw that it had no head. Its owner told them he'd bitten it off. The rooster had hurt his pet pigeon, he explained. The head was never recovered.[2] While doing yard work in Cheshire, Oregon, a man pulled his handgun and wasted his wife's pet chicken. The couple had been drinking, and he may not have meant to draw a bead on the bird, police said, but the wife certainly meant to shoot her husband in the back with a rifle. He lived to tell about it, if he so desired.[3]

The perpetrators of these chicken offings somehow lack the noble character of raptors whisking away their prey under thudding wings. The threat of hawks and owls and other birds of prey overhead may be what terrifies chickens more than anything that runs or climbs or slithers. A sudden shadow falling upon them can give them great pause. If hens see or hear a hawk, their eggs will spoil, the ancients believed. It seems chickens have to learn to fear the thing in the woods, but nature wires them to be wary of the thing in the sky.

Those that die by the talon have nonetheless fulfilled their destiny, which is to be consumed. From a chicken's perspective, better to perish in a meadow than in a processing plant. As the prey of human consumers, it dies shackled and hanging on the disassembly line. For the prey of raptors, the end comes in a swoop of wings, in a field, swiftly. This is death. It's part of life.

On the evening after the peep massacre in our yard, I couldn't find the seven survivors. I wondered whether they, too, had met their fate in the thickets. After a search, our daughter Gretel, home from college, heard a soft trilling coming from a pail next to the water pump, and she carried them into the kitchen—a bucket of chicken like none Colonel Sanders ever envisioned. They insisted on huddling inside their newfound fortress, and each ensuing evening they retreated into the bucket again.

They'd come to fear what might happen when darkness falls. They had a glimmer of the foresight with which humans are endowed. It's a blessing, I suppose, to learn from pain how to avoid it. But how simple life was before we understood so much. As the Scots bard Robert Burns observed, we cast an eye forward, our prospects drear, and because we canna see, we guess, and fear.

Desires of the Flesh

L ighthouse was covering himself with manure in a corner of a horse stall when we finally found him. Doubtless he wished he were dead, but it was not to be, not yet. I rousted the pathetic rooster and shooed him back out into the daylight to face his nemesis—Belikan, master of the coop.

It was midsummer of the first year we raised chickens. The rooster duo and their thirteen sisters were well into chicken adolescence when Suzanne and I left for a summer snorkeling vacation in the Central American nation of Belize, which boasts the best in barrier reefs and beers and encourages visitors to enjoy them simultaneously. We liked the full-bodied Belikan beer. We were less fond of the pilsnerish Lighthouse, the "effeminate" beer. (Our snorkeling guide used a different word as he explained this to us, flipping his wrist to demonstrate.)

Upon our return to Pennsylvania, we noticed that two of our young chickens were crowing. Or trying to crow, that is: Instead of a mature, undulating *doodle-do,* what came out was *caw-eek,* which left them winded. One seemed arrogant, the other timid. We named them after the Belizian beers.

No longer could we rightly call them peeps—they no longer made that sound, and besides, the word was too cute to describe these creatures that roamed the farmyard as June days lengthened. Those twittering fluffballs had turned lanky and awkward. Their eyes bulged over gangly necks.

And we suspected they were experimenting with sex. No longer did they seem content with bugs and grubs alone. It was not just butterflies the chickens chased now, but one another, like children on the playground learning the ways of the opposite sex.

When we bought them, the peeps had been sorted by gender. We ordered a "pullet run" of all females, as opposed to a "straight run," or take-'em-as-they-hatch. But even when peeps are professionally "sexed," mistakes happen, and cockerels sometimes slip into the mix. We wound up with two roosters, both of them Silver-Laced Wyandottes, and they had begun to try out their voices, and more.

And so ensued the summer of Belikan and Lighthouse. Their chirpy calls matured into robust crows, and they took notice of their sisters, who were busy learning to destroy the vegetable garden. As the pullets' ovaries ripened, they, too, played the field, such as it was.

The young roosters learned to accomplish the act in ten seconds flat and began jousting for dominance. Belikan soon laid claim to the hens, banishing his rival from the coop. But as the alpha chicken, he was so preoccupied with protecting his turf, so overwhelmed with his new roosterly responsibilities—so busy crowing—that he had little time to satisfy their inner needs.

The hens began canoodling with Lighthouse, who became a playboy of fleet foot. He would dodge in, jump a hen, and skitter away squawking in half-flight as Belikan rushed to her defense. Though Lighthouse got plenty of action, the hens gave him no respect afterward. They, too, pecked at him, chased him. He had to sleep in the barn rafters, a lonely lacewing, exiled. He disappeared for a few days—and that's when we found him in the horse stall, digging deep into the dung, disgraced.

Lighthouse did endure for a season or so after that, but he was a broken rooster. Soon he became embittered, and mean, hurling himself at me as I entered the barn as if it were all my fault. He skulked, for the rest of his short days, in the lilac shadows, fearful of the marauding hens. In the end, he went insane, trying to torpedo anyone entering the barn. Our friend Justino suggested that his wife would be happy to do something about the situation. I stuffed the poor deranged bird into a cardboard box and put it on the seat of his pickup truck. Justino drove off, licking his lips.

Chickens like sex. Daily I've watched their dance. The rooster likes to think the conquest is his, that he has impressed the hen into squawking submission with a dip and a wave of a wing and an offering of corn.

But often it's the hen who has set out to get the rooster of her choosing, manipulating the whole affair with feminine finesse. She waddles up close to her target, pecking fastidiously. She squats seductively. The rooster eventually notices. He makes his move, she runs, he chases.

It's over in a moment of back-clawing passion that begins with a squabble and ends in quiet rocking as he bites her neck—about ten seconds of splendor in the grass. He jumps off to strut. She shakes her feathers briskly and resumes pecking. And he raises his wattles high, already surveying the field, looking out not only for his hens but for any rooster that might challenge him.

"The eyes of these birds are shining and limpid," Aldrovandi wrote. "They say that they are endowed with a salacious and libidinous nature"—and you can tell by their facial features. "Indeed, whoever has a concave nose, a round forehead, and a round, prominent head like roosters is commonly considered to be fond of sex."

I think of Bob Hope and Alfred Hitchcock, and Aldrovandi himself as he was depicted—though it seems Bob was more the type. "So

great is the abundance of their semen," Aldrovandi wrote, referring
to roosters, "that they emit it not only when they see the females but
also when they hear their voice," as distressing to the female as that
might be.

The south wind moistens the feminine anus, he said, citing Albertus Magnus, a great German theologian and naturalist of the
Middle Ages: "They are stirred by the wind to lust, as also women
delight to open their wombs to the south wind by which their menstrual blood is attracted."

A brisk wind to a hen's rear turns her on, stirring up her excrement, Aldrovandi wrote, citing experts including Aristotle, who held
that in birds the "seed of generation" is in their excrement; it's their
menstrual flow, and they conceive by way of the anus. Other birds,
ones that can fly, he said, "desire the male in order to set the excrement in motion." But the earthbound hens need only the wind. And
the hen is so full of it that she can turn her excrement into an egg—
an infertile "wind egg."

By modern standards, such reasoning seems, in itself, a load of
excrement. Science, through centuries of discovery, has discredited
much of the ancient knowledge; in the future it will no doubt dismiss
many of today's certainties.

Some of the lapses into fantasy are based on valid observations. It
is true, for example, that hens need no rooster to make an egg. They
do just fine by themselves. Oh, they enjoy their rooster, and the
hottest hen gets to sit closest to him on the roost. But she doesn't
need him for a good lay—her egg comes out just as lovely, though infertile. No need for a southerly breeze, though, as refreshing as the
hen may find it.

Aldrovandi pointed out that a hen invariably shakes her feathers
with gusto after the rooster has had his way with her. It's because, he
said, "a vapor is stirred up in her by lust, which extends her limbs."
He cited Albertus: When a man's passions rise from lack of coitus,
he, too, becomes extended and needs to shake out those vapors.

Hens likewise can be overcome by lust—"especially those hens who willingly admit the male," those hussies.

Great men have even cautioned that one must therefore never let hens eat beans. According to Pythagoras' legume theory, "they generate an impure breath and humor in bodies and thus incite sexual lust." Cicero said so, too: "That food produces great flatulence and induces a condition at war with a soul in search of the truth." Many weighed in on the matter.

The rooster keeps coming back to his favorites in the harem: hens whose backs turn bare from his embrace, who roost closest to him in the pecking order. The hens do like the boys with the biggest wattles, according to research, but other things seem to matter more. Is he a good provider? Does he communicate? Is he trustworthy?

When a rooster encounters a supply of food—whether he finds it by his own ingenuity or it rains down from the farmer's hand—he announces his prowess as a provider by calling out to the hens, who come rushing over to partake of his largesse. He'll peck at a few grains, but by and large he luxuriates in being the hens' center of attention. He lets them eat first. With his hens so near, and so appreciative, what better time to suggest a little loving attention? ("After all I've done for you, baby . . .") He does the dance.

And she keeps pecking, with one eye on him and his moves. She's at a dinner theater. He'll have her squatting soon enough, but for now there's corn to be had, and what hen doesn't like to be pampered?

If no food is at hand, the rooster always has the option of just saying there is. He soon learns he can get the hens to rush over to him simply by announcing his "find." It doesn't seem to occur to him that such behavior might displease the hens. About 40 percent of the time, the rooster's food call is a lie, according to Dr. Chris Evans, an Australian researcher on animal behavior and communication, particularly among chickens and other birds.[4]

Any hen who heeds a prevaricating rooster is at risk of a wrongful encounter. If he's a liar, he's unlikely to waste much time in wooing.

Since that's not particularly to her liking, she learns to identify the deceitful males. In laboratory experiments, Evans and his colleagues observed hens as they listened to the recorded calls of the roosters they had known, the truthful ones and the liars, as well as roosters new to them.

Upon hearing a trusted call from the loudspeaker, they immediately lowered their heads close to the ground, as if searching—they began foraging for the corn they had learned would surely be there. If the food call came from an unfamiliar rooster, they also searched expectantly. But upon hearing a call from an established liar, Evans reported, the hens glanced at the loudspeaker but didn't bother looking down. They turned away. You might call it contempt.

The liars had lost all credibility. The hens wanted an honest rooster.

What they wanted even more was a brave one. Evans, who in 2006 became director of the Centre for the Integrative Study of Animal Behaviour at Macquarie University in Sydney, did experiments on how, when, and why roosters call out alarms.

When a predator such as a hawk soars overhead, a rooster screeches out a distinctive signal that means, "Watch out! Danger in sky!" The hens, wisely, believe him and take cover. The rooster's alarm is just an instinct, researchers had long believed, just a reflex—like the way you holler when you touch something hot.

To see for himself, Evans placed a rooster in an enclosure, all alone, and projected the image of a hawk flying past overhead—a computer-generated silhouette. The rooster tilted his head and looked up, but made not a sound. He apparently knew to lie low; he knew it would be folly to attract attention to himself.

Evans added a hen to the enclosure and ran the projection again. This time, with a hen by his side, the rooster had something to say. Something distinctive. He sounded an alarm to his hen—a stealthy one, as Evans described it, like an urgent whisper. The rooster still desired to minimize the risk to himself, but the hen came first.

Hens come to know which rooster is most reliable in sounding the aerial alarm. They take note of his diligence and bravery. And he's the one who turns them on. The research team found, unexpectedly, that such alarm calls were the strongest predictor of a rooster's success in mating. Hens want the male who's most willing to die for them, to take the big risks.[5]

A dog will fight just to be next in line to mount the bitch, Aldrovandi pointed out, but a rooster's struggle is often to protect the hen's honor. No one but he may tread her, the sage observed, and tread her he does, up to fifty times a day by Aldrovandi's count. One rooster can handle six hens, he advised. "If there are more hens than this, they wear out the rooster by too much copulation." (It's a simple formula: $\frac{6 \times 50}{24} = 12.5$ per hour, which means one happy rooster equals one happy hen every five minutes, and I'm feeling old.)

The rooster no doubt figures every hen is worth protecting. He comes to her defense, Aldrovandi noted, fearing no harm to himself and ready to war with the intruder. "Not only in battle does his exceeding courage shine forth, but also in copulation." Instead of drooping afterward like most animals, he bursts out crowing, showing his "alacrity of spirit."

Clearly, though, if the rooster wants some action, the hen has certain expectations. He has learned that he must be a good provider, a good leader, a rooster true to his word—and above all he must make her feel secure.

And there's something more.

A Canadian study explored whether hens showed a preference in which rooster they'd allow under their feathers.[6] Given a choice, would they go for a nice rooster, or would they seek out broiler cocks—the bad boys raised for the meat market? These tend to be rough-sex lotharios who can claw a chick's back until it's bloody, leading her to ruin. Other roosters, of the breeds developed for the egg market, tend to be gentle souls, faithful providers, vigilant guardians—all-around nice family guys.

The study, as reported in 2000 from the University of Guelph in Ontario, looked into the continuing problem that farmers were having with those rough broiler boys. Earlier studies had presumed the problem was a defect in their behavior. But it's possible, the researchers theorized, that the problem lies with their hens. Maybe they're too choosy, rejecting the rooster's advances to the point that an otherwise normal male is just frustrated beyond all good sense and propriety.

The big question, in other words: Are hard-to-get broiler hens driving their roosters crazy so they have no choice but to force sex upon them? Is it the hens' fault the roosters are rapists?

In the experiment, the researchers tethered a variety of roosters and let hens circulate among them, picking and choosing who would get lucky. (Imagine.) The study began with twenty-four broiler hens, all mature, at least in body, but sexually inexperienced. The researchers watched their every move.

Then the researchers made sure the hens got some real action. Each was housed with a rooster for six weeks, some with a broiler boy and some with a family guy. Thus trained, they were set loose among the captive cocks to practice their newly acquired wiles.

The study found evidence that the sexually knowledgeable hens preferred the gentler roosters of the laying breeds—but certainly didn't shun the broiler breeds, who still got enough sex to satisfy a reasonable rooster. No way were the hens starving them.

And the hens weren't choosing on looks alone: They wanted more than just a firm, plump wattle. Different hens showed different preferences, and the rooster's behavior seemed to make a lot of difference. Getting roughed up was either acceptable to the hen, or it wasn't.

The study's conclusion: Broiler hens don't go out of their way to frustrate their males. As a female gains experience, though, she's less impressed by the bad boys. It's the sexually naive hens who care more about whether their rooster is dominant.

Other research has also contradicted the notion that females always flock to the macho males—the bigger ones, or the aggressive ones, or those better endowed. A study of Japanese quail, for example, found that they, like the broiler hens, learned from experience that they're better off settling for a softer touch, according to a 2002 report in *The New York Times*.[7] The male quail are particularly harsh with each other, and they often treat the females badly, too, in the mating game.

In the study, from McMaster University in Ontario, females watched two males fight it out. Some of the females were virgins, others had been around. Winner and loser were then placed in opposite corners of a cage containing a female to see which she'd choose. The virgins generally went for the male who had won the fight. Those with sexual experience tended to choose the loser.

I have seen how a rooster entices his hen to crouch for him, how her eyes grow placid and accepting as she awaits his body heavy on her back, the grip of his beak, the clutch of his claws. His foreplay is wired into his circuitry: He flaps a wing and flaunts it, displaying it before her in a dance he never had to learn, one that the first rooster knew as well. Unless the hen sees his intentions so signaled, she'll have none of it.

Something went awry as technology created our designer birds of fleshy breast and luscious leg. Modern scientists, looking for ways to strengthen a chicken's heart and muscles to withstand its oppressive weight, fiddled with its genetics—and consequently, it seems, reprogrammed the snapping of its synapses. Ian Duncan, a Canadian biologist at the University of Guelph, examined how patterns of courtship had changed as scientists modified the chicken to perfect it. The roosters were losing the desire for the dance.[8]

But they were not losing their desire to mate. Slowly, over the years, farmers have come to accept a growing violence in the coops: here and there, a hen clawed bloody and left for dead by a rapist rooster. The change has been gradual. Violence is like that. We become inured to it, a little bit at a time. Hasn't it always been this way?

The aberrant roosters care nothing for seducing and winning their hens; they mate only by force, slashing their victims with their spurs as they try to escape. It is a shame, yes, but farmers can tell themselves that it's just an occasional hen, and that this happens. They can count the loss against the fabulous profits that science has engineered.

Suzanne T. Millman, a student of Duncan's, earned her doctorate by investigating the reports of the broiler breeders that were turning vicious. These were not just rough-sex roosters: They were attacking and even killing hens, which lived in fear of them and congregated way up on the high slats of the poultry houses. When a hen did jump down into the common area, mobs of roosters would try to gang-rape her. The stress and injuries were hurting productivity.[9]

Millman and Duncan, who did the research on hens' mating preferences, conducted another study in 2000 that asked, basically, this: Are such roosters nastier to hens if they had a deprived peephood, or are they just nasty to them by nature? Millman and Duncan compared three types of roosters: from the broiler breeds, from the layer breeds, and from the breeds raised for cockfighting. As they grew from hatchlings, some got their fill of feed, and some were kept constantly hungry. The researchers tracked their behavior.

They found that the layer roosters tended to be kindly toward the hens, even if they never had much when they were growing up. Their hens never suffered injuries, and male and female dust-bathed and foraged together peacefully. The cockfighting types weren't mean to their hens either, go figure. Ah, but those broiler boys—they were horrid to the females, forcing themselves on them without any attempt at courtship. Even in small groups of twenty hens and two roosters, the males corralled the females into corners and attacked them, leaving gashes on the backs of their heads and deep cuts into the muscles under their wings. A hen in such a predicament struggled to get away during the deed, but, oddly, acted all indignant if her boy then went after another girl.

Roosters aren't homicidal toward hens because they had it tough growing up, the researchers concluded. Nor because they were bred to fight in the ring. It seems their killer ways abide in their genes. The ones raised to face the ax within weeks after hatching seem surly by nature, for whatever reason. Those broiler boys are just plain bad.[10]

In a similar study, Millman and Duncan investigated whether broiler breeders were mean because of hunger. Commonly, producers cut their rations to keep them lean because fat roosters have more trouble with sex, somehow, and can grow lame. Hungry roosters are sure to feel frustrated. Do they take it out on the hens? The research involved watching sundry chickens mating at various ages.[11]

The broiler roosters were the most aggressive, both with the hens and with each other. The cocks forced themselves on the females and "displayed little courtship behavior compared with laying-strain males," and doesn't a girl deserve a little romancing? And get this: Those roosters that got as much feed as they wanted turned out to be even meaner than those that got limited rations, as if they had some sort of entitlement issue. Conclusion: It's not about the feed, or a life of privation. These are just rotten roosters. Smart chicks stay away— if they can.

It's time, I think, to impose a little simple discipline on these roosters. Any rooster, of broiler stock or not, can go bad. But raise them with a little backbone, teach them a thing or two about humility, and they'll be kinder to their hens, no matter how much we've messed with their heads. Go forth and do right. No more excuses.

I like the approach of Alan Stanford, an Ohio poultry breeder who raises Silkies and Araucanas and maintains a Web site, BrownEggBlueEgg. It's good form for a rooster to strut and show off, he says, but one just cannot tolerate hen abuse, nor handler abuse. If this happens, it's time to show who's boss.

Stanford tucks a truculent rooster under his arm and carries him around as he does his chicken chores, such as cleaning the coop and feeding the hens. It might take a week or more for results. If the rooster pecks and fusses, hold him firm and ignore him. Don't show him any aggression of your own. You're above that sort of thing.

"Carrying the bird around," Stanford says, "shows I am so very big I don't even have to fight. I just win." It no doubt demonstrates something to the hens, as well. Sometimes, he invents a special tune to sing to the rooster as he scoops him up for chores. Later, upon hearing just a few bars, the rooster will scoot away, wobbling his lower beak.[12]

And there you have it. No more mean rooster. And a coopful of disdainful hens.

There is a frighteningly large body of scholarly research about chickens' sex lives out there. Based on my own perusals of the literature, it seems to me that Canadians and Scots dominate the field. Why is anyone's guess. To accomplish these studies, somebody—no doubt several people, pens in hand—stood around counting copulations.

But such is the scientific method, and no doubt it was employed to research this pressing question: Do hens lose their virginity sooner when raised in the same pen with roosters? I bring you this scholarly intrigue from the library's musty stacks. The study, reported in 1998, also comes from Canada's University of Guelph. That's where the good Dr. Duncan, a product of Scotland and a longtime leader in animal welfare issues, is a professor in the Department of Animal and Poultry Science.

In their experiment, the researchers set up two dorms for their chickens: One was coed, the other for females only. They kept them thus sequestered from earliest peephood and watched the goings-on. The hens raised with a masculine presence began laying eggs sooner, and they laid more of them. The hens also developed bigger combs (and, I'm guessing, flaunted these fleshy appendages whenever a rooster was strutting about).

And a rooster strutting about was all it took to stimulate the hens—even if they could only look and not touch. The researchers tried letting roosters circulate outside the hens-only cages, so near but yet so far, and the results were the same as in the coed coops: More eggs, laid sooner. Gets the juices flowing.

The cloistered hens, however, eventually made up for lost time and managed just as good a lay rate. The researchers also noticed an unsettling behavior among them. When a human walked past, the hens often did a "sexual crouch," suddenly squatting down as if to say, "Here I am! Do me!" The researchers started keeping statistics on the squat rate and discovered that 80 percent of hens that were denied access to roosters did the squat around humans. The hens in the coed dorms didn't bother trying to impress the humans so much, presumably because they had a rooster to keep them happy: Only 20 percent ever showed the hots for their handlers.[13]

I'm not sure I want to know what this all means. At the time I read this study, we still had roosters in the coop, and the hens had extended no such indecent invitations to me, or at least not that I'd noticed—though I soon began to imagine strange yearnings in my Araucana's lonely cluck.

It was about that same time that I carted off all our roosters to the auction. Their numbers had grown to seven, including a weary Belikan, by the autumn of '06, and the sunrise cacophony was driving me and, no doubt, much of the county to madness. I've learned to sleep through the call of one rooster. What's most annoying isn't the cock-a-doodle-do itself, but the metronomic timing. The crow comes in maddeningly precise intervals. Put two or more roosters together, and they seem to conspire to challenge the daylight coming on, as if together they might force it to submit. One crows. Then another. And a third. Then, they raise their voices together in an ungodly harmony.

At the Perkiomenville Auction, a quiet man in the ramshackle poultry shed subjected them, indelicately, to the scale and consigned each to his own crate, while a group of buddies played cards around a table, arguing and laughing about something indiscernible. Belikan and the other roosters fetched about three dollars apiece, slightly more than we'd paid for them as hatchlings.

Left to a roosterless life, the hens came to regard me in a new light. They began squatting for me. If I surprised one as I walked suddenly around a corner, she'd begin to run, but then decide to seize the moment. She'd splay her body down to the earth as she peered up and sideways at me, awaiting my dance. It's a compliment, I suppose, to be considered a surrogate cock. They are telling me, in their own way, that I command their respect. I am the dominant force in their world. I am Rooster, the provider, the protector, and they'd do anything to please me.

They'll squat just as readily for Suzanne, too, though. And they squat for our daughter Allie, a sweet-sixteen beauty who would never think of leading a chicken on. They would squat, I believe, for a sudden stirring of the breeze.

But they don't give squat for B.B. King.

That's our peacock, which I bought from a neighboring farmer in December of '06 as a Christmas present for Suzanne, who had missed Groucho since his demise the year before. I acquired a peahen for her as well—they were a mating pair that had been together for eight years, inseparable. They were raised in a chicken coop, and had never been given names.

Allie eventually named them, in March, when she and Suzanne and several of our church brothers and sisters returned from Hattiesburg, Mississippi, where they'd helped to build homes for hurricane victims through a Habitat for Humanity project. They came home raving about a barbecue joint there called Leatha's, a plywood palace that'll slow cook anything you bring in, whose motto is "B.B. King is king of the blues . . . Miss Leatha is queen of the Bar-B-Que."

Come spring, our newly procured peafowl roamed barn and pasture together: B.B. would fan his feathers with regal step, as Leatha circled him, demurely, but with rapt attention. Peahens fall for that sort of thing, and they're particularly impressed by the number of "eye" patterns gazing out from that fabulous frock.

We had hoped some peachicks were in the offing, but Leatha had vanished by May. We wondered if somewhere deep in the brush, perhaps, she was nurturing a clutch. As the weeks passed into summer, we wondered if perhaps she had nourished a fox. She never returned. Baby done gone.

Forced to improvise, B.B. took a fancy to the hens. He raised his fan, rattled his rump, and strutted toward his intended paramours, who seemed not to notice: Maybe his old coopmates had been taken in by that sort of thing, but not these chicks. Once he tried to seduce Suzanne, who ducked behind him to his blind spot and tickled his downy pouf—a surefire way to deflate a peacock's ego, and feathers, too.

B.B. turned his attention to the younger brood of pullets pecking in the pasture. He saw himself as a dashing dandy. The hens, if they bothered looking up, saw a cheaply festooned harlequin. He flared and swaggered like a Mummer marching up Broad Street amid the drunken masses on New Year's Day. One day I saw him charging the truck's chrome bumper, his feathers hoisted, ready to take on his rival.

As summer faded, so did his tail: One by one, his glorious feathers fell out and he had only a short little stub to shake. He spent long hours alone, crying out like a banshee. The racket startled my nephew Blaine. "That came from the peacock? I just assumed it was Dad goofing around." Blaine knows how my brother is.

As the weeks went by, B.B. accepted his status, but now and then, even in the night, we heard his lunatic wail. When a woman up and leaves you, it's like to drive a body to act crazy that way. It makes you want to sing the blues.

Still in his prime, B.B. has passions aplenty. He'll live to lift another tail in a new season. Only old age will cure what ails him. One day we'll have a crotchety old peacock who couldn't get it up if he had a mind to.

Scottish researchers from the Roslin Institute in Edinburgh discovered in 2000 that, oddly enough, as roosters get older they, too, woo a wee bit less wildly.[14] The study compared the sex lives of males and females at various ages. The Scots roosters, young and old, all knew the dance steps, but the elder ones had less jiggle in their jig—they mated less often. As for the hens, they didn't seem to care that they got less action from an older cock. The female responded just the same to his amorous efforts, and she made sure to lay him a good fertile egg.

Aldrovandi had seen for himself what others before him had sworn was true: Hens mounting roosters. Roosters mounting roosters. Hens mounting hens, and crowing about it. Such things happen.

Hens have "a mutual imagination of lust among themselves," Pliny asserted, explaining the origin of "wind eggs," produced without benefit of rooster. Aldrovandi begged to differ: When a hen exposes her anus to the elements, he said, she imagines she has actually been serviced; a hen can produce an egg only after she's convinced that she has conceived, he believed. And if she has no rooster, she makes do.

"One female mounts another female, as sometimes happens," he said, producing "an itching and tickling in the genital parts." Thus deluded, the hen goes off to lay her egg. Sometimes, sure, she gets that tickling from taking an innocent dust bath, he said, but mostly it's that old lesbian itch.

"The ancients handed down the view," Aldrovandi said, citing Aristotle, as well as Julius Alexandrinus, personal physician to the Holy Roman emperors, "that a woman who practices lewdness with women, or one who does not blush to perform the function of a male, or one who attempts to dominate her husband, could be understood through the hen who erects crest and tail, and from whose feet small spurs stick out.

"When she has conquered a male in a fight, as some hens do, she begins to crow and tries to step upon him in coitus." Having put him in his place, "she entices the other hens as if she were really able to perform as a male and wearies them by leaping on top of them."

Nobody, he said, should tolerate a hen with spurs—Pliny said so, Lucius Columella, too. "This is a sign of maleness," he said. Such hens are rarely able to produce chicks "since when they incubate eggs, they break them with their spur points."

It's indecent for a hen to do the crowing, he said, quoting a proverb: "It is not proper for a woman to guide the helm instead of the man, because she is not strongly endowed with greatness of soul."

Out in the provinces, Aldrovandi said, farm women considered a crowing hen to be a bad omen, and they knew the only thing to do was kill her. Zero tolerance, there. In Plutarch's day, such antics were forbidden among chickens, and the Greeks were particularly rough on same-sex rooster unions.

"For so foul and horrible a deed," Aldrovandi said, the rooster was burned alive. If the Greeks would do that to a chicken, he reasoned, imagine what they would do to a man. (And I'd imagine it's hard to run an empire without any men.) "Infamous and worthless men who commit such a crime attack the force of human nature and bring about the destruction of the race, pouring their seed upon a sterile soil."

Some roosters, he continued, "are born so effeminate they neither crow nor tread the females. Yet they suffer willingly the love-making of those who attempt to mount them." An effeminate rooster lets himself feel the hen's pain—you'll even find him sitting on her eggs for her, he added, as the Greek poet Oppian observed.

A rooster like that should be castrated, Aldrovandi said—he *chooses* to do what he does. Nobody makes him. It's not as if you can give a rooster a potion to make him run after the boys—and some have tried. "Kiranides promises that if cinaedus stone with polenta is offered to the rooster, he will become a sodomite. Let the belief in this matter rest with Kiranides."

I can't say as I know what a cinaedus stone is, or why it goes so well with polenta, or why Kiranides, the king of Persia, would have wanted to work such alchemy upon a chicken's sexual identity. I'm suspicious of the motivation behind a professed desire to create an avian sodomite.

In the modern research lab, however, scientists have performed many such tricks with chickens. A rooster that had been king of his coop lost his charisma among the hens once he was castrated and reintroduced to the flock, one study found. Other hens pushed him around, and he sank way down in the pecking order, with only some of the meeker hens still below him. Understandably, he wasn't much interested in sex anymore.

The researchers perked him up with sex hormones, and he was hot as ever—but he didn't regain his top rank. Only the meek hens would entertain him, and he gave them quite a workout. He got nowhere with the hens that had recently outranked him. They chased him away, repulsed at the idea of sex with him. Conclusion: Among chickens, a female requires a male to dominate her before she'll accept him sexually. It seems that once a male loses rank, he's finished.[15]

As early as the Depression, researchers were having fun with prolactin, a female sex hormone common to many species. It's the one that makes a pregnant woman's breasts swell with milk, that makes birds gather twigs for a nest. Inject a hen with prolactin, and she soon becomes broody, staying in her nest box and insisting on trying to hatch eggs, real or imagined. Inject a rooster with prolactin, and, wouldn't you know, he does the same thing; he will even take over hen duties, nurturing and mothering the chicks.[16]

Imagine: Fathers actually taking care of their children, rather than just breeding and bolting and leaving it to the mother to raise them right. I know some men who could use a prolactin injection, with a king-size needle, in an appropriate spot.

In 1935, scientists also isolated the pure form of testosterone, the male sex hormone, the stuff that makes men grow beards and notice curves. To learn what wonders such a potent substance might produce, researchers tried injecting it into hens after removing their ovaries. The hens became more aggressive—from the testosterone, the researchers presumed, though I imagine the needles and scalpels weren't exactly cause for mirth. Souped up on male hormones, the hens rose in rank, some from bottom to top.[17]

Whether they started to crow, I can't say. I've never heard any of our own hens crow. But neither had I ever seen them squat for me until they got desperate, so I imagine this experience awaits me.

A backyard chicken farmer heard a crow while collecting eggs one morning near Bristol, England, in 2006. Odd, since there was no rooster in the coop. The farmer turned to see a hen, looking guilty— it was the same hen he'd noticed had mysteriously begun to grow a scarlet comb. For eight months she'd been a good layer but then had begun jousting with the roosters. She even tried to mount the girls with whom she once nested. The farmer renamed her Freaky.[18]

In 1954, a Canadian farmer took his hen—or what used to be his hen—to the Alberta veterinary laboratory.[19] He complained that the eighteen-month-old Leghorn had stopped laying eggs and, worse, two days earlier had taken to crowing. The good folks at the lab forthwith killed it (as they do in the provinces) and conducted a postmortem. Prominent comb, wattles, hackles. Looked like a rooster, all right. Upon further digging, they discovered what they believed was wrong. The chicken had a diseased ovary. As happens in cases of certain rare ovarian tumors documented in humans, the ovary had begun secreting male hormones. The girl had become boyish, though not quite a sodomite.

Spontaneous sex reversals do happen, but they're quite rare, according to a report from poultry specialists at the University of

Florida. The reversals are invariably of the female-to-male variety. The chicken remains a hen genetically, but it looks and acts like a rooster.

Here's what happens: Hens have only one functional ovary, the left one; the other is a shrunken, residual one. If a cyst or tumor damages the left ovary, the residual tissue in the right ovary some-times regenerates. The tissue may be ovarian or testicular in nature, or both. This newly energized gonad may secrete androgen as well as estrogen. The hen soon may notice a surge of affection for its sisters it never felt before. There are reports, the specialists said, of semen production, though most such hens will not father offspring, nor ever lay an egg again. They are in sexual limbo.[20]

I have to wonder, though, about the few who do manage to father offspring. It was long my understanding that a penis is useful for sex. I would expect that a rooster not only possess a penis, but that it be commensurate with his romantic reputation.

I will tell you now: He doesn't really have a penis. The cock, of all creatures, lacks one.

A rooster, of course, would deny this, and he does have a little button thing that might qualify. It's true that roosters are better en-dowed than other birds—which isn't saying much, because a lot of birds have no penis whatsoever. Both the male and female have an opening called the cloaca, which, when worked up, they press to-gether briefly for the transfer of sperm.[21] This may account for why the rooster is able to perform repeatedly and recover quickly, mas-terfully wielding his little button. Though his way might not sound like Casanova's way, it would appear he has more fun than, say, a worm, which couples with itself while mired in the muck, or the soli-tary fish fantasizing in his spawning bed, alone in the dark.

In his disdain for gay and lesbian chickens, Aldrovandi minced no words. Whether they were born that way, under the influence of hormones, or tainted by tumors, it was all turpitude to him. He seemed, however, to reserve an even greater contempt for birds that fancied other species. Our ever-hopeful B.B. King, who each day makes the rounds of the hens hoping one will succumb to the charms of his regal raiment, would have been quickly banished from Aldrovandi's villa.

The master's primary argument for the impropriety of inter-species sex was that Aristotle had said so. A gay rooster is bad enough, but "far more detestable" and utterly disgraceful is one so lost in lust that he "cohabits with other birds who are not of his genus, such as the pheasant and partridge," Aldrovandi wrote, citing the man. He did offer a spin, however: He blamed the females for allowing such a thing. "Perhaps this is to be regarded rather as the fault of the hens because they permit themselves to be trodden by these same birds to such an extent that they bid fair to hatch out a different progeny."

I shudder to think what Aldrovandi and his Aristotle, if only they knew, would do to my dear Araucanas, whose Chilean ancestors got it on with the local pheasants, or so the theory goes. To this day their progeny lay lovely blue and green eggs, evidence of the pheasant philandering.

An Araucana keeper in California suspected something was afoot when she began finding her prize hens drowned in an old bathtub she kept in the coop.[22] The prime suspect was a duck named Hansel who also lived in the coop. That was why the tub was there, installed at floor level: It was a swimming hole for Hansel and his mate, named (get ready) Gretel.

The backyard farmer had bought them together from a nearby breeder, who herself had housed the pair with chickens since they were ducklings. Within a few weeks, the breeder, Lisa Jansen Mathews of Far Out Farms in Nevada City, got a call from the ducks' new owner: "Would you take these things back, please? I don't even want my money back. They've got to go!"

Hansel had been murdering her Araucanas. The resident rooster, trying to protect his hens, had consequently been trying to murder Hansel. Unhappy times had befallen the coop. Mathews graciously welcomed the duck duo back to her farm.

Gretel, it seems, had taken ill after moving to her new digs. Hansel, distraught that his lover no longer desired to share amorous evenings in the sunken tub ("not tonight, dear"), had surveyed his options. He saw chickens.

Hansel had been raised with chickens and thought he knew something about chicken ways, the funny duck. But there was a detail that had escaped him: Chickens can't swim. He had nonetheless compelled them, one by one, to join him in the Jacuzzi.

Back at her farm, Mathews had a little talk with him. He needed to spend time by himself until he'd forgotten the whole ill-begotten idea and until Gretel was well enough to consort with him once more. But let's not come down too hard on Hansel. It might seem an unnatural act for a duck to try to do a hen, but it was what came quite naturally to him, considering his upbringing.

Something similar had happened before, right there on Far Out Farms—and if Mathews can tell two such tales, then either she's a good tale-teller or else such intrigue is playing out every day on a farm somewhere. Out on the pond one morning, the first rays of sunlight revealed something floating amid the ripples. A hen, drowned. The next morning, two more, and as the bodies mounted, it was clear a serial killer was at work.

This time the suspect was a goose named Clyde. He was a newcomer to the farm, having been brought there by his first owner, who had found it unsettling when Clyde, as he started to mature, began attacking her little boy. The boy found it unsettling, as well.

Clyde had a secret. He had been raised with chickens. They'd been together since their hatchery days. They ate together, foraged together, slept together in the same coop. Clyde and the girls. It was the life he knew.

Goslings become ganders as the seasons pass—big geese with big-goose urges. When he arrived at Far Out Farms, Clyde beheld all the possibilities and decided to play the field. Or in his case, the pond. He began escorting the hens one by one on moonlit excursions across the lake, where, not being proper geese, they drowned.[23]

Clyde's perversion, like Hansel's, had begun so innocently, on the day he arrived with the chicks from the hatchery.

It's called imprinting. It's a form of instant learning that happens in many animals, even humans, they say, but it's a classic characteristic among ducks and chickens and geese and other birds that leave the nest soon after hatching. The first moving thing they see, they'll follow, eager to learn worldly ways. Ordinarily, that's mama. Or a duck may see a hen—mama! A chicken sees the coop keeper—mama! A goose sees a bearded zoologist—mama! Some theorize that fetishes arise from the imprinting of inanimate objects: An infant sees a pair of stilettos—whoa, mama!

Konrad Lorenz (1903–1989), a bearded zoologist from Austria, studied the phenomenon extensively among geese.[24] Some considered his research tainted by Nazi sympathies (the Reich would not have been aghast at the concept of early racial stamping), but late in life he wrote that if mankind were to survive, we needed to choose our mates solely on the kindness in their hearts—hardly a genocidal sentiment.

Lorenz discovered a thirty-six-hour critical period after hatching in which the gosling was vulnerable to being led astray. And Lorenz did lead them far astray: His goslings imprinted on various stimuli, including Lorenz himself (they seemed enthralled with his tall boots, the devils) and baby carriages, which as grown geese they found particularly alluring, much to the apprehension of Viennese mothers strolling in the park.

Birds have been known to imprint on hang gliders. Eagles and cranes raised in captivity have learned the ways of the wild by following a glider as it rides the thermals. The 1996 movie *Fly Away Home* tells a tale, based on fact, of orphaned Canada geese learning their migratory route by following an ultralight plane.

Sexual imprinting apparently led to Clyde's and Hansel's problems. Each had fulfilled the theory that a young animal learns what "sexy" is by observing those it first encounters, particularly the one who raises it. I may never feel comfortable in the coop again.

In Clyde's case, his brain got the "chicken" imprimatur. In his world, the chicken was the image of Mother. She was Comforter. She was Provider. And, somehow, more. He began to see his coopmates in a new way as his hormones surged. Feeling aggressive, or frisky, at first he had taken it out on the boy. When that earned him a transfer, he took it out on the hens.

Hansel's predilections were more complex. He did have his Gretel. He knew the pleasures of duck. But with all those chickens pecking about when he was just a duckling, he had entertained secret desires that he had never shared with Gretel. When she became incapacitated, his fantasies flew—or, rather, drowned.

Mysteries solved.

Suzanne knows how it feels to be wooed by another species. She has owned many peacocks. Her first, Bellocq, named after the renowned photographer of New Orleans prostitutes, found her irresistible. He would roost on the fence outside her bedroom. He would try to peek in the bathroom window to catch a glimpse of his beloved in her natural state, and he would be waiting for her when she left the house. He would then follow her to the barn, displaying his feathers for her, as if to say, "Pick *me*, choose *me*, love *me!*"

As he was mooning over her one day, a man came to rent a horse stall, and he and Suzanne began talking and laughing. He wore a cowboy hat with a spray of fancy feathers on the front. The next day, Bellocq lay in wait and barreled into him like a cannonball. As this continued day by day, the burly wrangler took to clutching a pitchfork, in fear of the peacock.

Suzanne knew Bellocq had to go. As she called to make arrangements, her lovelorn peacock secretly listened at the window. On the day she was to take him to his reward, she found him already dead, way out at the end of the lane, hit by a truck. He had hurled himself into peril. His lover was sending him away.

It's tempting to imagine how an animal feels and compare its behavior with our own. I'm guilty of it. But Aesop also did it, and Chaucer. So did Aldrovandi, and likewise many thinkers of antiquity. Today, pop psychologists and sociologists spout specious profundities as they measure us against the species, tracing the evolution of behavior.

People are not animals, though, for the most part. If we have animal impulses, our responsibility is to rise above them, not revel in them as we make excuses for why we're acting like jackasses, or pigs, or weasels, or worse.

And chickens, lest we forget, are not people. They don't look like people, necessarily, nor act much like people, and they generally don't think like people. We therefore have no reason to conclude that the raft of research papers involving chicken behavior, particularly as it relates to their sexual peccadilloes, offers any insight into human behavior. In many of the scholarly studies, the focus is on improving poultry productivity and profits, not on finding the roots of our primal impulses.

Whether fish or chicken or three-toed sloth, animals do their thing in many different ways, and their ways are not ours. Consider the sex life of the stickleback fish, in which the female requires proof of good fatherhood. That would seem refreshing, were it not utterly weird. The male builds his nest to lure a female. If she sees eggs in the nest, she'll add her own, and swim away. Done with her, he scoots back inside, spills semen, and happily cleans house till the eggs hatch. But rival males, desperate to appear masculine, may steal his eggs to make their own nests more attractive. It's what the ladies require. The males of other species grow appendages around their heads that look like fish larvae, so sexy, or develop fake egg clusters on their fins.[25]

Murderous, deceitful, goofy: We can't predict how a man or a woman will act based on how animals act. We only know we can be far stranger. No beast could match our depths of malevolence, or heights of benevolence. We are capable of great good and great evil. Animals are capable of neither.

Chicken Noodle

><

As I watch the cultured crowds letting out after recitals at the Kimmel Center on Philadelphia's Avenue of the Arts, I see many a tight waistcoat stretching around the belly of someone exposed to classical music.

I may be on to something here. Because I can't resist the temptation to apply principles discovered in research to human affairs, here's my theory: What we've learned about chickens just might explain the preponderance of portly classical-music buffs, as well as the emaciated, hollow-eyed look sometimes observed among habitués of rock concerts.

Chickens gain weight faster when exposed to soft music, particularly classical, a researcher determined a generation ago in a study at Cornell University in Ithaca, New York. They also have a lower mortality rate. Loud rock music, he said, would have the opposite effect.

The researcher, Gadi Gvaryahu, an animal psychologist, had noticed what music does to chickens while he was a graduate student in Israel at Hebrew University. A poultry farmer nearby had reported his chickens were insisting on congregating in one corner of their pen and wouldn't budge. Gvaryahu investigated. The farmer had kept a radio playing in the corner; when it was moved, the chickens followed.

In his 1987 study at Cornell, Gvaryahu piped music into a pen of hatchlings for twelve hours a day (in an alternating pattern of an hour on, an hour off), seven days a week, and kept it going for eight weeks, which is how long it takes to raise a broiler.

He chose Vivaldi's *The Four Seasons*. The rhythm and dynamics of the Italian baroque composer's work are just what chickens dig, he explained. He said nothing about whether *Peter and the Wolf* would be appropriate punishment should the chickens not respond.

As they got into the seventeenth-century groove, the researcher reported, the chickens thrived. They also enjoyed other "environmental enrichment" tricks such as red mittens hung near the chicks—next best thing to mama.

During the eight weeks, the birds averaged a weight gain of 2 percent more than a control group's gain, he reported, and also had a lower mortality rate. At the time, he estimated an annual savings for the broiler industry nationwide of $57 million. Cornell forthwith sought a patent, recognizing the sobering implications of this discovery.[26]

It was there we had our chance. It was our opportunity to develop a worldwide society of highbrow chickens. We could have tried to make up for the things we've done to them.

Off came the rooster's head, but he kept running—and Lloyd Olsen couldn't catch him, so he put away his ax. "No chicken dinner tonight," he told his wife, Clara.

Next morning, September 11, 1945, Olsen was dumbfounded to find the poor beheaded creature milling about in his Fruita, Colorado, yard. Feeling a surge of compassion, he asked Clara to fetch him an eyedropper, mixed a little grain and water, snuck up on the rooster (easy enough), and held him tight while dribbling the feed down what remained of his gullet.

The Wyandotte rooster not only lived, but thrived. He gained weight, kept his balance on a perch, even tried to preen his feathers and peck the ground with the beak that wasn't there. The world must learn of this miracle, Olsen declared, and he took the rooster on a national sideshow tour. Step right up, folks, and see Mike the Head-less Chicken.

Suzanne related this Ripleyesque tale to me as we drove home from New Hampshire, where we had visited our friends Bill and Lori. She said Bill told her about it. I snickered.

"You don't believe Bill? He's not the sort to make up such a thing. He said it's absolutely true."

"Suzanne, it's probably like a game of tag. If you fall for this crock, you're 'it' until you find somebody else who swallows it."

She scoffed. But a half hour later, when Alexandra awoke in the backseat, Suzanne began earnestly telling her the story of Mike the Headless Chicken—"No, really, he lived, your mama wouldn't lie to you." Allie fluffed her pillow and went back to sleep.

No, really, friends, it's the true story of Mike the Headless Chicken. Since 1999, his hometown of Fruita has honored him with an annual festival that has included such events as the Run Like a Headless Chicken Race; a peep-eating contest, of the marshmallow kind; and Chicken Bingo, in which numbers are chosen by where droppings land on a grid. This, too, is true, all of it.

You can find numerous references to Mike in such sources as *The Guinness Book of World Records, The New York Times,* and *Life* maga-zine, which a month after the beheading ran a photo spread and the inside story, deep inside: "Headless Rooster—Beheaded Chicken Lives Normally After Freak Decapitation by Ax."

For a quarter, sideshow gawkers throughout the West got a good look at Mike, who raked in as much as $4,500 a month. Other farm-ers, hoping to cash in, sharpened their axes and tried to create their own headless rooster. None of the copycats lived more than several days. Mike survived about eighteen months, until the spring of 1947, when he suffocated on his esophageal mucus in a Phoenix motel room while on tour. Olsen searched for the syringe he used to clear Mike's throat, but he'd left it at the last stop.

A postmortem found that the ax had chopped precisely right to allow the chicken to survive. Olsen had aimed high—his mother-in-law liked neck meat, so he tried to leave a little extra—and his blow missed the jugular vein, leaving one ear. He'd lopped off the head but left the brain stem.

The rest of a chicken's brain, it seems, doesn't much matter.[27]

Which is why, perhaps, chickens are purported to be easily hypnotized. The illustrious Al Gore, who came within a few Floridian votes of becoming President of the United States and De Facto Leader of the Free World, told us all about it on *60 Minutes*. Later, on a televised chat with Regis Philbin, he elaborated that he learned as a child how to pin a chicken to the ground with one hand while using the other to encircle its head with a stick. Others who are experienced in this practice suggest tracing a line with a finger back and forth in front of the beak.

Such rhythmic motions jam the chicken's circuits, mesmerizing it so that it stays in place even when you remove your hand—or so say those inclined to do such a thing. I tried this at home (more than once, I'm afraid). *The Old Farmer's Almanac* suggests a variety of methods, but no matter which I tried, I failed. Each time, the hen jumped up and shook her feathers, as if my palm were a surrogate rooster, and not a particularly entrancing one. I washed my hands of the whole unseemly affair.

I did hit upon one hypnosis technique that seemed to work: Hold the chicken securely, positioning its head gently between thumb and forefinger so it is forced to meet your eyes. Lean close as you intone, "You are . . . now . . . a chicken." Say it twice, then release your grip. Results are immediate.

Some folks do claim that through traditional techniques they can zonk a chicken for up to half an hour. What's going on, I suspect, is a freeze instinct. The poor critter fears it's about to be killed, and so it feigns death hoping the wagging finger will lose interest and go away, just as the voting public tends to do.

Chickens and such just might be smarter than Al Gore thinks. Consider the case of Lily, the tic-tac-toe chicken of Chinatown. She lived in a cage amid pinball machines in a Manhattan amusement arcade for *four decades,* which would make her longevity as astounding as her perspicacity. A sign near her cage presented the fifty-cent challenge: "Bird Brain. Can you beat this bird?"

She never seemed to lose a game. When it was her turn, she pecked at a tic-tac-toe grid inside the cage. A computer program took over from there, translating her peck, wherever it landed, into a logical move that appeared on an indicator board.

When she died in 1993, the arcade owner conceded there had been a succession of Lilys, or Willys, and complained that a chicken trained to peck on cue cost over $1,000. It was chicken abuse, said animal rights activists, who campaigned to scuttle the Chinatown game, which had been featured in tourist guides to the Big Apple. In 1998, Lily was replaced by a robot chicken that laid plastic eggs with prizes inside.[28]

Lily was smarter than the robot chicken. I can say that categorically. She was a living creature, and somewhere north of her neck she had a swollen spot of nervous tissue called a brain.

Who gives the rooster the wisdom, God asked his servant Job, to discern when to crow at the approach of day? The Rev. Dixon, in his nineteenth-century writings on poultry history, declared that, yes, a creative power had produced the original jungle fowl.

He theorized, however, that modern domestic chickens might have resulted from interbreeding with relatives of other species, such as the grouse—and the dodo bird.[29] The long-gone dodo stood three feet tall, big and dumb as a bird can come, or so it was said. If those sleek little jungle tarts were having their fun with the big boy while he lasted, they weren't exactly advancing the cause of rooster wisdom.

In the years since the parson's speculations, chickens have no doubt gained in girth and receded in sense. But the dodo didn't do it. We did. God indeed gave the rooster discernment, but ever since, his smartest creation, of the genus *Homo,* species *sapiens*—meaning, when translated from the Latin, *the wise guy*—has been working diligently to take it away.

At Oregon State University, researchers polled faculty and students to find out whether they thought animals had minds and the ability to think, and how they ranked animals in relative intelligence when comparing cats, chickens, cows, dogs, horses, pigs, sheep, and turkeys.

In general, the respondents maintained that animals do have thinking minds, though those studying and teaching animal science and zoology were considerably less likely to believe so. When asked to rank the animals in intelligence, the participants all responded similarly, no matter their field of study. The dog was smartest, they said, then the cat, followed by the pig, horse, cow, sheep, chicken, and turkey.[30]

I'd put the pig first. Something in Sophie's eyes tells me that what's behind them is capable of outsmarting me. She anticipates, plots, and strategizes ways to finagle food from Suzanne and me, the chickens, and the garbage can, and when caught she feigns innocence in the wagging of her curly tail. And in her eyes I see something else: sadness, and fear.

Sophie, a Vietnamese potbelly, came to us from a nearby pig rescue farm that arranges adoptions. She had been found roaming the streets in North Philadelphia—perhaps that explains her affinity for Suzanne, who knows what that's like. How Sophie got there we don't know, but on her left flank she has a series of long scars. She was hit by a car, I thought, but the lines are straight and parallel. A knife blade? Sophie lacks the exuberance of some pigs. She's cautious about the world. She remembers abuse, if you ask me, but then, I don't have a zoology degree.

Most of those in the Oregon State survey believed animals should be treated humanely, though they conceded that mind, thought, and intelligence were relevant in that regard. And that makes sense to me: I give not a thought to whether the worm on my hook likes the water, not to mention body piercing. But I consider what happened to Sophie the cruelest of cuts.

It's hard to know what to make of the fact that those who had studied animals were less likely to deem them intelligent. A study from the University of Edinburgh made a similar finding: It took a look at the attitudes of veterinary students at two British universities over the course of three years of their schooling. The female students in the surveys (published in 2000) thought of themselves as more empathetic toward animals than the men did, and kept that empathy throughout their years of study, whereas the men began to lose what little empathy they started with. Overall, the longer the veterinary students had been in school, the less smart they considered animals to be.[31]

This may be a case of familiarity breeding contempt. I grew up around cows. Unlike those who ranked them high on the relative intelligence list, I'd place them well below the turkey, though I understand why the turkey would be last. The bovine head is mostly bone, and greed motivates the meager matter within. A cow in a stanchion with a generous pile of grain in front of it will stretch its neck and tongue to steal the grain from the cow beside it. As it does so, its own bounty is being lapped up by its equally covetous neighbor as they cross their straining necks.

Come to think of it, I've seen people do that—meaning either cows should be elevated closer in rank to human intelligence, or vice versa.

The chicken's brain, however, is indeed adroit, comparable to a dog's or cat's, according to some experts, whose own brains remain unranked. Chickens can remember dozens of faces in their pecking order, and they have a heart that nurtures and protects. I've seen behaviors that are playful, curious, deceitful, and loyal. I watch daily as one of my Rhode Island Reds sneaks away from the brood to rob the feeder on our back-porch rabbit hutch; she comes alone, guarding her secret. After a long winter, she picked up her vice again in the spring.

But mostly, chickens live by instinct—roosting, mating, mothering—and these behaviors demonstrate the collective intelligence of the flock, and, many would say, of the hand that created them.

God must often see his people behaving much like chickens, who learn early where they're unwanted, and go there. But chickens lack the brains to be truly contrarian: Once they find a routine, they'll faithfully follow it until distracted to another way. Train them in the way they should go, and their wanton ways they'll soon forget. Within minutes, sometimes. Give them a coop, lead them into it a time or two, and they won't know how not to retreat there.

If a chicken manages to make it across the road, it might be following the sun: Research has suggested that chickens, like migratory birds, use it to navigate, even when traveling just a few feet. Modern scientists, like ancient thinkers, have concluded that the chicken knows celestial matters.

Christine J. Nicol, a professor at the University of Bristol, England, and her colleagues set up an outdoor maze in which a chicken could only find food by going north. They made sure the chickens had no cues other than the sun to determine which way that was, and they regularly altered the maze. The chickens couldn't smell the food, see the landscape, or communicate. They consistently found their way in the right direction, the 2003 study discovered. They have an internal compass that apparently can compensate for the hour of the day.[32]

Chickens can learn not only quickly but also indirectly, through observation, according to Nicol. It's easy to train a chicken to press a button to open a door for food; it learns to choose, say, a red or green button as the correct one to get its reward. Experiments have found that other chickens, when allowed to watch this behavior, are much quicker to get the right button themselves when given the opportunity. The best "teacher" is a hen that is socially dominant and has the mothering instinct—the tendency to go broody.

But when hens watch a rooster trying to do the button trick, they don't learn much at all. For one thing, the rooster takes longer to figure out what to do, though he eventually masters it. And the rooster, Nicol speculated, may display other attributes that the hens find more interesting than his intellectual prowess.[33]

Though chickens clearly demonstrate that they have a remarkable noggin, any farmer, watching them peck through the manure pile in the rain, sometimes wonders if they're sentient at all. The domestication of *Gallus gallus* has not enhanced its wits. We have tried to build a better chicken, but we have not attended to its brain.

Evolutionary biologist Jared Diamond of the University of California in Los Angeles and colleague Sue Jackson compared various organs of the modern factory-line broiler chicken with those of the close descendents of its wild ancestor, the jungle fowl. After careful disassembly, weighing, and measuring, they made some predictable observations: The broiler's legs were scrawnier. Its small intestine was three times as massive. And its brain was significantly smaller.[34]

The researchers pointed out that breeders, selecting the genetic lines that would give them the fattest products as quickly as possible, chose chickens that put their energy into what was important: brawn, not brains. This new creation was greedier by nature and developed innards that could process all that extra feed. Standing around in a cage and pecking incessantly at a trough require little leg power, or brain power—a production chicken doesn't need wiles for the wild.

We decided it wasn't dumb enough to begin with and gave it some help. All the better to eat you, my dear.

Spend much time around chickens, and occasionally you'll see two hens standing head to head, as if sharing some delicious confidence. If you witness this, according to an old saw, it means somebody is gossiping about you.[35]

Chickens do communicate remarkably well. Through history, careful observers have heard their voices. A hen's distinct call after laying an egg was variously described by the ancients as cackling, or sobbing, or a shrill cry. Some said it was grieving. Or it was crying in pain from the cold air rushing into where the egg had come out. The same wind that brought those tickling thrills to the hen's eagerly up-lifted anus was quite a pain there, too, it would seem. Ill-begotten pleasures often end that way.

A German researcher, Dr. Erich Baeumer, spent hours recording and evaluating cackles and peeps and clucks. This country doctor from Weidenau told *Time* magazine in 1964 that he had grown up playing in a chicken yard, learning to imitate their sounds, and while in medical school had kept chickens in his garden and communed with them there. "They became brothers and sisters to me."

He began experimenting with them, raising some to believe he was their mother, and others in complete isolation. No matter: The rooster always learned to crow just right, the hen clucked for her peeps the same way, whatever the breed.

Baeumer teamed with a behavioral researcher and began recording the chickens' voices. They always spoke the same universal language made up of about thirty sentences uttered by chickens of every breed. He identified the peep's call to its mama and its cry of panic; the hen's clamor after laying an egg, which means, "Where is everybody?"; the rooster's battle alert and the soft cluck by which he rounds up the hens.[36]

Australian researchers, as well, identified the rooster's common *took-took-took* utterance as a food call to his hens. In the hens' minds the sound creates an image of the feed he offers, and they rush over to him, sometimes accepting it directly from his beak. The researchers, Chris and Linda Evans at Macquarie University in Sydney, played various recorded calls for a group of hens. Only the *took* sound, of the proper pitch, put them in feeding mode. The implication is that *took* is a word. It was functioning similarly to language.[37]

In some of their latest research, the couple discovered that hens utter distinct calls for particular kinds of food. Regular rations, for example, prompt a standard call, but when they find a goody such as corn, the call changes in rate and pitch. Upon hearing a call for food, hens start scratching to find it, but only if the call imparts new information. They ignore repeat calls for food they've recently been eating. They seem to be thinking, "So what else is new?"[38]

From time to time, news reports tell of feral children raised with chickens. A mentally deficient woman in Portugal, for example, locked her daughter, Isabel Quaresma, into the coop soon after birth, raising her on bread and chicken feed. In 1980, when Isabel was ten, a worker at a local hospital rescued her. She was placed in a Lisbon institution for the profoundly handicapped. The girl behaved like the chickens, flapping her arms in excitement, scratching at her food. And when she was alarmed, she squawked. She had learned their lingo.[39]

Seamus Heaney, the Irishman who won the 1995 Nobel Prize in Literature, reflected upon such a soul in his poem "Bye-Child," about Kevin Halfpenny, a seven-year-old whose mother had kept him since birth in the henhouse, on the far side of the garden. I weep for Kevin, wracked with rickets, cowering behind burlaped windows. Discovered by neighborhood boys and taken to a shelter, he perched on his cot and cawed like a hen. He should have been shooting marbles with them on sunny sidewalks. They should have called him Kev.

The world, wrote William Butler Yeats, another of the great Irish poets, is more full of weeping than we can understand.

Each night, upon closing up the coop, I hear from the roosts an inquisitive chorus of *brooook?* It means "whassup?" or perhaps "Are you here to kill me?" My Marans from France sound the same as my Welsumers from Holland. They all know the same words. Nobody taught them. Were I raised among the chickens, I imagine that I, too, would speak a universal language of maybe thirty expressions, such as "Eh?" and "Argh!" and "Eek!"—and, when my hen drew near, "Mmm."

Each chicken knows its place from peephood, and keeps it. Early on, chickens exhibit clear differences; some are bold, some meek, some dominant, some submissive. In the coop, they establish an austere social system, often violent, not unlike some human ones. This is the pecking order: It's a structure they instinctively accept, and it works.

The primacy of the pecking order makes it difficult to introduce immature pullets to a flock of older hens, which pick on the newcomers—sometimes fatally. Chickens, for all their maternal talents, can be nasty critters that pick favorites and peck the less fortunate. Still, there are proven ways to help them get along, as most parents know. Take things slow, give them plenty of room, don't accept nonsense.

And as far as possible, let them work things out for themselves. Those allowed to explore the world freely are less likely to feel the slash and peck of others trying to prove themselves. Tensions arise between generations, of course, and siblings have their rivalries. But it's only when they're cooped up, unable to get away, that the need to show who's boss becomes a problem.

The pecking order is intrinsically chicken. It was the way of life for the Red Jungle Fowl, father of the chicken diaspora, and therefore is deeply rooted in all descendents. Roosters and hens in the

Gallus gallus order each have their own rankings, which they begin establishing by sparring a week after hatching and settle by eight weeks. They raise head and tail in the presence of an inferior. To signal submission to a superior, they lower head and tail, tilt the head, and squat—as they do for me, but no thank you. The top cock has a range of influence of sixty to seventy feet, research has shown, and hens are prohibited from fighting within ten feet of him. When he dies, the number-two cock is promoted immediately.[40]

When strange new birds suddenly enter the flock—which would be weird in the wild but is common in the coop—the birds fuss and fight until they decide where the interlopers best fit in the order. Once they've been shown their place, stability prevails again and life is secure in the harem. It's not necessarily the smartest ones that climb their way to the top, researchers at Oregon State University reported in 2006. Other qualities, which the study didn't address, matter more.[41]

As I watch my flock, it's clear to me that so much depends on the quality of leadership and family values—that is, the values of the polygamous family. That's the type sanctioned by chickens, as well as by most societies throughout world history. (That's a tidbit I read recently in *The New York Times*,[42] and as Aristotle was to Aldrovandi, so *The New York Times* is to many journalists, for better or worse.)

A good, vigilant rooster summons his hens before he partakes of food. He fends off other roosters before they partake of his hens. He tells the world that the sun is about to rise, lest it not. Aldrovandi noticed what I, too, have often seen: A rooster will lower his head whenever he enters a door. Maybe it's to protect his comb, as the master suggested. I like to think the rooster is showing a touch of humility, deference toward those to whom he has nothing to prove.

A bad rooster abuses his hens and claws up their backs as he satisfies himself. He turns tail when challenged. He fails to provide for his charges. All his crowing, which seems to offer security, turns out to be a false promise; he looks out mostly for himself.

Like a man, a rooster either has character, or lacks it.

And not every pullet becomes a good mother hen. Certain hens clamber into the nest box just long enough to do their daily plop and they're off and pecking. Egg farmers love this sort of female, for she doesn't waste time and money on motherhood. A chicken such as this, if she does manage to hatch peeps, doesn't teach them well; she leaves them to fend for themselves as she preens and squats and attends to her own tail.

Other hens regularly retreat to the nest box and linger there, plaintively wishing to keep a clutch of eggs so they can become a mother, their heart's desire. They begin to waste away as they pine for peeps for a full cycle of the moon, after which they either devote themselves to their new brood or venture back to the roosts in resignation and wait to try again.

Once a hen gets her way, the bond of motherhood starts early. Even inside the eggshell, an unhatched peep begins to learn the language of chickendom, a research team from the City University of New York discovered. For four years, the team turned an eighth-floor lab into a high-tech chicken coop. In the two days before hatching, hen and embryo communicate, according to the scientists, who identified eleven calls.

Seven of those calls came from within the egg. Among them: a high-pitched distress peep, a screech signaling capture, a pleasure twitter, a feeding patter, and a huddle call to mama. From the hens, the scientists identified four vocalizations: a cluck for comforting, a food call, an intruder alarm, and an alert to unexpected situations. In the experiments, when a hen clucked, the embryo twittered in response. When the embryo screeched, the hen offered comfort till it stopped. A hen's alarm call got an alarmed answer from the egg.

Previous studies had found that unhatched peeps made sounds; the new research learned that the hens talked back. Thus begins the imprinting by which the hatchling recognizes its own kind, and particularly its mother, a developing bond so crucial to survival.[43]

And crucial, as well, to something that we humans might call self-esteem. The researchers compared peeps that had been incubated artificially with those hatched naturally and found that the ones that had a mother hovering over them in their egg days were quicker to adjust to the world and more secure about leaving the nest.

It would seem that encouraging and caring words, coming early and often from a parent who listens, are the best prescription for well-rounded chickens. There might be a lesson of value there for us, too.

FALL

A Season to Collect

I found Aldrovandi nodding by a dying fire in his library, with a book slipping from his lap, as he cradled his hen. He straightened and turned in his chair to greet me. The chair faced an open window overlooking the garden of Sampolo and the mountains beyond. Together we watched the last of a bright evening leaving the Apennines, the russet of beech and chestnut turning fast to gray. A breeze caught a wisp of his hair. The fire now was out.

"I have something for you here. Suzanne sent them. They're from our garden." I lit a candle on the table and opened a grocery bag, spilling five tomatoes onto the table. Aldrovandi sent his hen fluttering to the windowsill and struggled to his feet to inspect my gift.

"This one's an Oxheart," I said, pointing. "And this one is named Hillbilly Potato Loaf." He picked one up and held it inches from his eyes, running his thumb over its skin. His heir's heirs would still be centuries shy of these heirlooms. Italy was just awakening to the possibilities of the tomato.

"Golden apples? They are beautiful—but this one's red," he said, "and this one nearly black. They are from the New World?"

"They're from my world, yes," I said. "From yours, too, they're from all over." I reached into my pocket. "And here . . ." I held in my palm another gift from Lilyfield, the finest egg my hens could lay, large and lavender. "This is for you, too."

Aldrovandi accepted the egg and smiled, remarking just how lovely was the dye, but it was the tomato that still held him. He turned it in his hand, inspecting each flaw in its flesh, gently squeezing it, this new kind of eggplant from far across the sea.

"I should so much like to go there," he said.

"Ulisse, just a few steps through your gate . . ."

"I wanted to go, you know. I told them what they should look for. We should take good men, I said, men with the sharpest of eyes. And I would lead the way. But they wanted something else, not me, not then."

He turned to the window, gazing southward down the valley rolling toward the mountains and, beyond, Florence. "They asked me later if I would like to come along on one of their trips," he said, "but I didn't know if I'd make it. I'm an old man. It's harder now to see . . ."

"When was this?" I asked.

"It was half a lifetime ago that I still dreamed of an expedition. And when they asked me at last, my colleagues from Bologna—that must be twenty years gone, now. I told them no, that I was too frail, that I wouldn't survive it. It was best."

He set the tomato on the table and eased himself into his chair. "They brought me back so much."

I looked at him. Aldrovandi, at age twelve, had left for Rome, so very far from home, without money, telling no one, to learn what might be there. His father, a notary and secretary to the Senate of Bologna, had died when Ulisse was six, and his mother, a woman of noble blood whose cousin would become Pope Gregory XIII, had brought in tutors to educate her children. She fetched young Ulisse home from Rome and placed him with a merchant to learn about accounting and international commerce.

But at sixteen, he was gone again: He joined a band of pilgrims who set off for Santiago, Spain, and onward to *de finibus terrae*—the "end of the world"—where he stood high upon the rocks gazing westward to the sea. "I turned around," he wrote in his memoirs, "because I could not go forward any further." He told of seeing the serpents. On his return trip, he wrote, he was shipwrecked with his fellow pilgrims and pursued by pirates, who killed three of them. He grabbed an oar and rowed for his life. The boy had a sense of adventure.

When the youthful Ulisse finally returned from the high seas to the arms of his dismayed mother, he found himself the head of the household; his older brothers had died. He heeded her wishes and decided he'd seen enough perils, settling down to the scholar's life. But it wasn't money he wanted most, it was the world of nature and ideas, and he had much to see. He made other pilgrimages—to Jerusalem, notably—always taking intimate note of the plants, animals, and minerals he encountered. Dedicated to philosophy, he came to believe that the quest for truth required careful study of the natural sciences.

In his thirties, he embarked to the Sibillines to gather the mountain flora for study. As the years passed and explorers returned from the Americas, their journeys frequent by then, he counted all the curiosities they brought home, organized and classified them, labeled and sketched them, gave names to things unseen before. Such was Aldrovandi. It became his life's work, tallying these wonders, and wanderlust could wait.

He'd had high hopes, in his forties, of seeing the New World. In his letters, he deplored the lack of attention that explorers gave to the natural history of the regions being discovered. Historians, he complained, cared too much for conquest. He had a better idea. He would organize an expedition. He would have writers, and painters, and scholars, and they would bring back not only specimens but detailed drawings and descriptions of all they saw. He proposed it to heads of state—and Aldrovandi knew many famous men, with whom he corresponded. Nothing came of his dream.

Thirty years before Aldrovandi was born, Columbus had returned with tales from the Indies. Not until about thirty years after he died would there be an expedition such as Aldrovandi envisioned—organized by the Dutch East India Company. When his attempts failed, he went back to his books, and by the time he was offered passage, when he was about sixty, he had recently recovered from a year-long illness—he had a kidney stone. Though his health had otherwise been good, he chose to stay home and devoted himself instead to further developing his botanical garden at Bologna. And now, at eighty, his eyesight beginning to fail, he looked to the hills.

"Shall we go to pick the blueberries?" he asked. "The foothills must be thick with them just now. And it's the season for porcinis—take me to the bower, I keep my basket there. Will you come with me?"

"Tomorrow," I told him. "It's too late now, but tomorrow we'll see what we can find out there." I touched his shoulder. Aldrovandi's chin was on his chest.

I sat alone outside through the night, dozing on the bower seat, lulled by the sweet jasmine into fitful dreams. Tomatoes appeared, glistening on the vine, deeper reds and brighter yellows than any I had known, and they grew huge, then shrank and blinked away.

And in the morning I brought my friend his basket—it was time for the picking. I helped him out to his garden, and he stooped to pluck a *pomo d'oro* from the vine and presented it to me as I led him through the gate.

Joy of Eggs

The look in Tim's eye as she lays an egg tells me she knows she's on to something good. She squats and stares. I can tap her beak, wag her wattle—it's all the same to her. Suddenly she lifts and squeezes; her eyes bulge, then soften as she peers at what she's done, clucking inquisitively. She nudges her egg, rolls it, and settles proudly on top.

Thief that I am, I lift the lid to the nest box and grope within, and she cocks an eye at me, annoyed but resigned. I retrieve her egg. Most of the world's chickens lay brown eggs. Tim, who I thought was an Araucana, is supposed to lay blue eggs. She puts out white ones.

And that's okay. She's a hen named Tim. She was the first peep I lifted from the box that Suzanne brought home that March morning when our chicken days began. I named her Tim on the spot and still don't know why.

Evening falls, and I lift the nest box lid again. Tim is still there, but this time she's glaring at me and hissing, hackles raised. She fluffs her feathers, trying to make herself look big and menacing so that I might flee in fear. I retreat to the shadows inside the coop and watch her: She seems deep in concentration, and dour, as if nursing a grudge. She fusses over a piece of straw, trying to decide where to put it, then places it carefully on her back.

Tim wants to be a mother hen, and she knows that's unlikely if I keep depriving her of her eggs. She'll forget my transgressions soon enough. These are creatures not inclined to noble thought, nor much at all, yet I marvel at their maternal yearnings.

I've heard many theories about the best way to "break" a broody hen of her lament—methods as radical as putting ice cubes in her nest. Some coop keepers sentence her to solitary confinement; others roust her constantly, hoping she'll get over it; some even try to starve her into compliance.

None of these methods work. She'll get over it, indeed, but most attempts to hurry her along will merely madden her. Her angst is biological, and only time will cure what ails her. The egg cartel is working hard to quell this beautiful but annoying maternal instinct. The well-bred Leghorns seldom waste precious time fretting over their eggs.

A broody bird may sacrifice a third of her body weight while hatching her clutch, such is her dedication. She's determined. Rather than submit to daily egg thefts from one such as I, she may sneak off into the hostas to hide her handiwork and reappear twenty-one days later with peeps in tow. I'm told to expect this if I keep raising chickens.

And yet I have seen what happens when I drop an egg in the coop. It's the yolk they go for first. Squabbling, they rip it asunder— oh, mother hen, what led you to this? At times I'll find an egg pecked open in the straw, while from their roost the chickens eye me innocently. Once they've tasted of it, the habit dies hard. The ancients considered such a hen to be depraved—the prescribed cure was to replace the egg white with lime, and that'll teach her. Lime is also good for disposing of carcasses.

I think, however, that I understand this longing for the egg. Come morning at Lilyfield, shells pile high on the kitchen counter. Some in my family prefer scrambled, some sunny-side up, and what a sun it is: brilliant, radiant. Hens that eat cracked corn yield a yolk that redefines yellow. Farmers sometimes add marigolds to the feed mix, but the color needs no help.

Supermarket eggs are days or weeks old by the time you eat them, and they lie pale and flaccid in the pan. Their dissipated taste disappoints anyone who knows better. The farm-fresh variety, mere hours from coop to kitchen, is sublimely eggy. The yolk sits high and proud, beaming like a sun; the white clings close and thick.

Chickens are alchemists. I've seen what goes through those beaks. They'll eat nearly anything, given a chance. In Fairmont, Minnesota, last fall, a butcher found a child's shiny ID bracelet in a gizzard. The butcher tracked down the owner, now thirty-one and living in Massachusetts, who said he lost it when he was kindergarten age while playing hide-and-seek at his grandfather's farm. The barn where he had been hiding was torn down a few years ago. The materials were hauled to a nearby farm to build another barn—a farm that raised chickens, and had sent them to the Fairmont butcher.[1] A chicken will eat anything that glimmers, it would seem, but it finds the base elements more attractive. And these it turns into gold on the plate.

Tim looked as if she were dying. She stayed huddled on her nest and clucked her days and nights away, looking miserable. She barely took time to get up and eat or drink. This was my first experience with a determined broody hen, and I thought I had to do something to help her.

Others have made the same mistake. "That desire to incubate can be inhibited," Aldrovandi wrote, "by drawing a little feather through the hen's nostrils and by sprinkling it with cold water." Aristotle had a recipe: "Crush together an equal weight of cooked white of egg and dried grapes and offer this mixture to them instead of other food"—a method about as effective as the feather trick.

But going broody is a good thing: Too much laying can leave a girl exhausted, Aldrovandi said; excessive brooding is bad not only for the body but especially for the spirit. Some hens go broody more than others because of "their too great affection for their chicks." Deprived daily of their eggs, he wrote, hens can feel the same sorrow shown by a woman whose baby has died before birth.

Through history, people have gone to a lot of trouble to fill in for the chicken. Legend has it that the Roman empress Livia Augusta put her own heart into hatching an egg: She tucked it into her bosom and kept it cozy there until it hatched. According to ancient accounts by Pliny and Suetonius, she did this upon discovering that she was pregnant by her first husband, Tiberius. After hatching out a fine cock, she was confident she would bear him a son.[2]

Aldrovandi pointed out that folks recently had been hatching eggs by placing them on straw next to a gentle fire. In ancient Egypt, he wrote, eggs were incubated by burying them in mud. "I gather as much also from the testimony of Aristotle, who tells the story about a certain toper at Syracuse who used to put eggs in the earth under his straw mat and to keep on drinking until he hatched them."

Those who went to such trouble avoided the risk of getting less than the best from the unscrupulous, such as those who would pass off unfertilized eggs as the real deal. Since no rooster had come near the hen that laid them, such eggs wouldn't hatch even in the most bounteous of bosoms. To test an egg for fertility in the market, Aldrovandi suggested, a customer should taste a sample. "He should first eat one so that from its sweet flavor he can judge the other shares of the semen."

And take care, he said, to put them under the hen—or in whatever cozy spot—after the new moon, from the tenth to the fifteenth day. "This practice," he said he'd heard, "even now is practiced by farm girls in Germany." It ensures the chicks will hatch as the moon is waxing, when nature tends to thrive.

My electrician told me that very thing. A lanky man who sizes up circuits brilliantly, he was impressed by our chickens; he wants to keep a flock himself when he disappears into the West Virginia woods. He warned me that the government was thrusting needles into the brains of baby chicks and that goons would soon be coming over the rise from Norristown to steal my water. No doubt Aldrovandi would think my alectryomancer a wise man—such souls have long professed to know the ways of chickens and God.

Aldrovandi believed that womenfolk, too, had a knack when it came to chickens, knowing, for example, that eggs that are elongated and come to a sharp point would produce roosters, while rounder eggs with blunt ends would produce hens. "Who does not see," the master wrote, "that in the round eggs the heat is more diffused, but is gathered together in the long eggs in one part?" Not I, but I do see this: Debating the matter seems silly, like something from a Swiftian fantasy.

Aldrovandi conceded that Aristotle—"the most imposing author of all in the secrets of nature"—seemed to have declared that roosters came from round eggs. But rest assured: Aristotle would not have made such a mistake. The man did have bad, "crabbed" handwriting, and some have speculated that it might have been misinterpreted or poorly translated—but he would not have been simply wrong, Aldrovandi insisted. He was too wise about egg ways.

In his *Ornithology*, Aldrovandi celebrates the miracles that happen inside the egg. A loving God makes the unhatched chick begin peeping for its mama two or three days before it breaks the shell, he points out. And he weighs in on the wrong side of a controversy, insisting that the chick forms from the white, not the yolk, despite the insistence of many learned men.

"In order to search out the truth in this trivial controversy between medical men and philosophers," he said, "I took twenty-two eggs which a hen had incubated. Each day, with the greatest care and curiosity, I dissected one of them. I found Aristotle's doctrine to be the true one."

He did not say whether he got royalties from Aristotle.

Though conceding the matter was trivial, Aldrovandi kept to his nature and devoted copious attention to it. His *Ornithology* also includes fascinating drawings, day by day, of growing veins and fibers and huddled embryos, as well as pages of other drawings of dissected chicken innards.

The ancient Greeks, such as Hippocrates, thought the egg grew from the yolk and was nourished by the white albumen, and when the albumen was used up, the chick wanted out. Hippocrates was wrong, it's vice versa, Aldrovandi wrote, and he suggested that his readers think of it this way: When you fry an egg, what happens? The egg white turns hard, while the yolk stays liquid. What does this tell the observant man? The heat of incubation, he said, renders the chick's body out of the part that it can harden—namely, the white. Furthermore, he argued, "Who does not see that it is more easy for the white than for the yolk to be mixed with semen?"

Aldrovandi advised his readers not to be fooled by the yolk theorists—not only Hippocrates but also the likes of Jerome Cardan. "We must not listen to Cardanus," he said, cloaking the name in Latin. He had known the man. A physician and mathematician from Pavia, Cardan had trouble finding a job because he was of illegitimate birth—and nasty to the core. He was smart—perhaps too smart. He produced many lasting insights in his fields, biographers agree. But he dared to write Jesus' horoscope, and it nearly cost him his career. He was a genius with numbers, but he couldn't keep his finances straight. Chronically broke, he used his math skills for gambling, calculating probabilities.[3]

And not only that, but he thought chicks formed from the yolk.

Let's set the record straight: Aldrovandi and Aristotle were wrong. Hippocrates was right, and so was Cardan, the bastard, or at least they were closer to the truth we know today.

"Do chickens have an assembly line going in there?" my friend Ted asked me as I stood at the sink in the *Inquirer* newsroom pantry, cleaning the day's take of eggs before delivering them to my customers. "I mean, how do they do it? That's what I want to know."

Inside a hen's body, wonders must occur each time she lays an egg. No other bird lays an egg a day. Most lay only a few eggs a year, during the mating season. Aristotle maintained that some chickens lay two eggs a day. Aristotle, again, was wrong. Even our prodigious factory fowl aren't there yet.

In her monthly egg cycle, the hen is attuned to the moon. And she observes another celestial cycle, that of the sun. She knows the seasons well, and when she detects the waning light of a winter coming on, her brain tells her pituitary gland to shut down the hormonal signal for egg production, lest her chicks hatch in a subzero blizzard. This has little to do with temperature; a light left shining in the coop will satisfy her that balmy days prevail, and she'll keep on pumping out the product.

Here's what happens on that assembly line. This is how she does it:[4]

After the rooster wham-bams the hen's anus with his small, inconsequential penis, his sperm go dashing through her all-purpose chute and up her oviduct in search of a friendly egg cell. The sperm can hang around in there for several weeks, so a hen can produce a fertile egg even if she hasn't let a rooster near in a while.

The oviduct connects to the ovary. Here the hen makes yolks, adds a single egg cell to each, and releases them down the funnel, one every day or two. If the egg finds a sperm waiting in the oviduct, they dance on down the line.

Only a single sperm cell makes it to the germ spot on the yolk; the rest of the rooster stuff doesn't get inside the egg, no matter what you might fear when you crack it open. That stringy white clump near the center is the chalaza, which holds the yolk in place; the fresher the egg, the more prominent it is. You can't see the sperm cell. You can see the germ spot, though, if you examine the yolk: It's a circular spot on the yolk, usually near the edge. If it's just a whitish speck, the egg isn't fertile. If it is larger—say, an eighth of an inch across—and translucent, the embryo has begun dividing and the egg is fertile. It's edible, though: A chick cannot begin to develop unless the egg is kept at a relatively constant 101 degrees Fahrenheit.

If no sperm come calling in the oviduct, the egg cell waits around about twenty minutes, sighs, and pretends it had a fling anyway. A hen doesn't need a rooster to lay an egg; the construction project commences regardless. All along the oviduct during the egg's day-long descent, the assembly line kicks into gear. The egg white forms around the yolk. Membranes grow between them. Minerals are deposited to make the shell, with pigment applied in the outermost layer—the color depends on the breed and serves no purpose other than decoration. Muscular contractions move the package along, turning it through spiral folds and defining its contours—and out comes the egg through the hen's pulsing cloaca.

If the egg cell was fertilized, the embryo will be dividing happily by now, but the action stops abruptly outside the hen's body unless things heat up—mama settles down on top of her prize, or the farmer plunks it into an incubator, or maybe an empress tucks it in her cleavage, if she's hot enough. After twenty-one days, if all goes well, the chick is ready to make its break. But if the egg cell never wed with a sperm, nothing more can happen—except, perhaps, sunny-side up for breakfast.

As soon as the first day of incubation, the next wave of wonders begins. At first, the changes are visible only under a microscope. The brain crease forms in the nineteenth hour, then the rudiments of the backbone. At twenty-four hours, the eyes start to develop; the next day, ears. Veins form. At thirty hours, the heart beats; when mature, it will tick away at about three hundred beats per minute, at rest. Wings and legs begin taking shape on the third day, and the chick stirs on the sixth. Feathers emerge on the twelfth day, then claws, and soon the chick turns its head looking for the blunt end of the egg.

At this point, the albumen (the egg white) is nearly gone, having nourished the growing life. Sorry, Ulisse, but the chick didn't form from the white, and that sweet semen never mixed with it. Nor did the chick form from the yolk, really, though there's a speck of truth to the argument—the speck being the yolk's tiny germ spot, the only living part of the egg, which carries the DNA guidebook on how to make a chicken. From there the veins pushed forth and the chicken came to be.

With the albumen depleted, the embryo begins depending on the yolk for nutrients. By the seventeenth day, the chick is thinking about hatching, though it doesn't know why, or what awaits. By the twentieth day, it has sucked the yolk sac into its body through the umbilical cord attached to it. It starts breathing the scant air inside the egg, and begins hacking out of its prison with an egg tooth it grew just for that purpose.

Within a day, out comes the peep. It can live several days without food or water—that's why its body absorbed the remaining yolk. This trick allows the mother hen to stay on her nest to finish hatching the stragglers in her clutch without having to immediately care for the first ones to hatch. It also allows hatcheries to ship peeps long distances through the mail.

We have inherited a uniquely human trait from our ancestors: We sometimes kill the things we love and admire. It was for the greater good, the ancients argued. Many was the chicken that the soothsayers eviscerated to learn, from the patterns of the spill, what the future held. By studying the chicken's innards, we believed, we could obtain wisdom.

In 2004, the chicken spilled its secrets again: An international team of scientists cracked its genome, fully mapping its recipe for life. The project was the latest in a series of genome mapping initiatives, which for a decade had been striving to "sequence" the DNA—identify which genes do what by logging the entire letter code—of life forms as diverse as humans and germs. Rampant technology had given us abilities that had seemed beyond our dreams.[5]

When they turned their attention to the chicken, the genome crackers had already mastered the puffer fish, which till then had been the species closest to the mammals to be sequenced. Fish are among the earliest of creatures, far more primitive than birds. The scientists reasoned that chickens, though no less silly looking than puffer fish, came along much later, and therefore their genome would reveal more about human genetics. The chicken's middling position on the tree of life between fish and mammals promised new insights into the shaping of our genes. It was the first bird, and the first agricultural animal, to have its genome analyzed.

The chicken team, led by Richard K. Wilson of the Washington University School of Medicine in St. Louis, assembled the genome of the Red Jungle Fowl, which still exists much as it did when we started messing with it. It has a billion letters in its DNA code—a third as many letters as the human code has. The work was funded by the National Human Genome Research Institute.

This was more than just a project to figure out what makes a chicken tick. It offered the prospect of developing disease-resistant flocks that would be meatier and produce more eggs. The chicken is a mainstay of agricultural and biomedical research; anything more we learn about it could help to feed a healthier world. The genome project could track down traits so that producers could enhance the commercially lucrative ones and eliminate those that cut into profits. By better understanding the genes, scientists could alter them and turn the chicken into a better research tool.

The research came as avian flu was threatening to spread throughout the world. The viral disease, which often appears first in chickens and hitchhikes from nation to nation along the routes of migratory birds, had clearly shown it could jump to human hosts. The strain seemed limited in its ability to do so, though it had claimed lives throughout Asia and was spreading into Europe. The fear was that the virus might do what germs do so well—mutate, into a strain of plague potential.

The flu outbreak didn't prompt the chicken genome project, but researchers did hope to reveal details of the avian genetic portrait that would help us understand what makes birds, and humans, vulnerable to the avian flu. Sequencing a genome is a major step but only the first of many—the researchers are able to list words from the genetic alphabet, but it's another arduous task to learn to speak in sentences.

In a separate project, the research institute had already parsed the human DNA code. With an avian code conquered, scientists were able to compare human and chicken sequences to see similarities and differences—and learn to better fight human diseases, including the viral connection to cancer, in which mutations run amok. The new research produced insights into what humans share with the lower vertebrates.

About 60 percent of the chicken's genes are similar to those in humans, the researchers discovered. The analysis, for example, discovered a correlation between a human gene and the one that regulates a chicken's eggshell proteins. In humans, the gene helps to govern the growth of bone.

Chickens have fewer genes for sensing tastes than mammals do. Considering the kinds of things they'll eat, I'd consider their tasteless nature a godsend. And chickens can smell far better than scientists had believed, the researchers reported. Can't say as I've noticed. I'm the one who cleans the coop, and chickens still don't smell so good to me.

Equipped with the newfound knowledge of the genome, German scientists have made a disconcerting discovery: Hens, it seems, once had teeth, and they could grow them again.[6] Apparently, some already have—and I don't relish the thought of saber-toothed Silkies hissing at me from the nest box. The researchers identified a mutant tooth gene in some chickens and coaxed them into growing what chickens are renowned for not having. The teeth were conical, like an alligator's. Imagine.

The experiments, reported in 2006, enhanced genetic vestiges of the formidable teeth sported by some birdlike dinosaurs, according to the researchers from the Max Planck Institute for Developmental Biology. Those dinosaurs eventually turned toothless, seventy to eighty million years ago, and developed beaks. The genome project found that modern chickens lack any counterpart to the human gene for tooth enamel.

The German research suggests, however, that primal genes are still there in some birds and can be switched on. The scientists identified a chemical in the mutant chickens that could stimulate the growth of teeth; they exposed the chickens to a virus that increased the levels of that chemical.

I would think that chickens with a virus would be something we'd want to avoid right about now. Equipped with teeth, such birds could be truly bad news. Until this latest development, researchers had been able to sprout teeth in birds only by grafting jaw tissue from mice into their beaks. Now we know that some chickens have the capacity to grow teeth from their own tissues.

Listen up, folks: Chickens, in their heart of hearts, are vicious and inclined to use any teeth we might give them. Some farmers see fit to cut the beaks off chickens so they don't destroy one another; next, they'll have to take a file to their teeth. And we risk ruining a perfectly good platitude. I'd hate to see "as scarce as hens' teeth" used to describe the expression itself, come the day when chickens prowl around with fangs.

It wouldn't be the first time we fooled around with the chicken's genes to create birds that have little resemblance to their ancestors. We have made chickens pretty, or plump, or mean-spirited for the cockfighting ring. Today's chickens are products of our puttering. If we insist on asking whether the chicken or egg came first, here are the facts: Many of the modern chicken breeds were concocted in the last century and a half, the result of selective breeding. Eggs with shells have been around for nearly 300 million years, the result of natural selection.

The very first eggs developed in the primordial ocean. Fish, and later amphibians, laid their eggs in water to keep them from drying out. When creatures sought out dry land, the amniotic egg was one of their many brilliant accommodations. The shell enabled the reptiles to take the water with them, and they began to lay nests of eggs. The dinosaurs laid eggs, too—with tough, leathery shells that protected the egg cell as it floated in its own microcosmic sea.

Among those dinosaurs was the birdlike one that developed a beak—the one whose toothy genetic vestiges waited to be reawakened by the German researchers. All birds evolved from dinosaurs, according to evolutionary biologists.[7] One of the dinosaurs, a meat-eating biped named Archaeopteryx, had wings and feathers, and among its feathery descendents was the Red Jungle Fowl, which begat all modern chickens.[8]

Such is the beauty of evolution. Through the ages, life has been divinely equipped to adapt and survive and thrive—the qualities we admire in ourselves. And measured against eternity, those ages passed in an instant. The evolution of species was a sudden creative flourish. It happened in a twinkling.

It goes like this, then: The egg came before the dinosaur, which came before the bird, which came before the jungle fowl, which came before the domestic chicken, which came before the production-line hybrids or the Frankenfowl or whatever you want to call some of these things we have today—but at least they don't have teeth. Yet.

I found the first eggs on a stormy September morning, six months after Suzanne had fetched our first peeps home. There, in the hinged nest box, was the payoff. Two eggs. One was the size of an olive. The other had a rubbery shell. But the fourteen hens soon yielded six to eight perfect eggs a day, brown beauties that I began peddling to coworkers at the *Inquirer*.

"You're selling them too cheap," Suzanne declared after about a week at two dollars a dozen. I protested that I couldn't ask much more than the price of supermarket eggs, or I wouldn't have any customers.

But as the months passed, a few of my customers tried to palm me an extra buck here and there and hinted that I should ask for more—after all, I hand-inspected each of the eggs and delivered them to the customer's desk.

"Have you seen what those so-called organic eggs and free-range eggs are going for at Genuardi's? Four bucks, buddy," a business-desk regular told me. "Make sure you get what your girls are worth," she said.

Such is the demand for fresh eggs. It seems everyone has known them somewhere, sometime. New customers were seeking me out, stopping me in the elevator. They were nostalgic for the taste, and once they tried fresh eggs again, there was no turning back.

I was not alone. I learned that a reporter, too, had been selling eggs, as well as someone in advertising. An online editor, admiring my basket in the elevator, told me that his wife carried eggs to work. A friend of a friend, I heard, kept a backyard coop and peddled the eggs at her job with the Vanguard investment company, near my home. I wondered how much those eggs had accrued.

Within months, I had thirty regular customers in the newsroom. They included the parking-lot attendant and the fine-arts editor, the obituary writer and the handyman, the books editor and real-estate writer, assorted clerks and technicians. The restaurant reviewer asked for half a dozen for his grandmother, and I made sure he got the best. The food editor asked me to write a feature piece about my little egg enterprise and the tide of backyard coop-keeping, and the day after it ran, my e-mail inbox was flooded.

"We were selling them too cheap," I eventually advised Suzanne.

I hiked the price to three dollars and still had folks waiting for deliveries.

And the questions came—not just about the eggs, but about chickens and all they do and have ever done and why. Conversations came easily. Peddling eggs was an opportunity not only for petty cash but for small talk with people I'd never met, though I'd seen them around for years.

"Is it true the dinosaurs turned into chickens?"

"Why don't hens have teeth?"

"So, hey—which came first, then, your eggs or your chickens?"

Good questions, predictable questions, sometimes annoying ones. And the most basic question of all: "Why do you do this, anyway?"

I can say with some assurance that my motivation for keeping chickens is purer than Socrates' motive for keeping his wife, Xanthippe. It seems she was a shrew, quarrelsome and quick-tempered, and everyone in Athens knew it.

"Why don't you kick her out?" an associate asked of the philosopher.

Socrates answered, as usual, with a question: "Why don't you drive away your noisy hens?"

"Because they lay eggs for me."

"My wife," said the sage, "bears children for me."[9]

Upon hearing about this, Xanthippe, if she wasn't a shrew already, had reason to become one. Socrates joked that if he could learn to get along with her, he could get along with the most gnarly of people. He had a habit of making annoying points like that to the authorities, as well, who eventually did him in with a snootful of hemlock, even before he could pay that last cock to Asclepius. Xanthippe, maybe, mourned.

One Basket

ᗷ ᗷ

"Five dozen lovelies, fresh from the coop—what do you say?" My question leaves Dave scratching his chin only a moment. "I'd say you have a deal," he says, and we shake hands. In exchange for the eggs, he'll give me two huge bags of sawdust and a load of wood scraps.

Whenever he sees my pickup truck coming up the driveway to his one-man sawmill in a glade a half mile from Lilyfield, Dave knows I'm there for his leftovers. I need his premium sawdust for bedding in the chicken coop and the horse stalls. The log scraps will heat our farmhouse for days, come fall.

It's the last day of August, and though summer still hangs thick amid the maples as we talk, something is changing. The cicadas chatter desperately, and the afternoon light feels tenuous, as if it's trying too hard. I can smell a chilly evening coming on.

Many of those who visit Spacht's Sawmill on a busy weekend are woodworkers and hobbyists searching for the perfect pattern of grains among the planks sawn from the Pennsylvania hardwoods he harvests locally, within thirty miles. He cuts them on his vintage mill, down the hill, where a four-foot circular saw glides through the logs. His customers come to peruse ash and oak, walnut and sycamore.

In his shop, where he planes and displays the boards, I've met guitar designers and cabinetmakers and an assortment of other characters. It's a warm place to visit, and not just for the camaraderie: A fire snaps in the stove when I return with his eggs, on a leaden afternoon in November, to consummate the deal.

I hand over the eggs, and I've brought my best: They're mostly green and blue ones from the Araucanas and some black ones from the Marans. One is a wonderful shade of rose, anonymous artistry from a hen unknown.

"Better than brownies, by far," I tell him. Suzanne has been trying to barter with Dave for years by offering him a plate of her luxurious brownies in exchange for his sawdust. He always delights at the prospect, but the deal hasn't happened. He's bartered with his dentist, but not yet with Suzanne. Today, he's bartering with me.

"Brown or white or any color, they're all great," he says, opening each carton to admire our hens' creative touch.

I point to one of his planks and tell him it looks like the image on the Shroud of Turin. "Man, you could have folks making pilgrimages to your mill from all over the world," I tell him. "Just imagine."

Dave has done his share of imagining, and dreaming. When he and his wife, Carol, bought the property as newlyweds in 1983, it was abandoned and forlorn, the equipment rusty, the buildings so derelict that they swayed to his push. Built in the Roaring Twenties, the mill had made it through the Depression and seen many tough years since.

He had earned an economics degree several years earlier, but Dave's style wasn't professorial. If he was going to count beans, he'd rather they be real ones. His dream waited here, amid the weeds and mud and rotting piles of wood that he and his family and friends slowly began to clear. A generation later, schoolchildren come on field trips to the tidy grounds to watch him work.

At home in our farmhouse, with a fire flaring in the woodstove, I'm dozing within minutes in the Morris rocker that Suzanne reupholstered for me as a Christmas present. Outside, from the field-stone chimney that rises over a wide colonial fireplace, a plume of maple smoke curls into a heavy autumn sky.

When I awaken from my nap, I peer out the window into the sullen dusk. Across the pasture, the coop windows glow from the lightbulb that helps to keep the chickens cozy. The drizzle turns to a cloudburst, drumming the metal roof of the farmhouse. In the coop, the noise must be thunderous. The chickens hardly notice. I've watched them when the sky opens: They merely edge closer together on the roosts, their eyes glazing.

I pull on my boots and rain slicker and head out to the barn. There are chores to do, yes, but mostly I just want to inhale the smell of hay and hear the rain pounding the tin roof. It's good for the soul.

We long for the homespun, many of us, and dream about building things from scratch, the way Dave did, as do all those creative souls who buy his lumber. Gardening and cooking, in particular, soothe our souls by reacquainting us with a primal need to touch the earth and taste of it. And in both pursuits, we embrace the do-it-yourself ethic of self-reliance. It's why Martha Stewart and her canon of domestic wisdom are so popular.

Even finances can be homespun: Bartering is commerce at its most fundamental. Not only do we exchange goods and services but we give something of ourselves, as well—our talents and our assets, as God has endowed us. We know our own worth more than an accountant ever will, and bartering renews our pride in what we can offer others.

I'm pleased to have a few chickens around to boost my self-worth. I can now say that we heat the farmhouse on chicken power, since I traded their eggs for the wood to fire the stove. My desk in the newsroom is cluttered with cartons, and though I generally accept enough lucre for my eggs to buy a hoagie or cheesesteak for lunch, I'd do as well to trade them for a smile.

It's what I like best about peddling my eggs at the *Inquirer:* It gets me talking. Editing news reports and writing headlines can consume silent hours. My little side gig gets me up on my feet now and then and chatting with security guards and janitors and bosses big and small, not just harried reporters on the phone.

Once, it was the queen who got everyone talking about chickens. Victoria's poultry palace at Windsor was the inspiration for the nineteenth-century surge in backyard fanciers worldwide. It has happened again: Martha Stewart likes chickens, too. Her royal touch has renewed a widespread interest in show birds. She's particularly partial to Araucanas, those South American beauties that lay the Easter eggs that I traded at the sawmill to make our house so warm. Stewart raised them at her fabled Turkey Hill home in Westport, New York, featuring them prominently in her books, magazine, and television show.

Chickens were part of her scheme, as well, when Stewart, in 2000, began renovating a 150-acre farm estate of tall sycamores and gentle hills in Bedford, where the old money meets the new just north of New York City. Shades of gray dominate the clapboard sidings and interiors of the houses, barns, stables, and even fences (she calls it Bedford Gray). In keeping with the color scheme, Stewart decided to keep only black animals on the property—her five Friesian horses, her sheep, the farm dog, too. And black chickens.

Stewart maintains a dream that's not to be dispelled, whatever troubles she encounters. "I want to have a new kind of house, a smart house," she told a writer for *Vanity Fair.* "This is going to be the future. That's what I'm trying to do here." She's striving to create a model for the self-sufficient life, on acreage that provides fruit and vegetables, milk and eggs, meat for the table. It can take money, these days, to re-create the simple so thoroughly, and she's earned the right to try.[10]

Stewart hardly sees the world in shades of gray: Self-sufficient homesteaders find many uses for the amenities at hand, and she

seizes opportunities as they come. So enamored was she of her Araucanas that she introduced a line of house paints inspired by the color
of their eggs. If the Araucanas' variegated plumage and pastel eggs
don't quite fit her personal home decorating vision, I have news for
her: Among my latest chicken acquisitions are a few Black Marans
whose eggs are as dark as chocolate.

Though she admires show birds, she knows chickens are also ex-
traordinary with the right seasonings. Chickens give their all for the
cook. The egg is the ultimate food, she says, and she insists on fresh
ones; the meat is a dietary staple and a cookbook standard that can
be prepared in many not-so-standard ways.

In explaining her drive for the ultimate in excellence, Stewart says
that in running her business enterprise, she has insisted on "the high-
est standards of perfection." She adopted the phrase, she says, from
the American Poultry Association's handbook.

Stewart told this to a judge she visited a few years ago—he wanted
to hear the inside story on how she got so good at bartering. Stewart
has since gotten back to the business of catering to our competing
desires for simplicity and elegance, for the latest in living tradition-
ally. She offers life the way we worry it might never be again.

"All hail to the chicken, who offers himself a delicious sacrifice on the
household shrine!" Charles Wyllys Elliott wrote in an 1869 article
called "The Poultry Lovers" in the periodical *The Galaxy*. "All hail to
the hen who lays the matutinal egg." I don't know what *matutinal* means,
but I understand his excitement. The culinary possibilities seem endless.

There's no accounting for taste, however. Through history, what
one culture finds delectable another finds revolting. Whether we consider a particular food to be tantalizing or terrible has often been
influenced by dietary sanctions that seek to control what's good for
us. Such restrictions may be motivated by health concerns, or a distaste
for excess, or both.

Joey Chestnut is king of the wings. He's the two-time champion of an event that does my town proud: the annual chicken-wing scarfing contest in Philadelphia. In 2006, he emerged as the Wing Bowl winner, having eaten 173 wings in the beer-soaked competition featuring dozens of voluptuous "wingettes" leading the cheers. In 2007, at age twenty-three, he defended his title by eating 182—all in half an hour. He has also done well with burgers, waffles, bratwurst, and, praise be, asparagus.[11]

All hail to Joey. He saved ninety-one birds the humility of demonstrating how poorly they use those wings, weak from generations of disuse.

Philadelphia, where ordering a cheesesteak "whiz, wit" means you want it with the traditional Cheez Whiz and fried onions, is a natural for such a contest. In 2000, *Men's Fitness* magazine designated it the fattest city in America, taking the honor away from New Orleans. My fair city has yet to develop a reputation for healthful living and avoiding excess. Great restaurants, though.

The desire for a safe and healthful meal may be the root of a dietary peculiarity known in the Pacific Islands and Southeast Asia.[12] When humans were first acquiring a taste for the egg, they took what was available: the clutch that they found under a hen as she lay on her nest in the wild. The hens of yore didn't lay eggs daily, but rather tended to wait for mating season. A clutch was likely days old by the time it was raided. Unless the eggs were fertilized and growing, they would soon spoil in the heat—and the only way to be sure an egg would be safe and tasty was to crack it open. If a fetus was forming, what a treat: delicious, with a little crunch, and earthy accents. If I could get past the gagging, I suppose I'd learn to appreciate a fetal egg. It's no more distasteful than a barbecued chicken wing, when you think about it.

But I'll stick with the wings for my lunch, thank you, or the wonderful "whiz, wit" served from the food truck parked out on Broad Street, where my friend Ahmad, an ever-smiling Pakistani, makes

one of the finest sandwiches in town—or so it seems to a hungry journalist on lunch break. "Would you like to buy some of my eggs for
your breakfast crowd?" I asked him once. He smiled and nodded
buoyantly, which he would also have done had I asked, "Would you
like me to pelt your truck with my eggs?" Ahmad knows enough English to ask me regularly how my family fares. He calls all women
and children "baby," which sometimes takes his customers aback,
and one day maybe I'll correct him. But I like him pretty much the
way he is. It's his smile, more than anything, that keeps me coming
back.

Another kind of specialty egg—once a down-home favorite, still
known in Italy and France, and making inroads into American
restaurants—is one that never was laid. They are called immature
eggs, or embryonic (though the latter term tends to suppress appetites), and they are often found among the innards of retired hens
when they are slaughtered.

When their productive laying lives are through, such hens are
routinely rendered into chicken soup or stew, their flesh too tough
for tenders. Their final egg, still up the chute, usually goes to
waste—but not for those in the know. Back when most families got
their poultry from the butcher, housewives made sure that egg didn't
get tossed. An unlaid egg can be small as a marble or full-size. It may
have no shell, merely a membrane. It's velvety and sweet, mellow and
creamy—like an egg fresh from the coop, but richer.[13]

The chicken and eggs on most menus, of course, are the more
traditional variety. The products of the henhouse are among the
most ubiquitous fare in restaurants around the world, where chefs
prepare them in endlessly interesting ways. They have to. The mass
production of meat and eggs has turned what was once a luxury into
one of the cheapest of entrees—and has robbed it of much of its
taste, as well.

For that reason, cooks in many cultures have added flavors to
make chicken once again pleasing to the palate.[14] Chicken became a

canvas on which chefs could practice their artistry. Barbecue sauce once enhanced the meat; now, the meat seems almost incidental, as most of the flavor lies in the alchemy of the sauce.

In the *Inquirer* newsroom, where food abounds, I arrived at work one weekend afternoon to find a heaping plate of marinated chicken strips on the credenza in front of my friend Addam's desk. We weren't sure how it got there—leftovers from some seminar, probably—but it was disappearing fast, with no help from Addam. Having just read a treatise on factory farming, I found myself empathizing with his distaste for meat. As we commiserated about what humans have done to chickens to satisfy fleshly cravings, I popped a piece of one in my mouth and found it delightful—then realized that it was all in the spicy marinade.

The chicken itself might as well be tofu, I told Addam. In my western Pennsylvania hometown of Mercer, I used to hear about "city chicken," a Pittsburgh regional specialty. It wasn't really chicken at all, but rather cubes of veal and pork, often on a skewer, rolled in breading and shaped and seasoned to look and taste like chicken. It dates to the day when veal, never an American favorite, was far cheaper than chicken, which cost a pretty penny before the factory farms.

City chicken is part of a long tradition, dating to the Middle Ages, of mock foods, named for an ingredient that isn't in the recipe. The Victorians had their mock turtle soup, made from the parts of a calf that were often discarded, such as the tail and hooves. In New Hampshire, our friend Lori uses the ubiquitous zucchini to make mock apple pie. When chicken finally got cheap, in the 1940s, it was used to mock the breaded veal of the German Wiener schnitzel. A cheap cutlet of beef, prepared similarly, became known as chicken-fried steak, common in the South.

This amounts to mind over meat. If veal can masquerade as chicken, and vice versa, then maybe meat can be anything. Close your eyes, open your yap, and your veggies turn savory. You can buy a "tofu turkey" shaped like a little roast bird, ready for slicing. If I were to turn vegetarian, I think I'd want to give up the meat illusion as well, or what's the point? It would be like staying faithful to your spouse while drooling over whatever walked past—if you could call that faithful.

My vegetarian musings, however, ended the day after my talk with Addam. Suzanne brought home some ribs and chicken from the smoker out by the highway, a place called Bones—and I was a goner once again. I'm a Philadelphian with a taste for New Orleans, seduced by the spicy sauces.

Spices were big in the Middle Ages, as well, at a time when refrigeration was not big. But the spices weren't just a cover-up; the cultivated palette relished them, and a single dish would often meld a dozen or more exotic flavors, balancing the "humors" to keep the body in good health. Among the spicy medieval delights was chicken dressed in a peacock's feathers. This was an era of colorful cuisine— for the wealthy, that is. Let the peasants eat their porridge and cheese; the food of the privileged was pheasant and venison, elegantly seasoned, worth sailing afar in search of the best. The lust for spices was the impetus for explorations and conquests. Spices, like gold, became instruments of commerce.[15]

Still, ice could be hard to find during a hot spell, and if the taste went bad, or bland, the spices could make up for it; the hotter the better. Spices served that purpose then, and they serve it now in this tasteless age of sweatshop chickens.

The fattening of chickens is really nothing new. The practice displeased Pliny, too, who denounced the "revolting practice of devouring fat birds basted in their own gravy." Roman law officially forbade it. No fowl was to be served at a banquet except for one solitary hen—and it could not be fattened for the occasion. Such sumptuary laws were meant to control excess and extravagance among the masses, particularly in matters of food and dress. Roman gourmands got around the fat-chicken prohibition, Pliny wrote, by surreptitiously soaking the feed in milk.

Dutch farmers once believed that chickens would get delectably fat if blinded by needles. Those same farmers, Aldrovandi related, were also known to keep their chickens in their kitchens in large boxes divided into tiny compartments. Each unit had only two holes, one for the head to thrust through for feeding and the other to let out the excrement. Beer and beer dregs were among the recommended sustenance, and of these the chickens could partake constantly, for a maximum of two weeks—any longer and they might burst, the experts warned.

The more conventional way, in Aldrovandi's day, was to keep each bird immobile in a separate two-hole box for up to twenty-five days. The feathers were plucked from her wings and tail. She might have preferred they stick needles in her eyes.

The kind keeper, however, did give her soft hay to lie upon, lest the box's hard floor make her uncomfortable. And she was allowed to peck at will from a generous supply of the finest feed—barley meal and flaxseed sprinkled with honey and rolled into sweet little balls. Some even recommended wheat bread soaked in the best sweet wine. Any feather that hadn't been plucked was kept scrupulously clean. If a coop keeper started all this at the new moon, an erstwhile scrawny chicken would soon be plump and ready for the table. No telling how it tasted.

Like cardboard, perhaps. That's how traditional Chinatown shoppers in New York City would describe the taste of meat from brawny supermarket hens, sometimes far from farm-fresh. Pumped full of enriched feeds, discouraged from exercising, such chickens produce meat that's tender but pallid. Plant pigments have sometimes been added to their feed to make the skin the normal yellow that shoppers expect. And with the meat rendered into cutlets, you can't even look the chicken in the eye to ask it where it came from, one shopper told *The New York Times,* explaining why she preferred to buy scrawnier birds sold in one piece from purveyors catering to the ethnic market.[16]

The regular supermarket fare is just not "finger-lickin' good," to use Colonel Sanders's slogan for Kentucky Fried Chicken—which in the early days of the company's forays into China was mistranslated into Cantonese characters that meant "eat your fingers off."[17]

Tasty or not, chicken has gone mainstream in the culture of China. In a nation where famine has been endemic for centuries, the obesity rate among children in prosperous cities is beginning to rival that of America's kids, though hunger remains widespread in rural areas. Nearly 8 percent of ten- to twelve-year-olds in Chinese cities are obese, and an additional 15 percent are overweight, according to health ministry authorities there.[18]

They have warned parents not to let their children pig out at fast-food places such as KFC and McDonald's, which proliferated as the Chinese economy boomed, even though the avian flu alert later hurt chicken sales. The marketers play the crowd well: In China, the chicken nuggets come with chili garlic sauce—further evidence that it's not really the meat the consumer is relishing.

And so it goes around the globe: Ronald McDonald was recognized by 96 percent of American schoolchildren in a survey reported by Eric Schlosser in his book *Fast Food Nation* in 2001. Ronald did nearly as well as Santa Claus. A survey in Japan (where the Teriyaki McBurger, made of pork, and the Ebi Filet-O, or shrimp burger, top the menu) found that almost as many children recognized him there. They knew him well in Britain, too. China seems destined to join the elite.

In the 1960s, Walt Disney and McDonald's founder, Ray Kroc, were the first to separate children from adults as a marketing demographic. Today, McDonald's is a major marketer of Disney toys, with which Ronald lures the children in. Fast-food giants are buttering up the next generation to be their kind of consumers.

McDonald's has infiltrated the exotic isle of Tahiti, where a depressed Paul Gauguin sailed in 1891 hoping to live on fish and fruit and escape "everything that is artificial and conventional." Overcome by excesses, in European culture and in himself, he removed himself to Polynesia, which he captured in paints as brilliant as the golden arches rising over a scintillating sea.

It's the nature of marketers to try new things and take advantage of the amenities at hand, as did Gauguin, a master at his craft who, dissipated by alcohol, sadly died of syphilis. In the South Pacific, where cows are uncommon but where the natives told the first explorers that chickens had been there forever, the smiling and waving Ronald McDonald sells far more fried chicken than hamburgers. He also dishes out a chicken-flavored McSoup and a McRice burger. Chicken sells well, also, in India, where fast-food outlets serve no sacred beef. Fish and veggie burgers do well there, too.

Kentucky Fried Chicken also has a Polynesian presence, and it's well that the locals like fried chicken, because the chain has a tough time dissociating itself from it. Not that it hasn't tried. In 1991, the chain officially changed its name to KFC, explaining that it needed to be sensitive to a crop of health-conscious consumers who associated *fried* with *died.*

However, the company proudly restored its full name in 2007, bringing back the famous bucket it abandoned in the 1990s and once again declaring its food "finger-lickin' good." The company was licking its wounds over the failure of a healthful "oven-roasted" line it introduced in 2004. Discouraged, it explored the idea of restoring the old name, greasy as it might seem to some. In a test run in Washington, D.C., sales increased 20 percent.[19]

As marketers study trends to decide which way their knees should jerk, they perceive a public fixated on health and diet. Designer and imitation eggs are proliferating. A poultry producer in India recently introduced yet another one. This premium egg is aimed at beauty-conscious customers and those with diabetes and heart conditions. The hens' enriched diet is the key to the quality, the company says. The egg is touted as being high in protein. Such a special attribute, the producer says, is not injected or chemically induced.[20] This is, in fact, a genuine egg. A pricey one, too.

A hen's diet can indeed influence, somewhat, the food value of her eggs as her body transfers the nutrients into the albumen and yolk that will nourish the developing chick—or the consumer. But of all those choices on the supermarket shelf, many are of dubious value.

You can procure, for a price, the coveted omega-3 eggs, from hens that eat fortified algae and flaxseed.[21] Recent research has found that special diets can even infuse the hen's flesh with the omega-3 acid. The fatty acid is proclaimed to be good for the heart, and the body, too. And that would be good news, except omega-3 eggs can be budget-busters and a lot of other foods are better sources of the nutrient, such as salmon and tuna.

Thrilled at the thought I could sell these omega-3 eggs myself, I priced a sack of flaxseed at the gristmill, then came home and told the chickens the good news: They could keep pecking through the horse manure. They do just fine on bugs and grubs.

You can fall for the organic and free-range egg hype, if you must, though what you'll be eating is unlikely to be any different nutritionally than the economy eggs at the supermarket. You can buy your eggs pasteurized these days. And you can even get yolk-free eggs, if you're worried about cholesterol, but make sure you talk to your doctor about which cholesterols are good for you. Who's to know? Eggs are good, I do know that.

Some people say a fertilized egg has far less cholesterol, though I've yet to see a scintilla of research evidence in support of their theory. People say a lot of things about eggs. They also say Araucana eggs have less cholesterol. Research shows they actually have a higher concentration than regular supermarket eggs.[22] Araucanas do indeed lay low-cholesterol eggs, but that's because their eggs are smaller.

Or try one of those vegetarian eggs. It's made of dried soy, with egg flavoring added. Typically, it has a fifth the protein and seven times the carbohydrates of a real egg. And the protein in an egg's white and yolk is among nature's best. No wonder the Indian designer egg is so good for you.

Internet blogs recently gasped about a story from Handan, China, in which a street vendor supposedly sold strange eggs to a customer, who cracked one open in the frying pan to find an odd jumble of colors and chemical smells. Tests found the eggs to be fake, synthesized from calcium carbonate, starch, gelatin, and a varnish resin, the bloggers wrote. They reported that authorities found a case of such eggs for sale at a farmers' market and uncovered a network of counterfeiters selling their manufacturing secret to eager opportunists—and others making soy sauce from human hair.

There's something artificial here, all right. Eggs are cheap in China, too, and the way counterfeiting generally works is that the fake is worth far less than the genuine item. All those chemicals and the technical training would cost a bundle. And if that's not enough evidence of a counterfeit story, then consider that the reports identified "Queers Network Research" as the organization that studied the phenomenon in Hong Kong.

The mainstream media carried no mention of the story. They were busy reporting other problems in China's food industry. But bloggers copied and pasted the tale without substantiation. One writer who had fallen for the story proclaimed proudly that the Chinese had blocked his blog in reaction to his investigative journalism. Here's another story for the blogs: I heard tell that somebody fed a chicken an odd jumble of chemicals until it was so fat its legs bowed and then tried to pass off its eggs and flesh as the real thing.

I feel like Gauguin. I'd go hide in Tahiti, except they're trying to ruin it. Take me home to the farm, to the land, where I can delude myself with a few chickens and a garden, and if, like Gauguin, my mind wanders, I'll be all right. I had a little piece of paradise, once, and I wouldn't have bartered it away for the life of me.

In Xinjiang province in the late 1990s, the Chinese trained ten thousand chickens to wage a war against locusts. The Chinese have had their share of locust plagues through history, and this was the worst in a decade, covering nearly half a million acres, according to the Xinhua News Agency. The chickens were willing soldiers, hungry for battle. They underwent a sixty-day training period, the report said, and tens of thousands of starlings were sent in to augment the troops. The chickens weren't quite up to the task of conquering a plague of locusts and did little to slow the onslaught. In 2007, facing another infestation, the Chinese tried an all-starling brigade.[23]

I have less ambitious expectations for my chickens. I wouldn't ask them to turn back a plague. I just want them to eat a few bugs and leave the garden alone.

After we began raising chickens, Suzanne reported that she was finding far fewer ticks on Sophie the pig when she came back to the house to be let into the kitchen after a day of grazing. Ticks are troubling pests in these parts; they can infect humans with the debilitating Lyme disease. I've yet to see a scorpion hereabouts, but I heard from a farmer in Texas that the venomous little vermin has no chance against his chickens—they peck off the stinger first, then work over the rest. In the barnyard, chickens spread and sift manure, drying it out as they feast on the myriad bits of undigested grain that attract mice and rats and the maggots that become flies. All these delights the hens turn into eggs. And for their good deeds, they need no training.

Even the finest dung heap isn't all nourishment to a chicken. Some things even a chicken's digestive tract can't put to use. These get redeposited, daintily, as some of the richest fertilizer known to mankind. Each chicken produces six or seven pounds of manure per year,[24] great for gardening—an avocation that their keepers often eagerly pursue.

Coops and crops can coexist, even thrive together, though the symbiosis requires nurturing. Chickens can destroy gardens with their incessant digging, strutting in and kicking as if they owned the place. And their manure is hot stuff, too: It's so potent with nitrates that it will burn any plant it touches unless composted for several months and mixed well with the soil. It's exceptionally high in nitrogen, and rich in phosphoric acid and potash. Think of it as manure concentrate.

A backyard chicken farmer in Oklahoma used five hens and a rooster from his flock to weed and de-thatch his lawn: He made a lightweight cage, four by eight feet, and put the chickens inside, moving the cage every few days. Within a week they'd not only tilled the soil but fertilized it, too.[25] Another Texas farmer designed what he called a "moat," a tall, fenced chicken run surrounding his garden, to foil a plague of grasshoppers. To get to the garden, the hoppers had to run a gamut of hungry chickens.[26] A North Carolina man divided his garden into three fenced sections, with a coop in the center to which each section had access. He let the chickens use one area and closed off the others for gardening, rotating the chicken run in ensuing years. Season to season, year to year, they fertilized his garden, and paid him in eggs for the privilege.[27]

Chickens can drive you to do things like that. But it's only fair. For millennia, chickens have had to put up with our crap. The least we can do is put up with theirs—and even try to appreciate it.

A farmer and inventor in Devonshire, England, turned chicken manure into fuel that he used for years to run his '53 Hillman. An article in *Mother Earth News* back in 1971 told the story of Harold Bate, who presaged the poop-to-power pundits of today. Bate, sixty-one, tinkered in his cottage with odds and ends until he concocted a methane "digester" that looked like a home fruit canner. He bottled the liquid methane under pressure and connected it through a converter to the car's carburetor. Saying it was ten times cheaper than running a car on gasoline, he proclaimed the technology simple and inexpensive— but you needed plenty of raw materials. He preferred a chicken-pig blend but had no particular brand loyalty. Even one's own manure would do, in a pinch.

How much manure did he need? From three hundred pounds, he said, he could bottle up the methane equivalent of sixty-two gallons of gasoline. Preparing five gallons' worth took him half an hour of steady pumping, he figured.[28]

Let me do some figuring of my own. If my fifty chickens each pooped six pounds a year, their sixty-two-gallon gasoline equivalent would be worth $190 at today's prices. But I'd have to spend over six hours at the methane pump, time that I could have devoted to earning extra pay. And I'd only get enough fuel to drive about 1,500 miles. My chickens could keep me commuting to Philly for about a month, but I'd save nothing.

Now, if I gathered up Sophie the pig's manure and added it to the brew, I could make enough methane to circle the globe. I've had a few roommates in my day who could power a jumbo jet, but I'd prefer not to ask them to contribute to the cause. I'm just figuring chickens here. And they're not going to put Big Oil out of business.

I find it hard, as well, to work up much enthusiasm for chickens in the garden. As fertilizer, their manure seems more trouble than it's worth; give me horse dung any day. They do know how to till, for sure. Their feet are remarkable implements, and they use them relentlessly to scratch and dig and kick the soil in search of grubs and other snacks. Whatever greenery gets in their way, the chickens will mow through it. I tell them, in various ways, some more effective than others, not to do this, but they don't respect me. They are not good gardeners. They come to destroy.

I know this too well. In the autumn of 2005, we embarked on another project: We planted daylilies. Not just a patch beside the garden, not just a few accents next to the porch, but lilies along the road, along the lane, behind the springhouse. We transplanted the entire stock that we purchased from a couple who were retiring from their daylily business. We rechristened our farm as Lilyfield.

The chickens liked what they saw. They delighted in the freshly turned soil. I spent hours replanting and grading in their wake, and shaking my rake so they might see the gravity of their sin. What they saw was a madman flailing about. They believed, of course, that the rich, fresh soil was a treasure placed there just for them.

Lilyfield is ours to tend as long as it pleases God. I think of what Jesus told his disciples after teaching them how to pray, how to praise God for each day's bread, how to ask forgiveness and forgive others. We needn't fear, he added, for our father surely will provide for his people even more abundantly than he has endowed all creation. "Consider the lilies of the field, how they grow," he told them. "They toil not, neither do they spin. And yet I say to you that even Solomon in all his glory was not arrayed like one of these."

I've been toiling aplenty, till my head spins. And a few years down the road, we'll have daylilies to peddle, too, or barter, and then we'll be off to other ventures and adventures. The self-sufficient life awaits us. No need to keep all our eggs in one basket.

WINTER

A Season to Reflect

The sunflowers drooped over brown vines as a warm breeze played through the garden at Lilyfield, rattling what was left of the year. The sun belied the season this December day, the kind so fine it hurts the heart and lulls a man to dream he'll see things through till spring.

Aldrovandi and I stepped through my rustic gate to see the sunflowers tall now, and glorious, stretching high as they might go. Suzanne knelt by the newly tilled beds, planting sweet basil and lemon thyme, and stood to accept my friend's hand.

I reached into my jacket and gave Suzanne the gift from his garden. She smiled at Aldrovandi, wiped her brow, and settled back to pulling out the tall, determined weeds.

Time had come undone in our dreams. Winter was summer, autumn was spring, and time seemed to swirl and loop back upon itself, as it does in those surreal moments before one awakens to the blare of the alarm and the parade of appointments.

We sat in Adirondack chairs in the center of the patch, where eggplant vines entwined the poles that Suzanne had meant for beans.

The beans had been willing to share, and the morning glory climbed high, too, to crown the poles in bursts of yellow and blue.

What a lovely mess we make. "Ulisse," I said, "welcome to the New World."

Aldrovandi seemed far younger here, in our weedy retreat. Our garden, overgrown from not enough hours in a day, didn't match his ordered grounds, but he liked it just the same, he said. Even now he was cataloguing all he saw, as we circled through the seasons.

I named each plant for him. He looked at the pen and the torn envelope I gave him for his notes and shrugged as he began to write.

"This is curly parsley," I said. "I love it in Latin, *Petroselinum crispum*. And these . . ." Suzanne helped me: "These are mustard greens," she said, "and there's my spicy Thai, and rosemary, and oregano. Over there—that's Ronde de Nice squash; one taste and it'll blow you away." She eased open the gate and told us she'd be back.

Aldrovandi pointed. "Your eggplant's doing well."

"It is, indeed," I said, but he was admiring the tomato vines. "Old-time varieties," I said. "Brandywine, there." I stood and picked a handful of tiny Sungolds and popped one in my mouth, offering one to him.

A hen tilled the soil outside the gate, pausing to inspect her work. "Is she the author of the colored egg you brought for me?" he asked.

"One of the Araucanas laid that egg," I said, and I explained to him one more wonder the New World would bring to the Old. "If an egg has two yolks, they say, you get a wish." He nodded. He'd heard the very same.

"What were you writing in your library?" I asked.

He was thrilled that I'd noticed. It was his latest, he said, on the world of insects, all there was to know. His eyes widened in his enthusiasm. I nodded politely as he regaled me with insect tales and trivia—and then he paused, pensive.

"I do have a wish," he said. "An old man's wish." He was eighty.

He would die soon, he knew. He should hope, he said, that people would want to know about the things he counted important. He wanted his life's work preserved. A museum, a library—his papers someday published. He hoped the world would not forget about him.

I thought of a young man dribbling a basketball, alone in a Philadelphia lot, the bounce echoing over crumbling pavement as he tried his shot again, and yet again. I touched Aldrovandi's hand: "You'll make it," I said.

Spring, summer, fall, winter—the months meld here in our garden, into one season, a perfect one. Here, I can see snowflakes powdering the cleome in full bloom, and the corn turning to tassel as we plant the first spring peas. And I know another garden now, of a man whose words I heard so well that I came to know him, too. Mostly, he wanted to get it all down. When he was right, he was very right, and if he had some things wrong—well, so do we. I'll barter my own dragons for a unicorn, any day.

The gate swung open, and Suzanne set a plate on the table between us. *"Pomodori!"* she said, in her best Italian. "Five varieties, including the oldest heirloom ever known. Enjoy." She turned to fill his basket with the bounty of our garden—herbs and vegetables, a squash, a russet daylily delicate and delicious as lettuce. And on top, one of our own tomatoes, an Italian variety called *Cuore de Toro,* "heart of the bull," so very far from home.

Kinder, Gentler

The very things we love most can do us harm, and that's why the "Pekker Protector" attracted plenty of interest after a New Mexico woman came up with the idea. She even sold T-shirts emblazoned with her invention's logo. Tyson Foods was among the biggest customers for the device—a pair of long, fingerless leather gloves to be worn when collecting eggs or rounding up chickens. It keeps those angry beaks from turning a forearm into mincemeat.[1]

You can hardly blame chickens for being surly. They've put up with a lot from us, for thousands of years.

To protect the grape harvest, for example, ancient vintners sacrificed roosters. Aldrovandi related how it was done: Two men grasped the bird and pulled in opposite directions until it gave way, then each paced through the vineyards purifying the grounds with his portion of the carcass; they reunited at ground zero to bury the halves together. I'm sure the other chickens watched, and grew cautious.

Fast-forward a few millennia to modern China, in the summer of 2008. As a proud Beijing preens in Olympic glory, hungry lions pace in pits in a zoo outside the city. Visitors who want a special thrill can plunk down their cash and get a live chicken tied to a bamboo pole.

"Fishing" for a lion, they tease it as it jumps for the bobbing bait until jaw or claw finally connects, and the squawking stops. From a restaurant overlooking the slaughter arena, the crowd applauds. Pay a little extra, and one of the staff will toss in a goat of your choice. Or take a safari though the compound: You can shove chickens down special chutes in the tour bus and watch the lions mince them.[2]

From antiquity to our enlightened age, we've been at times unkind. I retrieved the following three tales from the newspaper "morgue," which used to be a musty room overstuffed with yellowed newspaper clippings but which is now surfable on the World Wide Web, and I guess that's good:

Flint, Wales, 1997: Marauding schoolchildren, some as young as nine, club and kick two chickens to death on a sports field. As a finishing touch, they yank the heads off.

Te Awamutu, New Zealand, 2003: A family returns from vacation to find three of their pet chickens stabbed to death with colored pencils and felt-tipped pens. One chicken has been skewered eleven times, including the fatal thrust through the back. Police think teenagers did it.

Torquay, England, 2006: A coop keeper notices the latch is broken on the henhouse. Inside, she finds most of her birds bludgeoned to death and others dying, their eggs smashed. Nearby is a bloodied shovel.

Sickening, disgusting—words such as those were how the victims and the authorities described these sadistic acts.

Here's one more news story. It's a gentler tale:

Guffey, Colorado, 2003: Townsfolk hold their annual "chicken fly" to raise money for charities. Contestants pay for the privilege of launching chickens from twelve feet up, using a toilet plunger to compel them to take flight, if they can. Some just drop. None are hurt, organizers insist, or they wouldn't hold the event.

It's kind of funny, isn't it, to see a chicken go squawking at the end of a toilet plunger. The kids get a good laugh. It's good, clean, family fun, the participants say, and it helps the community. They see nothing sickening and disgusting about it.

And there are other ways that people can amuse themselves with chickens—like a good old-fashioned cockfight. They've been staged for ages in cultures too diverse to list. Cockfights do get bloody. But it's the roosters themselves that are spilling the blood, with some help from those who equip them with the cutting edge in battle gear to ensure a good show. The birds get to display their natural fighting spirit. From those who bait the combatants, you hear words such as "nature's way" and "they're just chickens." Hardly disgusting, if you put it that way.

An Oklahoma state senator thought he had a solution to appease those who found that distasteful: If it's the slashing that has everybody upset, just give the roosters little boxing gloves and protective vests, he suggested in 2005, two years after the state became one of the last to ban cockfights. The honorable pecker protector even introduced legislation that would have required the sparring mitts—if only the cherished cockfights could return to his fair state. It was a sarcastic salvo against those who had ruined what he considered a perfectly fine pastime.[3]

No doubt about it: Chickens can be mean. They'll draw blood, given a chance, from their keepers and from one another, and whether they do so because they're unhappy or just vicious doesn't matter to those who raise them for profit. It just has to stop. To prevent their birds from cannibalizing one another in the poultry house, U.S. chicken farmers often resort to "debeaking"—the removal of as much as half the upper beak and part of the lower beak, typically by searing it off with a hot blade or wire.

Now, it's true I could spare some of my own beak, or so I've been told, but I'd prefer to keep all of it, and my chickens feel the same way about theirs.

"Whar'd ye git that nose?" a pirate asked me as I took an evening stroll along the beach on Ambergris Caye in Belize three years ago.

He looked like a pirate, anyway—a snaggletoothed coot with an eye patch. Though he had no peg leg, he wobbled nonetheless as he leaned close, pointing a filthy finger at my face and muttering about my nose. I begged his pardon. He rolled his eyes and shuffled off toward the sea, raising his arms in exasperation. "I said whar'd ye *git that nose*!" he shouted into the black surf. I should have hauled off and debeaked him on the spot.

Increasing incidents of henhouse mayhem led to the introduction of the debeaking practice in the 1930s, at the dawn of the factory farm age. It was suggested as a temporary solution for the problem of cannibalism, which has been part of coop life since we rounded up the Red Jungle Fowl; the only way to avoid it would be to let chickens rove and ramble and roost in the willows if they wished, and you can be the one to fetch the eggs. So producers began routinely removing beaks. It became a final solution. Activists call it mutilation. Farmers call it trimming.

Ian Duncan, the Canadian biologist who studied the phenomenon of rapist roosters, compared behaviors of chickens that had been debeaked with those that got to keep theirs. He observed that birds without beaks do indeed peck less, for obvious reasons, but they also preen less, and they stand idle and doze more, too. He attributed the changes in behavior to chronic pain from the debeaking.[4] Other researchers have concluded that the initial pain is brief and the soreness may go away, eventually, as it would if their noses were sliced off.

British researchers offered test chickens two types of feed—a regular mix, and grain laden with the painkiller carprofen—and let them choose their own diet. The chickens were selected from commercial flocks; some were normal, others were lame. The researchers noted that the lame birds soon began eating much more of the drugged feed—and the worse their condition, the more of it they consumed. The normal birds didn't care which they ate.[5]

The crippled chickens, aware of their pain, had learned to give themselves medication. They would prefer not to be hurting. Chickens also would rather not be shackled by the feet as they're fed into the disassembly line for slaughter, a French study discovered in 2005. It causes them stress, the researchers concluded after careful observation,[6] though I can't imagine an alternative that would stress them less, other than forgoing the whole affair, which the chickens would prefer even more.

The point is this: These are feeling creatures. They get upset, and they strike back.

In the mid-1990s, after a dozen years of trying, a Purdue University geneticist managed to breed a kinder, gentler chicken. Bill Muir had concluded that when hens didn't get along, it was because of their competitive spirit driven by their focus on egg laying. By selectively breeding for social cooperation, he found he could engineer a significant increase in egg production and decrease in mortality in the henhouse. With the more recent scientific enlightenments of the genome project, scientists should be able to selectively breed even more effectively. We have tapped the power to create a truly chicken chicken.

If survival of the fittest were the only law governing evolution, Muir said, how do we explain the communal relationships within a beehive, where many are willing to die for the benefit of all? Survival of species, he suggests, has much to do with behaving socially, with showing the community spirit—with getting along. He applied the principle to developing more peaceable chickens.

Though the ancestral Red Jungle Fowl is highly territorial, its modern descendent has been compelled to put up with other chickens in an egg-laying cooperative. The focus on production, however, increased the need for food and water, and the modern chicken is highly competitive. Its totalitarian social system, the pecking order, can be fatal to weaklings. That's why farmers trim those beaks and keep the lights down low.

In his research, Muir chose birds with mild temperaments and others with a reputation for laying plenty of eggs, and he selectively bred them to bring out the desired traits. He kept the lay rate as high as possible while finessing a much lower mortality rate, improving the flock's total egg production dramatically. During his experiments, a power failure in one of the coops spiked the temperature, and some chickens died—but not his gentler birds. He concluded that his chickens, bred to handle social stress, were also more able to withstand physical stress.[7]

Laid-back chickens do well, it would seem. All the better to endure the shackles.

For every chicken whose beak is trimmed, you can be sure there will be a human squawking about it. Animal lovers abound, and they've extended their embrace to the chicken.

In Liverpool a few years ago, police removed the remains of a chicken from an alley. Later, passersby noticed that somebody had dropped off a bouquet of flowers, then someone else left a card, signed "a loving mother," with the words "safe in the arms of Jesus." Several other bouquets appeared, and more cards, even teddy bears. The police felt it behooved them to issue a statement to the public: "Stop grieving. It's only a chicken." As the news had spread through the neighborhood, they explained, the chicken carcass had become a dead baby.[8]

It's only a chicken.

In Philadelphia, the bustling Matthew J. Ryan Veterinary Hospital at the University of Pennsylvania gets eleven thousand visits a year to its emergency room from pet owners bringing in their ailing charges. Among the recent visitors was the owner of a pet chicken that had tangled with a dog and lost. The hospital folks didn't try to tell the chicken's distraught owner what the police told the befuddled Liverpudlians. Its leg and beak were broken. There was a job to do. The treatment cost about $3,000.[9]

When an Arkansas preacher found one of his hens, Boo Boo, floating in the pond, he fished her out and began giving her the Heimlich maneuver: He pushed her belly, he said, patted her back, and told her to live in the name of Jesus. His wife worked her over with a hairdryer and wrapped her in a towel.

His sister, a nurse, arrived and immediately began mouth-to-beak resuscitation.

"I breathed into its beak, and its dad-gum eyes popped open," she told the local newspaper, *The Daily Siftings Herald*. The next day they found Boo Boo perching on the edge of her box, in the sunshine of the porch. They took her back to the coop, but the other chickens were a little less loving, so she got her own quarters. The family had named her Boo Boo because she was a timid bird, easily spooked. They rechristened her Lazarette, the feminine of Lazarus, whom Jesus raised from the dead.[10]

Some folks may treat animals like humans, yes. Or they may forgo all flesh if they're vegetarians. I don't need to understand. It's their business, really, and I respect them infinitely more than those who mistreat what they deem to be "only" animals.

"You sell eggs?" a reporter asked as I sorted and cleaned my daily dozen in the pantry sink at the *Inquirer*.

"I do indeed. You buy eggs?" I asked.

He looked into the sink and grimaced. "I'm not into eating embryos," he said.

I'm into eating barbecue—or I was. Having read more than a few reports about the meat industry, I'm finding my pulled-pork sandwich and slow-smoked drumstick to be a little less tasty. There was a time when I felt at liberty to tease my friend Addam about his daily bran muffin. I don't anymore. I tasted some vegetarian chili one winter day that nearly converted me, so savory were its flavors.

Some animal lovers and vegetable killers have evolved into activists, raising our collective consciousness. The animal rights movement is alive and kicking in the United States and has won sweeping changes through protests, public awareness campaigns, and political and economic pressure. Since the '60s, it has ranged far and wide, moving well beyond its initial concern for cuddly pets and barnyard animals. Today it is pushing for reforms in animal husbandry such as those that have been instituted in Europe since the late 1990s.

Among the European reforms is a ban on forced molting, which is still routine in the United States. A hen naturally undergoes an annual molt, usually in the fall as the days are shortening, but it can happen at any time if she is under stress. She loses her old feathers and grows fresh ones while tissues regenerate in her oviduct. This saps much of her energy, and her egg production temporarily stops—but it rallies afterward. Early in the twentieth century, farmers learned how to control the molt to their own advantage. By regulating it, they could keep egg production at optimum levels and lengthen the hen's lay life, boosting profits. To get the hen to lose her feathers, they needed to stress her out. An obvious way: withholding feed.

The American Veterinary Medical Association recently approved a resolution, after rejecting it for several years, to cease its support of the practice. The activists call it starvation; the farmers call it fasting. Whatever it's called, there are alternatives.

A 1996 study from the United Arab Emirates compared several methods for inducing molt.[11] Most of the methods require hens to lose a quarter to a third of their weight while molting, which gears up their bodies to lay the most eggs afterward. The conventional feed restriction was most prevalent, the researchers reported, because it was simple and easily combined with water deprivation and manipulation of light for best results. Molting can also be induced by minerals in the diet such as aluminum or zinc. The hens lay just as many eggs afterward and fewer die, the researchers said, but the method was considered to be impractical for large-scale production.

Hormone therapy effectively induces molt, too, they found, and the method doesn't require the initial severe loss in body weight. A Ukraine study had reported on the hormone method back in 1976 and found that not only does it work but that more hens survive. But the hens got depressed. They adopted a "penguin" stance for three or four days, the report said, without explaining,[12] and Lord knows what they were thinking. Here's what I'm thinking: It's a bad idea to mess with a female's hormones.

In the conventional method, the hens go hungry for a solid week or more. A University of Georgia study found a way to reduce that time to a single day, if the hens afterward consumed a "molt diet" low in energy and density. When the hens in the study resumed laying, they pumped out just as many eggs as those that had gone unfed for a week.[13] Other studies have examined how hens respond to dietary imbalances caused by iodine and sodium.

As producers feel the pressure to find alternatives, researchers have increasingly been evaluating which methods cause the hens the least stress. It can't be eliminated. A hen's natural molt leaves her looking rather strung out, sometimes as bedraggled as a pterodactyl. The studies are considering whether the forced methods actually cause her any worse stress than nature deals her.

The conventional tiers of battery cages, in which hens have little room to move, are another front in the chicken-rights campaign. Germany, Austria, Switzerland, and Sweden are among nations that have already banned the rows of cages that long have characterized poultry production. The entire European Union is phasing them out by 2012, requiring "enriched" cages that are a third larger than those now used in the United States. The chickens' fancy new digs will have roosts and nest boxes and litter where they can dust-bathe.

Even these cages are not good enough for Switzerland and Germany, which require birds to be raised on free range or in aviary systems—much larger cages in which the hens move freely and lay their eggs in communal nests. Switzerland, which banned battery cages for layers in the 1990s, found that egg production costs doubled.[14]

Animal rights activists have long called for at least the aviary systems. Critics have said that too many eggs would be laid on the aviary floor or otherwise lost, and that the chickens would peck one another to pieces. A Canadian study in 1996, however, compared birds raised three to a cage in a battery system with those raised in an aviary with nests and tiers of shared feeders and drinking trays. Over three years, the study found no difference in the size of the eggs, how many were deformed or cracked, and the total number of eggs laid. Very few eggs ended up on the aviary floor. And no more hens died in the aviary than in the cages.[15]

Though the animal rights campaigners have found their victories fewer in the United States, activists have persuaded fast-food chains such as McDonald's and supermarkets such as Whole Foods Market to adopt standards for treatment of animals. By staging highly visible public protests, the animal rights groups brought pressure on the marketers to protect their image. By changing their standards, the marketers brought pressure on the meat industry for concessions that the activists could not hope to have achieved alone.

Whole Foods Market, a purveyor of all things organic and natural, decided in 2003 to become a little more humane, as well. It was the first major grocery chain to accept new standards, advocated with passion by groups such as People for the Ethical Treatment of Animals (PETA), Animal Rights International, Vita, and the Animal Welfare Institute. The company knew its upscale shoppers would cringe at how the animals it sold were treated before and during slaughter, and it instituted new policies even at the risk of meat prices rising. Ducks, for example, had to have access to sunshine and fresh air and a clean place to swim. The company forbade debeaking.[16]

McDonald's was among the first major corporations to change its buying practices, and Ronald, that clown, has a way of getting what he wants. The fast-food behemoth agreed in 2000 to buy eggs only from suppliers who provided twice the average cage space per bird. For economy of scale, most cages allowed each bird only about six-by-seven inches. McDonald's called for about eight-by-nine. The company also told farmers it wouldn't buy their eggs if they forced their hens to molt. It denounced debeaking, too, but called for it to be phased out gradually, acknowledging that the practice was endemic. Burger King and Wendy's soon followed with similar requirements.

McDonald's began requiring annual audits of its meat suppliers to assess their attention to animal welfare. More recently, in 2001, the National Council of Chain Restaurants and the Food Marketing Initiative, working closely with animal welfare experts, also began audits for beef, dairy, poultry, eggs, and other farm products.[17]

The retailers and restaurateurs want to be able to demonstrate to consumers that they're doing what's right, which may be something other than selling the cheapest subsidized burger possible. For help in developing its standards and devising the audits, McDonald's appealed in 1999 to Temple Grandin, a renowned animal behaviorist and professor at Colorado State University who has designed many of the livestock holding facilities in use in the United States and throughout the world.

"I think in pictures. Words are like a second language to me." Those are the opening words to Grandin's book *Thinking in Pictures,* in which she invites her readers on a journey with her through the nearly inscrutable world of autism. Until well after her third birthday, she couldn't speak as she struggled and raged in a lonely land where few can visit: "I screamed because it was the only way I could communicate." In time, she learned to interpret the "ways of the natives."

At sixteen, plagued by anxiety attacks, she noticed at her aunt's ranch how cattle grew calm in a chute used to hold them immobile for veterinary work. She ventured into the chute and found that it calmed her, too. People with autism often find physical pressure reassuring; they sometimes want to wear very tight belts and clothes. But a cattle chute just wouldn't do, her psychologists admonished. They felt she was fixating on it. Her science teacher and mentor encouraged her to use it, but only if she would try to explain how it worked. With his guidance, she investigated the science behind why pressure calms nerves.

Grandin later devised a "squeeze machine" for humans that applied pressure with foam pads and compressed air. Her early "fixation" on the cattle chute, she said, became the foundation of her career. She turned her attention to the needs of animals, excelling as a scientist with an uncanny empathy for how they feel, how they communicate what they need.

With her visual mind, a hallmark of autism, she found she could conceive designs that work best for corrals and holding pens. Her ideas helped the livestock industry set higher standards for humane treatment. She came to understand the nature of beasts destined for slaughter, what scared them most, and how their terror and their pain could be lessened.[18]

By the turn of the millennium, the public was taking notice of industry conditions that seemed deplorable. The disassembly line was moving ever faster, and the animals had been stunned so haphazardly that some were alive, awake, and bellowing as the knives began dismembering them. Grandin had already assessed the situation for the Department of Agriculture. Hired by McDonald's, she helped set more rigorous treatment standards for animals, including broilers and layers.

Grandin developed an audit check sheet for assessing the treatment of poultry from hatchery to slaughterhouse, with standards she considers stronger than the audit used by the National Chicken Council. Her audit includes core criteria that she says warrant automatic failure if violated.

In the hatchery, mechanical sorters must never dispose of live chicks along with the eggshell fragments, crush or injure them, or toss them out onto the floor. Half the hatchlings are deemed worthless in a facility that supplies chicks for the egg industry. The males have it tough. They'll never lay an egg, and they're the wrong breed to be cold for meat. As the chirruping masses proceed down the production line, the human "sexers" pluck out the males and weaklings. The only two acceptable ways to destroy them, by Grandin's standards, are by gassing them with carbon dioxide or feeding them into a macerator, which instantly minces them with spinning blades. They may not be heaped into bags and left to smother.

On the farm where birds are raised to the correct weight for slaughter, wet litter and ammonia levels must be kept to strict minimums. The ventilation system must have a backup—either a generator or a telephone warning system if it fails—and birds must be able to move freely without piling atop one another. They must be able to walk freely for at least ten steps.

In the slaughter plant, the holding cages must be in good repair and roomy enough for all birds to lie down at the same time. No more than 3 percent of the birds can end up with broken or dislocated wings. The stunning device, whether it uses electricity or gas, must knock out 99 percent of the birds, and the same efficiency is expected of the cutters in the bleed machine. For any bird that does miss the cutters, a backup bleeder person must be available with a knife to dispatch it so that it does not enter the scalder alive. Only one hapless bird per day may be scalded alive.

In addition, Grandin's standards strictly forbid keeping poultry in near-darkness, and it's just not acceptable for anybody to be throwing or stomping on the birds. If too many of them are dead on arrival at the slaughterhouse (meaning more than one per two hundred received), she suggests that the catchers who round them up at the farm be paid a financial incentive to encourage them to be gentler.[19]

To reduce such deaths and bruising, some producers have turned to mechanical chicken catchers. The machine is a garden tractor that pushes a rolling barrel lined with rubber fingers to snatch the birds and whisk them away through chutes and conveyors into boxes, ready to be stacked on a truck bound for the processing plant. Perdue Farms tried the machines and reported that bruising was reduced 14 percent, increasing meat profits significantly. The human catchers, who had sued Perdue for overtime payment, complained that the machine was introduced to intimidate them and to thwart their drive to unionize.[20] As for the chickens, they don't really care whether humans chase them down on foot or behind the wheel. They regard both methods as disconcerting.

Even before the McDonald's initiative, United Egg Producers had drafted and issued its own guidelines for how producers should treat chickens. The industry group, heeding the public's increasing concern with the battery-cage issue, called for more cage space per chicken.[21] Since the newer, roomier ways were being endorsed by the fast-food giants and marketing groups, the egg industry had little choice but to accept reform, even if it raised production costs, because nothing costs more than lost business.

If the public continues to crave more humane farming, it seems inevitable that the industry will progressively invest in kindness. Though chickens are mainly raised for foodstuff, it still pays to treat them well.

And it pays to treat people well, too. For the industry, that means making sure working conditions for employees in the processing plants are tolerable and fair—that is, humane. For the activists, that means not losing sight of the fact that people are animals, too.

Most animal rights activists have little or no farm experience, according to surveys[22]—just like the average citizen, which is what they are. You can't conclude that their urban leanings and general lack of farm background render them clueless. As a cross section of society, their opinions matter.

When I was small, my classmates and I saved our dimes for a "Send a Mouse to College" drive to provide mice for medical research. The collection envelopes pictured a cute little rodent in a mortarboard. The idea was to save human lives. I cannot imagine such a fund-raiser today. The use of animals in laboratory experiments was one focus of the newly mobilized activists. The mice mattered. Human lives could wait.

Civil disobedience is a time-tested method of getting your way, and some activists have risked arrest by conducting raids on poultry farms to steal their property, "rescuing" the animals while videotaping what they maintain are abusive operations. But some activists have morphed into vandals and terrorists, particularly those who have come down hard on trappers and hunters.

I recall writing a headline for a news story in Allentown, Pennsylvania, in the late '80s in which somebody, in the wee hours, had hurled red paint over the front door and windows of a downtown furrier. It was one example of violence that got much worse. In Bloomington, Minnesota, somebody firebombed a fur shop in 1996, and a radical animal rights group applauded the crime. A spokesman denounced the killers who exploited animals.

Nothing was said about the risk to the firefighters who battled the fire, a Minneapolis newspaper columnist pointed out at the time. Nor did anyone mention how many furry creatures have perished, their habitats destroyed, their wetlands drained, to make way for suburban homes.[23]

At Valley Forge Park, just a few miles from Lilyfield, animal rights demonstrators have rallied in attempts to thwart controlled hunts of the deer that devastate the trees and foliage. Along our own roadfront, I see hoofprints by the dozens where the deer have ambled through and stopped to lop off the succulent daylily blooms. Though I haven't hunted since I was a teenager, there are days when my mouth waters for the gamey flavor of venison.

It's hard to hate deer. They are adorable. Tourists line the trails at Valley Forge to admire them as they do their damage in the evening mist. And the poor things have a right to get hungry. There are so many of them, heaven knows, and only so many trees left for them to destroy. Something has disturbed the natural order of predator and prey. Something like subdivisions. And something seems to be disturbing our natural ability to use common sense.

I like chickens. They're beautiful, intriguing creatures. I don't want to see them suffer needlessly. So many humane measures can be taken, at minimal cost, to ease their pathetic lot. But cruelty is relative. Do we only care about animals we perceive to be beautiful, or intelligent? Shall we protect chimpanzees and elevate them to human heights while remaining indifferent to fish? How about mussels?

Humans are sentient, mostly, often intelligent, and sometimes beautiful. Many of them are poor, too, and they can't afford the heightened price of those free-range or organic eggs in cartons stacked high in the supermarket. And let me say this again: Most of those aren't truly free-range; only a tiny percentage of chickens live in anything other than factory farms. If we returned all chickens to bucolic barnyards, eggs might rival caviar in price. Or perhaps we should release all the chickens back into the jungle. Some people would applaud—mostly people who can afford their grocery bills— though the chickens would inevitably die.

All of nature is interrelated and worth preserving, as Aldrovandi made clear in his fervor to chronicle it all. If we care about the masses of hungry people in a needy world, we need to keep prices within range of their budgets, and that's a challenge that agribusiness eagerly seeks to fulfill. Whenever we assert that an animal has rights, it's fitting to count the cost. If we can find ways to take better care of our fellow creatures—through science and innovation with a generous portion of empathy—while not condemning what agriculture has done to take care of people, we'll have found the delicate balance between animal rights and human compassion.

In Sickness and Health

⋋⋌ ⋋⋌

The five-year-old boy, playing in his yard in central Thailand in 2005, beheld his neighbor's magnificent roosters waiting to be chased, and he did what children everywhere do: He ran, he played. Soon he fell ill, and died, as did the roosters.[24]

A year earlier, in another province, an eighteen-year-old man died a week after entering his rooster in a cockfight. The man had noticed that as his prize bird struggled in the pit it seemed to be having trouble breathing, and he mercifully stopped the fight. He sucked mucus and blood from its beak,[25] a common practice, then let it get back to business. A man must do what a man must do. He soon fell ill.

The suspect, in both cases, was avian influenza, wrought by the H5N1 virus that was sweeping Southeast Asia. Thailand banned cockfighting temporarily after the man's death, and health teams killed every rooster within ten kilometers of where the boy was infected.

Confined mostly to birds, the disease has advanced to threaten more and more humans, killing more than half of those it has been known to infect, according to the World Health Organization. As of March 2008, avian flu had killed 236 people, most of them in

Indonesia and Vietnam, out of 373 known infections worldwide, the agency reported.[26] That number was almost certain to rise.

Avian flu emerged as a public health threat in 1997 with an outbreak among humans in Hong Kong. Six of the eighteen victims succumbed, but the disease seemed to disappear after the entire Hong Kong chicken population was put to death. That was about 1.5 million birds—a drastic measure, but some experts believe it averted a pandemic. A few years later, however, the flu reappeared in Hong Kong, then surfaced in Thailand, Vietnam, Indonesia, and Cambodia, which took varying degrees of protective action.[27]

As the death toll rose in Indonesia, the government responded to harsh criticism that it was doing little to stop the spread of the virus: It embarked on a major effort to vaccinate the nation's chickens. In Jakarta, authorities decreed early in 2007 that poultry must be removed from residential areas and certified as healthy. As inspectors searched for contraband, people hid their birds. One man, insisting his goose would stay, held a knife to an officer's face.[28]

Such resistance has been a major problem in Indonesia, where impoverished families struggle for every day's sustenance and will often slaughter dying poultry rather than lose a meal. Industrial biosecurity measures in developing nations have often been lacking or poorly enforced. Indonesia, trying to overcome lagging sales, has tried to face the issue by opening regional avian flu centers to fight the outbreak on a more local level and perhaps reassure consumers.[29] Anticipating that demand for poultry would rebound with a respite from flu deaths, some Indonesian agribusinesses increased their investments in the industry.[30] Meanwhile, the authorities were snatching birds from the locals—some of whom depend on their flocks as a sole source of income.[31]

In 2006, the flu spread to Turkey and Russia, then to Africa and Europe, carried by migrating waterfowl, which can harbor the viruses without symptoms. The waterfowls' feces infect flocks of chickens and other poultry that come in contact with it. The ravaged poultry then infect pigs, which can pass it to humans, though scientists believe the virus has mutated enough to leap without a bridge.[32] Besides mouth-to-beak contact at cockfights, cases in Asia have been attributed to the practice of consuming raw duck blood. A traditional Vietnamese dish called *tiet canh vit,* a pudding served on death anniversaries and other special occasions, is made from a duck's blood, stomach, and intestines. Health investigators suspect several people who contracted bird flu near Hanoi in 2005 had dined on the delicacy.[33]

Scientists and governments, bracing for the possibility that the virus would mutate into a highly contagious strain, have strived to develop and stockpile vaccines and antiviral drugs and to contain the spread of the virus. Numerous countries have eradicated flocks on large scales. Worldwide, more than 200 million chickens had been killed as of 2007.[34] Carbon dioxide gassing has been the preferred method, though the U.S. government has approved use of firefighting foam to suffocate the birds.

Import and export bans are in force. U.S. authorities, for example, forbid imports of birds and unprocessed bird products from a long list of nations in Asia, Europe, Africa, and the Middle East. The flu struck a turkey farm in southeast France in 2006, the first incidence at a commercial poultry farm in the European Union, and dozens of nations blocked poultry imports from the country, the biggest producer on the continent. International efforts to coordinate the containment and to plan for a pandemic have had mixed results, however, with some nations lacking the resources or the political will.[35]

Because the disease has jumped to humans in Southeast Asia, where the impoverished mingle with poultry and pigs in crowded conditions, news reports have focused on the risk from family flocks and on the few people who are dying from contact with infected birds. The large poultry operations nearby attract less attention. There, birds are packed into tight quarters; viral mutations have plenty of opportunity to take hold, and biosecurity may be nil.

Some media accounts have turned apocalyptic, imagining populations worldwide devastated by the killer from the East. A television movie dramatized such a doomsday. Another threat to the poultry industry that could turn out to be bigger than the avian flu is the publicity that attends it.

In 2006, as the virus and the news of it spread, poultry consumption fell in Europe and Asia. In China, where Kentucky Fried Chicken has had high hopes of tapping into the buoyant economy, sales turned bleak: Fearing the flu, consumers kept their distance. In some European nations, poultry sales dropped by more than half, and they didn't pick up until the news alerts slowed down. "Lottery Win More Likely Than Asian Flu," *The Times* of London claimed, and similar sentiments began to win back consumers. Kentucky Fried Chicken outlets put up posters trying to reassure customers that their food was safe.

Major producers in the United States see how much is at stake. Though nobody has contracted avian flu from eating poultry—cooking kills the virus—the perception of danger could devastate the business. In a Harvard survey, nearly half the respondents said they would stop eating chicken if avian flu struck the American poultry industry. If sales do decline, producers and restaurant chains say, they are ready with ad campaigns to educate the public. Meanwhile, caution prevails. Some farms require testing of birds before they are sent to slaughter, and anyone entering or leaving poultry houses must wear plastic booties and walk through disinfectant baths.[36]

How consumers would actually react, however, is hard to predict. They might blame peasants and squalor and look askance at backyard coops not only in Asia but anywhere, and insist on getting their chicken and eggs from federally inspected sources. Others, already wary of faraway food and inclined to enjoy the local bounty, could set up their own coop or buy directly from the farmer at the market, who seems healthy enough.

Backyard flocks, however, should be brought indoors at any sign that the avian flu has entered the United States, health authorities advise.[37] Left to forage in the dirty outdoors, chickens risk contact with the feces of migrating species, according to the official word; the biosecurity controls of factory farms are far more likely to ward off the virus. Should a pandemic arise, the learned ones say, it will surely be traced to some ramshackle coop in a developing nation, not to a health-conscious poultry parlor. To deal with the threat, several nations in Europe and Asia banned outdoor flocks and "village chickens," creating a hardship for families that depend on chickens for their livelihood or their next meal.

Never mind that the poultry industry exports its products and its wastes far and wide. If the virus rears its head, people such as me could be among the villains. Just as some consumers are beginning to remember the succulent taste of a free-living chicken and the ecstasy of its eggs, farmers are once again being encouraged to lock it inside, where it can forage in front of a hopper and soon begin to taste like . . . something other than chicken.

I guess I understand. It's hard for me to find anything menacing in the crisp autumn air at Lilyfield, but the migrating risk is real. Avian influenza fears are hardly a phobia. A precedent of devastation was set ninety years ago, when the Spanish flu felled millions around the globe. Humanity had yet to discover the lowly but mighty virus. Recent genetic analysis confirmed that the killer was the avian flu.[38]

One of its hallmarks was who it killed: healthy young adults, in whom it triggered a lethal immune reaction, rather than the very young and old. And it killed swiftly after onset of symptoms. The H1N1 strain of that flu had mutated so that it could easily infect humans and spread from person to person. So far, H5N1 hasn't done that. The fear is this: It will.

The chicken, as portrayed during the avian flu alert, has seemed both victim and villain. In the very lands where it originated, where the chicken first fell into human hands, a virus arose with the potential to lay it low and wreak destruction. It would seem the chicken is crossing a perilous road—but I'm having a hard time imagining that it's out to waste the world.

It's not the first time the chicken has been killed and feared for matters beyond its control. People often blame it, for example, as the source of the common chicken pox: The sores look like chicken pecks, for one, and, after all, why else would the disease be so named? Here's why: The ancients likened the lesions to chickpeas, or *cicer* in Latin, and the name stuck, though not the association.

Once upon the Internet, I found a list of how famous people—authors, celebrities, and the like—would answer the eternal question about a chicken's ulterior motive. I remember laughing at only one of the responses, and it still cracks me up, though lately it gives me pause:

"Why did the chicken cross the road?"

Ernest Hemingway: "To die. In the rain."

Far from being a killer, the chicken has been a healer for millennia, as the ancients well knew. Not only was the chicken considered good for what ailed us, but we were good for the ailing hen as well. Common folk soothed a sick hen by inserting a feather through her nostrils, moving it a little each day. Her dignity suffered, however, and "though this method sometimes cured the hens," Aldrovandi said, "it has been found that frequently it kills many of them."

He listed a few alternatives for his learned readers: "Some people . . . boil garlic in human urine and bathe the hen's beak in it, taking the greatest possible care that none of the liquid flows into the hen's eyes."

Thoughtful.

"Others bathe her mouth with tepid urine and press it until the bitterness forces the nausea of the pip to pass through the nostrils." He cited Columella. But if the chicken is dreadfully sick, "recourse must be had to the steel"—the ancients suggested cutting the cheeks, pressing out the pus, and then pausing "to rub a little pounded salt into the wound," all the while leading the chicken into the shade. In the shade, at least, it would be relatively comfortable as it died anyway.

In the age of fossil fuels, the treatments became more sophisticated. A 1920 agricultural primer called *The School-Book of Farming* advised that chickens aren't worth the cost of medicine, but it did offer the following home cure: "If the bird sneezes and shows a slight mucus discharge from the nose, mouth, or eyes, then it is possible to cure her. The easiest and surest method is to plunge the entire head into kerosene, holding it there but a moment. The fowl should then be removed to a comfortable place and receive wholesome food. A slight film of kerosene should be kept on her drinking water for three days. Usually one treatment cures."[39]

Leave sick chickens alone, Dixon recommended in his Victorian-era treatise on their care. In the morning, you'll find them either thriving "or as flat as pancakes and dried hiffins." We have done far worse to chickens than the feather torture and the salt rub and all those pissy treatments. They survive despite us, as they help ease our pains.

We owe the chicken quite a debt for the role it has played in fighting disease. Chicken eggs have long been used to develop flu vaccines, and research continues into other ways that the chicken can assist in human health issues. Recent work at Virginia Tech, for example, has attempted to modify the virus that causes the deadly Newcastle disease in poultry so that it can be used to treat prostate cancer in humans.[40]

Ironically, the chicken and its eggs may play a key role in halting the avian flu. Because the virus, unlike many others, infects both humans and poultry, studies of the chicken's immune system can help us understand how the disease spreads in humans. From the intelligence gathered in the human and chicken genome projects, scientists can compare the genes that we share to look for cures we might share.

Through biotechnology, scientists can now harvest wondrous things—like compounds such as insulin for diabetics—from the eggs of genetically modified hens. And when exposed to viruses and bacteria, a hen produces antibodies in her blood that end up concentrated inside the egg to protect her chick. This little trick has been giving immunologists plenty of opportunity to play with needles. They've jabbed an array of unseemly things into the hen's body to see what defenses she puts into her eggs. With new research comes new hope for fighting numerous human maladies, whether tooth decay or a flu pandemic.[41]

As a boy during the Depression, Maurice Hilleman tended the chickens at the farm where he grew up on the Montana plains, near the Little Bighorn battlefield. As a young microbiologist in the late 1940s, he discovered mutation patterns in the flu virus, helping to anticipate outbreaks that could lead to pandemics such as the Spanish flu and the one now feared from avian influenza. According to colleagues, by the time he died in April 2005, Hilleman, through the vaccines he developed, had saved more lives than any other modern scientist.[42]

Reflecting on his career in his later years, he attributed much of his success to the chickens and their eggs: "Coming from a farm, I always had a good friend called the chicken." Relatives raised him there after his mother died giving birth to him and his twin sister, who also didn't survive the birth. This was during the time the Spanish flu pandemic raged, and he blamed it for their deaths.

Attending college on a scholarship, he won acclaim for a graduate thesis at the University of Chicago that reported, for the first time, how to identify strains of chlamydia, which cause venereal disease. He did it by producing antibodies in chickens that he injected with the microorganism. He had accomplished what had been considered impossible.

Through his career, most of it at Merck & Co. in Philadelphia, he developed twenty-seven vaccines that spared millions from dread childhood diseases including measles and mumps, chicken pox and rubella, as well as hepatitis, pneumonia, and meningitis. Once, mumps infected two hundred thousand children a year in the United States alone; when Hilleman's five-year-old daughter came down with the disease in 1963, he swabbed her throat and isolated the mumps virus. His total career achievement, Merck's president said upon his death, "dwarfs that of any other scientist working today."

When it came to safely culturing large amounts of pathogens that could be weakened for use in mass production of vaccines, Hilleman was an artist, colleagues said. The chicken's embryo is essential for developing sufficient quantities of microorganisms—and the gratitude that Hilleman expressed toward his boyhood chickens reflected his appreciation for their lifesaving eggs.

After he had developed the measles vaccine, Hilleman soon discovered that the embryos in which it was grown also harbored a chicken virus that caused leukemia. He needed a supply of chickens certified to be free of the leukemia virus. A California poultry operation had such specimens but refused to part with the birds—until the research director learned that Hilleman was a fellow Montanan. "Montana blood runs very thick," Hilleman later commented.

When a vaccine was needed to fight the influenza threat of 1957, he mobilized the production, pushing for poultry breeders to keep a supply of willing roosters on hand to fertilize the forty million eggs needed to meet the demand. In his early research, he had discovered the genetic "drift" in the flu virus that makes it necessary to develop a new vaccine each year. But in the latest outbreak of flu, originating in Hong Kong, he noted that the virus had undergone a "shift" to a new strain, and blood tests showed the U.S. public had no resistance. His massive vaccine production effort, in collaboration with the chicken, may have averted a scenario rivaling the outbreak of the Spanish flu.

Hilleman saved countless chicken lives as well as human ones. By developing a vaccine against Marek's disease, a devastating chicken lymphoma caused by a herpes virus, he revolutionized the poultry industry and saved producers millions of dollars in losses a year. When his vaccine was licensed in 1971, it was the first for use against a viral cancer—one of his career goals.

"I figured I owed it to the chickens," Hilleman later said.

Home to Roost

T hey don't like the sun, these mutant chickens that Avigdor Cahaner has made. Like spiders, they shy away from it. The rays threaten to sear their already-red skin, devoid of feathers. As they flap their barren wings, they look like escapees from the meat counter.[43]

He calls them naked chickens, fittingly, and the professor believes they could be a savior for a hungry world. The climate is hot in much of the developing world, where farms are rising to the challenge of feeding the masses. Regular chickens, the feathered kind, have trouble keeping their cool. The naked birds would fare better in family coops, where air-conditioning is not an option. Fewer people would go hungry.

Imagine: naked chickens jumping for bugs, fanning their wing joints, and copulating, if they can. They'd be cheap entertainment, too.

As a farm boy, Cahaner once helped slaughter dozens of his family's flock when a heat wave threatened to extinguish them near Passover time. As a professor at Hebrew University, he began looking for a better way, and in 2000 he conceived the idea of a chicken for the new age—one that could withstand more abuse in hot sheds, one that would never need plucking, saving all that time and trouble and waste.

The contribution to humanity seems staggering.

He found an existing mutant strain with a naked-neck gene, but the bird was small and scrawny. He set to work, and no genetic engineering was required: Like the chicken fanciers of the Victorian age, Cahaner cross-bred the best prospects to see what hatched. Unlike them, however, he was not exactly looking for plush plumage. By breeding the mutant strain with brawny broilers, he eventually crafted his creation, coaxing it to shed what few feathers it still had and to get plump and ready to grill in six weeks, like a commercial bird. It got fatter quicker partly because it didn't spend energy growing feathers.

How does it taste? You tell me. His naked chicken, the professor says, is nearly ready for market.

Great achievements don't come without sacrifice—or that's what our parents' parents were taught around the hearth. The hungry masses clamor to be fed, as do hungry investors, stomping at the trough. If we are to satisfy such appetites, something must give—and it has. Science and business have re-engineered the chicken for the modern economy. They have changed our very lives. So much the better. We were bumpkins once.

You'll still find real chickens out there. A privileged few still dart about in barnyards and backyards, reveling in horse manure and marigolds, oblivious to the yammering masses huddled in the poultry sheds across the county line. But the heirloom hens can't compete with a factory chicken, and bloodlines have faded away for lack of interest.

Many of the historic breeds of chickens are endangered, according to the American Livestock Breeds Conservancy, which tracks their status through a periodic census of poultry breeders. The conservancy lists twenty breeds as "critical" (close to extinction) and several others as threatened. These are birds that may have superior immune systems that could be crucial if the tiered-cage system falls further from favor and more chickens are raised outdoors.

Among the old farmyard favorites that are slipping into history are the Buckeye, Delaware, Holland, Chantecler, and Java. Some of these are old-time meat birds, succulent and rare, that don't have a chance against today's superbirds. Many of the hatcheries that once produced them have closed and given up their breeding flocks.

To save rare chickens, people need to eat them: An economic fundamental is that supply meets demand. A consumer taste for heirlooms would help to ensure their survival, according to the authors of *Counting Our Chickens,* a conservancy report on the endangered breeds.[44] But don't look for them at the supermarket. Instead, the report says, try farmers' markets, community supported agriculture, and Internet directories of local food sources. Or raise a flock of rare chickens yourself, and let them reproduce—you'll eat well and sleep well.

There's hope: Numerous rare-breed clubs are saving lines such as the Black Java. Developed in the early 1800s, it is one of the earliest American varieties, a meaty breed with a long, broad back and deep chest. The last commercial Java supplier, in Minnesota, closed in the late 1950s, and for half a century the breed was thought to be extinct. But a small flock endured at Garfield Farm, a prairie farmstead in Illinois now working actively to cultivate the breed. Genetic testing certified the Garfield flock as purebred.[45]

Small family farms where such rare birds might rebound, however, are themselves threatened with extinction. Barnyards are few these days. In the agricultural revolution of the past century, family farms began to vanish—and gone, too, was the self-reliance that defined them.

In 1932, when my father escaped Brooklyn to a Pennsylvania farm, he joined a rural force that defined the nation. A quarter of the population lived on six million farms.[46]

Mercer County was no Brooklyn. In the city, most homes had dial telephones. In Coolspring Township, the nearest phone was in a general store at the end of the dirt road, and young Burton Leroy Sheasley, who at twenty-one fancied himself wise to the world, had to prevail upon the long-suffering locals to show him how to crank it.

But this was the Depression, and my grandparents had dreamed, like many, of having a little place of their own, away from the insidious city. The extended family endured the hard times there, sold timber from the woods when they nearly lost the mortgage, raised cows and chickens and pigs—and subsisted. The family got through.

Two-thirds of those farms are gone, now, and the remaining ones show little resemblance to the patches where so many scratched and toiled. Small family farms have yielded to large commercial operations. By 1960, the farm population had plummeted to 8 percent. Today only about 2 percent of America's population lives on farms.

Most of the loss came as technology transformed agriculture after the Depression and World War II. Few could afford the fancy machinery of the new age, in which farmers became debtors. Those who tried to compete began to specialize, focusing on efficiencies. Machines meant less labor: Buy a baler, fire the hired hand.

Multitudes of the rural jobless fled to the cities after the Depression, lured by the war boom, and they weren't coming back. Later in the century, the surviving small farmers found prices stagnating as their costs got ever higher. They took second jobs, or gave up. Their children observed this, and left—and they, too, were gone to stay.[47]

I didn't go back to Mercer County.

My father and uncle had managed their dairy farm frugally, eschewing much of modernity. They plowed with horses till well into the 1950s. They were snowbound on the day I was born, February 19, 1958. Hitching a buckboard to their new Farmall Model H tractor, my father bundled my mother up on the seat and pulled her out to the main road. My cousin Jim waited there in his car, the heater on high, and drove her to the hospital, shooting the drifts into the city of Sharon. His was among the last of the cars to get through the blizzard, or so I was told. I made it.

It was a time of transition, and our family was slowly adapting. We didn't get a combine till the 1970s, when my father found a good used one. Throughout my youth we had bindered oats as the Amish still do, stacking sheaves into shocks to cure golden in the field, then hauling them into the barn to feed the thresher's saber-toothed maw. My job was to man the oats auger. Bucket ready, I watched the counterweight gradually tilt on the hopper, until it dumped the load. When it did, I hustled with the full bushel to the granary and back, barely in time to receive the next outpouring. On deadline now at *The Inquirer*, as the stories and headline assignments flow into the virtual hopper, I feel I'm at the auger once again, scurrying to catch what I can.

When I was five, I watched from my perch on a fence as my father and uncle led a cow into the bull's pen to play piggyback. "Did he get 'er yet, Burt?" asked Uncle Bill, holding the tether tight as the cow's eyes bulged. "Can't seem to find her," my dad answered. Maybe the game was blindman's buff, I thought.

Whatever the game, a few years later it was over. The shortcomings of the old ways became clear on a rainy August afternoon. A cow had plodded into the barn at milking time, discouraged, her afterbirth trailing in the mud, and my father had sent out the search party to find the missing calf. It was my cousin Dave, I think, who found the thing, covered with flies at the edge of the woods—a cyclops, hairless, its tail growing from its forehead. We stood around it in yellow slickers, my brother and sister and cousins and I—a pastoral tableau.

By 1969, we had acceded reproduction to science. Next to the stanchion of a needy Holstein, my father would affix a bright yellow tag that said BREED THIS COW and wait for the man in the blue jumpsuit. It was high entertainment for me, and for my cousins, too—several, of assorted sizes, from Pittsburgh and nearby towns, who visited so often they seemed like siblings. We liked to watch: The man stretched a huge latex condom onto his arm and inserted it, up to the shoulder, into the cow. Her back rose into an arch and her eyes widened as he primed her with slow, languid thrusts, gradually picking up speed, before delivering the payload with a syringe through a long tube.

I studied this ritual numerous times, mesmerized. I don't imagine the young technicians had much to say about their workday when they got home at night. Nor was it likely they tried to impress young women at the tavern with their occupational prowess. "It's what you'd call a job with a high turnover," Uncle Bill once observed.

Discouraged by stillbirths and freaks, the result of too many generations sired by the same bull, my father had begun using this artificial breeding service. He picked the bull from a catalogue. The breeding service harvested the semen by a method which I did not know. To this day, I do not know, and, friend, I'm content in my ignorance.

As prepubescent boys, we debated just where the gloved arm had probed, pondering the matter over cigarettes behind the machine shed. We had witnessed the mysterious. My cousins would go home to the city from their summer visit with something to tell their buddies about what they do up Mercer way.

Meanwhile, my father and uncle cursed their old machinery, paid their bills in cash, and held on till 1988, two faltering farmers in their seventies who had made all their living from the land. A typical farmer these days is fifty-five or older, and he gets little more than a tenth of his income from farming.[48]

You'll still find farmers out there. Some even have barnyards that smell. They don't bother putting little signs on the animal pens saying PIG and GOAT and LLAMA. Dairymen mostly do it in a big way today, with high-tech milking parlors that vacuum the cows into drained, satiated bliss. If you go to one of those recreational farms where city folks can taste the country ways and play in a corn maze and go on hayrides to haunted pumpkin patches and such, you can watch the milking from behind a glass viewing window. I took my brother's family to such a place for ice cream on a rainy day. The milking wasn't much as I remembered it, and I didn't see any flyspecks, but farmers do still spit about the same.

Chicken farmers are a different breed today, too. Many are contractors who raise the company's peeps, feed them the company's special mix, pump them full of the company's antibiotics and vitamins and growth stimulants. At slaughter time, the company dispatches its catchers long past midnight to collect the fat bounty, and the cycle ensues.

Big Chicken provides the birds and supplies, and the farmers provide the coops and the care. They are paid per bird. It's not a lavish living—and increasingly the company, ever more integrated, is playing farmer itself rather than hiring out the work.

As chicken farmers shifted from running their own businesses to accepting contract pay from the large producers, they did find a degree of freedom. They wrestled less with the whims of the market and nature.

"A farmer runs a business but has to take what somebody else tells him his trouble is worth," my father explained to me, at age ten, during a 1960s milk strike. As the adults talked of hundredweights, I felt their heartache: Nobody sane wastes milk.

My mother, gentle Irishwoman, had heard that men were dumping milk down streams. She, too, was city-turned-country: The daughter of immigrants from County Tyrone, she grew up in Pittsburgh and after World War II moved with her family to a small farm in Mercer County, where she nursed her parents through their cancers. Their land was next to my father's. She met him when she came calling for eggs and milk—and kept on calling, pail in hand.

And now she was awash in milk again. For several weeks she made pudding aplenty, and she brought down the old jar churn from the attic. I cranked it each evening during the strike, watching slabs of butter congeal amid the foaming paddles. To me it was a magical time; to my parents, I'm sure, a troubling one. "Oh, I wish I was in heaven, eating oranges," my mother often remarked during the slightest stress, a saying I've heard from no other soul.

If it wasn't a milk strike, it was a March so mad with mud that my father couldn't plow; or it was Agnes, the spring hurricane of '72 that settled in to stay; or those July cloudbursts that rendered raked rows of cured clover into a sodden mess fit only for bedding in the stalls. Weather has no special mercy on a farmer.

Nor do the forces of the marketplace. Price fluctuations don't respect his budget, such as it is. Just getting by can be all-consuming. Back when we ventured away from the farm, agribusiness promised us a bright future. Big Chicken came strutting into town with promises of prosperity, like a talent scout slapping a young athlete's shoulder when the lights still seemed bright.

Donald Stull and Michael Broadway, anthropologists who for two decades have studied what the meat industry has done to people and places, describe what happened in *Slaughterhouse Blues: The Meat and Poultry Industry in North America*. Most of the benefits went into corporate coffers. What the rural communities got was low-paying jobs, and conflicts with the newcomers brought in to take those jobs. They got housing shortages, and inadequate schools and health care. They got labor strife and crime. And they got pollution.[49]

These are wounds that need to heal, and the scars could last generations. Some would say it's impossible: We are a people who love meat, poultry, and eggs, and we're not easily going to give up the bargain prices that production-line farming sustains. Despite the buy-local trend, we generally haven't given much thought to the source of our sustenance.

Our own appetite for cheap food, fed by the machinery of marketing, created conditions that helped to doom the family farm. And now it seems to take a corporate farm to satisfy our cravings. You can see how chicken farmers would find safety and survival in accepting contract pay. But in doing so they ceded control over their livelihood.

They worked hard but gave up a measure of independence, a farmer's staple.

It's the much-vaunted Protestant work ethic: By your own hand, endure. Or call it the Yankee spirit. Or call it neither, since it fits no creed or country: The Mexican immigrants I've known are keener to succeed by their wits and hard work than many other Americans I've met. They still dream.

Hispanic laborers have long manned the major mushroom farming operations in Chester County, to the southwest of Lilyfield. They immigrate here to work on the production lines, living frugally and often sending as much money as they can back home—to Mexico, to Puerto Rico, to wherever their loved ones wait. In the nearby city of Norristown, Mexican immigrants have built a thriving community, opening restaurants and starting businesses and contributing a colorful and honored culture to the mix of other immigrants of generations or centuries ago—people such as the Irish (that's me) and the Italians and the Poles and all the other breeds we call Americans. They came far, they worked hard, they endured.

The rooster and the hen embodied those values—they foraged afield, industrious and self-reliant. Creatures great and small share this need. Stripped of independence and dignity, we soon wither into servile complacency. But when we feel our sinews stretch as we pursue our own fortunes, when our hands get dirty from our own initiative, hard times seem like a challenge to overcome. Unfettered, we flourish.

It's the philosophy of a charity called Heifer International, which provides struggling rural families in diverse lands with cows and chickens and pigs so they might learn to farm and better feed themselves. For years on Christmas Eve, I've gone down to the barn at midnight, hoping to witness the animals kneeling. I've yet to see it happen—chickens, it seems, don't have knees—but I can hope for miracles on a holy night. On Christmas morning of 2007, our daughter

Gretel handed me an envelope: She had donated a flock of chickens to an impoverished family, in my name. No finer present have I ever received—a gift of hope for someone else. Dignity survives. But it no longer dwells in the chicken products that fatten in the poultry house. They know no barnyard.

As the animals of the convoluted cortex, we have been granted dominion over beast and fowl and creeping things, and we honor God not only by surviving but by thriving in harmony with his creation.

"Dominion" doesn't mean brute authority to kick animals in their pens, or zap them gleefully with prods the way I saw an Amish youth make a recalcitrant cow move along years ago at the New Wilmington livestock auction. The word implies good husbandry, kindness, respect. These the Amish have in abundance—never mind that nasty kid.

We must treat our subjects well, even as we prepare to eat them. So it goes. If you tell me beasts have human rights, I'll smile and maybe rub my eyetooth. But they do have rights. And if you treat them cruelly, if you waste their lives, I hope it takes less than a prod on your own rump to teach you humility.

Take it from no less an authority than Cicero: "He was no less at fault who killed the rooster when there was no need to do so than he who choked his father to death."

People seldom kill chickens needlessly, of course, except for the ones that cockfighters toss into the pit—and at least that gives the birds a fighting chance to hold on to their roosterhood. Cocks fight. I don't see any reason to cheer them on, or to arm them like gladiators, but fighting is what they will do when allowed to exhibit their nature. Under the lilacs the other day, I watched two of our birds settling some rooster business, hackles raised high as they slammed their breasts together. I wouldn't have dreamed of trying to stop them. Nor can I stop the hens from dealing one another savage pecks as they manipulate for position in the harem, or keep them from moping all day in the nest box till their hormones subside.

If I presumed the power to stop such things, I might as well tell the wind not to blow, or the sun not to shine. Others have done just that. No wind blows in the massive poultry sheds, and the chickens there don't know what a sun is. They can't move around much to peck one another, and without a beak, what's the point? Mass production has stolen their identity. In peephood, they tumble by the thousands down a conveyor belt to meet their fate, sorted and consigned to either the macerator or the market. From then until they enter the slaughterhouse, they know nothing of what the jungle fowl knew.

Once, we thought of chickens as breeds. At the market, you could buy a Wyandotte, a barnyard beauty developed in the 1870s to be both meaty and a good layer. Or a Rhode Island Red, a prolific layer also bred in the late 1800s whose rich hues originated in the ancient Malay strain that contributed to its bloodline. You could choose from dozens of breeds. They came from the farm to the butcher and were sold in one piece, plucked and gutted and ready. Today, consumers go to the market and buy a package of legs, or wings, or boneless breasts. There's no spine under that plastic wrap, just cutlets. Over in the freezer bin are bags of breaded nuggets. This is the chicken's identity now, for most consumers. The breed doesn't matter; few have even heard the names.

In his essay "Making the Chicken of Tomorrow," historian Roger Horowitz describes how industry has reworked the meaning of poultry in our culture. The true history of the chicken, I believe, ended in the 1940s as technology was transforming the bird into a manufacturing unit. Horowitz picks it up from there.[50]

Most of the change, he points out, has been since World War II. Until then, broilers had been a by-product of the egg industry, and chicken therefore was more expensive than other meats. Families sat down around it for dinner only on special Sundays. Today, chicken is cheap and more popular among American consumers than beef. The fast-food industry has established it as a quick munch for lunch. It has developed a reputation as better for you than fat-laden red meat. A typical American enjoys chicken for four or five meals a week.

As technology was making poultry production possible on a large scale, eager markets waited. New York City, for example, was not only a huge market, but also a Jewish one. By the 1930s, two million Jews lived in New York, and kosher dietary rules forbade many of them to eat pork. They eagerly sought to purchase chicken. To the south, in the Delmarva Peninsula of Delaware, the supply arose to meet the demand, at the same time that better roads and refrigeration were decreasing dependency on the rail.

Small farms discovered the market. One story tells of a farm woman ordering fifty chicks from a hatchery but mistakenly receiving five hundred—and reaping a fortune when she raised them to sell. Such examples weren't lost on others. Small farms began focusing on broilers, with the women usually running the business.

When businessmen get a whiff of a good thing, they respond, and processing plants soon opened on the Delmarva, shipping meat that was acceptable to Jewish consumers to New York City. A similar symbiosis between city and country was arising in many areas of the nation. Mostly, the processing plants employed workers who did everything by hand—hanging, slicing, plucking. Eventually, machines took over many of the duties. The military's consumption of poultry during the war also increased demand tremendously, and consumers were putting a chicken in more and more pots. With so much money to be made, the industry wanted to build a better chicken.

In the 1940s, the USDA and the A&P grocery chain promoted a "Chicken of Tomorrow" contest and awarded cash prizes for production of superior meat chickens that were plumper and could get to market faster. Farmers no longer talked of breeds—they left such talk for the fanciers who flaunted their birds at the county fairs. What mattered was function. As Horowitz explains, a chicken became a layer, a broiler, a roaster. Poultry for every purpose.

In that spirit, the county agents came and had a talk with the farmers and producers. Agricultural extension services, established in every state in the 1880s, were given the task of helping to improve farm economies. After the war, the agriculture experts persuaded farmers throughout the country to switch to poultry production and to do it right, with the latest methods. Many did it wrong, and failed, but some figured out the secret to profits beyond their dreams.

In his essay, Horowitz points out that a major obstacle to the industry's growth was the persistent attitude that chicken was a special weekend meal. A survey of the Delmarva market after the war found, strange as it might seem, that people would buy more chicken if it were cheaper. The perception of luxury had to change, marketers knew, and it could only happen if the price came down—and that could only happen if science could make a meatier bird and the producers could make it consumer-friendly: fully plucked and cleaned and ready to cook.

Hybrids soon came to the fore, and their feathers were white, mostly, so that consumers couldn't see any pinfeathers not removed during processing. Science had yet to invent a featherless bird, but this was a first step. The hybrid chickens were ever plumper and seemed healthier. All of these wonders were expensive for the farmer, who nonetheless went into debt to keep up with the new ways. Those that didn't were doomed to mediocrity or bankruptcy. To survive, many chicken farmers began to sign contracts to raise chickens on behalf of hatcheries and feed suppliers, who reclaimed them when grown. The farmer had to use the company's supplies and follow its dictates, but it was a less manic living. Somebody else took the risk, and most of the profits.

Soon, major corporations were pulling the strings of all aspects of the poultry industry. Perdue, Tyson, Townsend, and many others focused attention on the need to streamline processing, and led the industry away from the typical practice of producing plucked but ungutted chickens to be cleaned by the butcher or the homemaker.

Processing plants expanded, and hundreds of new workers were hired for the new evisceration duties. To keep costs and wages down, the plants hired mostly African-American women, who had fewer choices in the job market. The strategy worked: In a generation, chicken consumption doubled as prices fell, attracting new customers.

Surveys in the 1960s, however, found that chicken was still far too special a treat for consumers. Beef and pork were still the staples for the table—the "real" meats, in the view of housewives. Chicken was relatively boring unless served in moderation, or so the perception went. This "inferiority complex," as one study put it, had to go, and only then would the poultry market truly boom. Chicken had to be reinvented and marketed in different forms, to be served in a variety of ways.

The marketers weighed their advantages. The public saw chicken as healthful, low in fat; as economical, with little of the weight going to waste; and as easy to prepare for the increasingly harried home-maker. Advertising campaigns by Perdue and Tyson began to capitalize on such perceptions. Tyson went after the fast-food market, peddling pre-cooked nuggets and patties, as well as chicken hot dogs and other products for supermarkets, and it expanded Asian markets for the dark meat that American consumers tended to turn down.

Frank Perdue's strategy was to foster consumer loyalty; he tried to distinguish his chickens as the finest. "It takes a tough man to make a tender chicken," he repeated endlessly in advertisements, suggesting to listeners that he personally monitored quality. He proclaimed his chickens a boon for dieters and extolled their "healthy, golden yellow color"—not mentioning that it was enhanced by adding xanthophyll to the chickens' feed. Under the Perdue marketing, whole birds became an increasingly smaller share of sales; cut-up parts and processed chicken, packaged conveniently, became the bestsellers.

To meet the demand, processing plants expanded dramatically with thousands of new hires to handle the new products. The work was nonstop: The line moved at ninety birds a minute, a hundred thousand chickens per day. Many workers suffered repetitive stress injuries to their wrists; at the same time that unions were losing their grip because of the rapid changes.

The processing plants were increasingly rural, far from cities and their ready labor supply. The workforce had been predominantly black; in the 1980s, it was becoming dominated by immigrants from Mexico and Central America. Wages were set as low as possible. African-American workers, with better English language skills, had higher expectations and took jobs elsewhere.[51]

The nature of communities changed rapidly, with ripples throughout the rural culture and economy. Schools found basic literacy a new challenge, and decent housing was a crucial need. And communities also found that the processing plants could be major polluters.

Not the least of the problems was the need to dispose of feathers. The American poultry industry alone produces two billion pounds of feather waste a year. Some of this mountain is reprocessed into animal feed or fertilizer, and researchers have experimented with blending feathers with plastic or fiberglass for building materials or using their fibers for insulation, textiles, even diapers.[52] Much of the waste, however, goes to landfills, and the plucking operation produces foul water that poses its own pollution problem. The spread of salmonella is a constant risk as feather dust fills the air in the processing plant and carcasses come in close contact with one another during washing procedures.

A featherless bird would seem a welcome development in the continuing quest to reinvent the chicken. If it turns out to be tasteless, I hear there's a booming market for barbecue sauce. The ideal factory chicken would be featherless, witless, listless, spiritless. We're well on our way to the chicken of tomorrow. This, we have decided, is our dominion.

We the enlightened ones took away the cycle of light from a creature that had lived by it. The bedazzled hen, forced to live by production efficiencies, came to know only a couple of hours of darkness in the controlled world of the poultry house. Gone was the unindustrious night.

Gone, too, were the meadows, the sunrises, the sunsets. What did they profit a man? No more breezes—except such as a circulation fan could provide. No more seasons.

Suzanne and I often cross the plank bridge by the crabapple trees to the far side of the pond, where we share a cigar and watch the catfish gliding ghostly under the ripples. We await the sunset and the arrival of the mallards. They splash into the shimmer when the light falls precisely right. Day by day, the mallards come minutes earlier until it's time for other ponds.

Like the wild swans that Yeats first saw at twilight, the mallards know something I fear I'm forgetting year by year. The seasons attend them. They live by the slow and silent oscillation of the shadows, unharried by the clocks and alarums of illuminated man.

We humans dice and divvy up time into days and years, seconds and hours that we base on the eminently divisible number 360, also handy for partitioning circles. That's also close to how many times our sphere spins as it swings round at full tilt to fulfill the seasons. With atomic accuracy we calibrate and calculate.

Mesmerized by the pendulum, we keep track of beginnings and ends. We try to establish which things came first. But time is as immense and capricious as an ocean, with waves and riptides and deep rolling swells. It ebbs and flows and crashes with our joys and pains and boredoms.

The Mayan week was thirteen days; the pharaohs favored ten. Modern man has mostly settled on seven, because seven heavenly bodies mystified the astronomers of old. They assigned them to their gods and named the days we know now: the sun day and the moon day, the Tiwas, Woden, Thor, Freya, and Saturnus days.

Into our seven ordered transits of the sun we try to condense all creation, but God alone measured the expanse between those evenings and mornings. Whether twenty-four hours or twenty-four epochs, he alone knows. He takes the measure of our lives, as well, knowing how very long our day can be. He walked the earth himself, feeling what we feel, showing us he understood, inviting us home.

Once we trusted the rooster, who fathomed the night by his own unknown devices. Well before dawn, his first call came, and again just before the light broke. "Before the cock crows twice" meant "early" or "imminently" long before Jesus foretold how his faithful Peter would soon deny ever knowing him. Aldrovandi traced the expression to Aristophanes.

Since antiquity, farmers and philosophers have respected the rooster's raucous good timing. How they could suffer him to live, I can't say, but they arose to his call.

Aldrovandi wondered at depictions he had seen of the Egyptian sun god holding a finger to his lips while pressing his elbow into the throat of a rooster. To the Greek and Roman poets, this god was Harpocrates, whom they interpreted as the guardian of silence and secrecy.

Now, I'm no god, but I can appreciate the divine desire to throttle a rooster, particularly when our boy's wake-up call comes but a few hours after I roll into bed. I relish a hard day's work, but first things first—like sleep. I'm a child of Thomas Edison. I live and love and learn by artificial light.

And I confess: In our coop I keep one bare, dim bulb on a timer that distorts the seasons and keeps the eggs coming—more than I can use, with plenty to sell. I, too, manipulate chickens for profit.

We have forsaken our kinship with the chicken. We divested it of sun and moon. We took away the rooster's strut and his dominion over daylight, the hen's maternal longings and her protective wing, and turned them into instruments of production. The chicken became a pod creature, driven only to consume and reproduce. We lost a symbol of what we were and gained an omen of what we risk becoming.

Golden Dreams

I am tired, as evening falls, of deadlines and headlines and too many turnings of the clock. Beyond the arching maples of Frog Hollow, I pull into a gravel lane embraced by oaken arms, and there lies Lilyfield.

Come to the garden now with me, while the fading sunlight angles across the farmyard. Chores can wait. Night is closing in, and the rooster crows—a trumpet to the morn, indeed, and evening, too. He tries so hard to master the day.

Let me show you our sundial. I made it. The markers and the gnomon are shards of slate. More accurate than quartz, it keeps the perfect timing of the sun. On its face, these words: "A time for every purpose."

Soon enough the mallards will return to the pond, as they always have at sunset, guided by the light to splash ungainly in the shallows. Their quarreling voices rise, then soften to harmonize with the crickets and the night sounds—a truck shifting gears on the highway; a child crying far off.

And listen: Other voices grace this garden, sweeping in from the hollow. They come, at first, like the breeze itself, in a rush of whispers, until the quiet distills them. Each word distinct:

"When they're the size of a baseball, they're just right for picking," Suzanne is saying. Among the vines and weeds, she searches for the Ronde de Nice squash she loves so much.

"Play ball!" calls her grandfather as his teammates take the field. He's winning now but wincing as his knees give way from too many games.

"Just rest here awhile, Pop," says Suzanne, who helped him round the bases back to home, who caught him as he fell. The murmur of their voices rises to a rustling in the cherry tree.

I need your help with the chores tonight—it's time to close the gates. The first stars are forming. Stay, until they fade away again. You can sleep in the hammock across the pond, if you wish. The birds will wake you. I'll make blueberry pancakes, and Suzanne will fry up omelets, with fresh mushrooms—joy in the morning.

We'll have eggs aplenty, gold on the plate, and for us I've saved the very best, from my Blue Cochin. She's a special sort of hen. She keeps me company, late at night, as I write. I call her Blue.

"You're beautiful," says my uncle to a dead bird in his glove. A voice adrift in the cool of night.

"You pray, too?" I hear my kneeling father ask of me. I do. I must. When the places and the faces that you counted on have left, it's time to dream for life anew.

"The barn is gone, there's nothing there," my brother says, and we search in the rubble for anything we might keep, something to take back.

My sister nods. "This is how we'll say it was."

"An old man's wish," says Aldrovandi, going blind and praying he'll be counted, too, among the chickens and flowers, the bugs and dragons, and the marvels of a world unfolding so fast it's hard to keep track. "Nothing is sweeter than to know all things."

Let's go down to shut the chickens in. Beyond the coop where the night begins, there are things circling that don't mean them well, that would usher them away in the dark. The full moon rises to the strains of Vivaldi. The rooster cries to the firmament, because he can.

"We owe a cock to Asclepius," the dying Socrates tells his weeping friend. "See that it is paid?" For all my God has done for me, I'd pay him two, but it's not what he wants—he knows my heart is his.

"I wish I was in heaven, eating oranges," my mother declares, and she offers me one with a smile. The dewfall smells of citrus.

"Golden dreams," Suzanne whispers, as I slip from her hands into the tomato vines to rest in a patch of Sungolds gleaming in the moonlight.

"And golden dreams to you," I hear myself say, as another breeze swells in the hollow, and she comes to lie by my side.

Notes

⚔ ⚔

YOU COME, TOO

1. Lind, *Aldrovandi on Chickens*. All of Aldrovandi's observations and citations, except where noted otherwise, are from this English translation of the chicken volume of *The Ornithology of Ulisse Aldrovandi*, published in 1600 in Bologna, Italy.

2. Letter from Martha Stewart to U.S. District Judge Miriam Goldman Cedarbaum, July 15, 2004. Full text has been posted on various Web sites, including the archives of WestportNow (www.westportnow.com).

3. Perrins, *Firefly Encyclopedia of Birds*.

4. William Boyd and Michael Watts, "Agro-Industrial Just-in-Time," in Goodman and Watts, *Globalising Food*.

5. USDA, Economic Research Service, Poultry Yearbook, Table 002.xls: Eggs: Production, Disposition, and Value. Posted at usda.mannlib.cornell.edu/MannUsda/viewDocumentInfo.do?documentID=1367.

6. Greene, *The Bird Flu Pandemic*.

7. *Encyclopedia Britannica*, 9:967 (1994); *Encyclopedia Americana*, 8:463, 18:627–28 (1991).

8. Michael Purdy, senior medical sciences writer, "First Analysis of Chicken Genome Offers Many New Insights," Washington University in St. Louis, School of Medicine, Medical Public Affairs (January 28, 2005), mednews.wustl.edu.

9. Richard Orr, "Music in Chicken Coop May Be Money in Bank," *Chicago Tribune*, November 2, 1987.

10. USDA, Economic Research Service, "Policy Options for a Changing Rural America," *Amber Waves,* May 2007, www.ers.usda.gov.

11. USDA, Economic Research Service (see n. 5).

SPRING: A SEASON TO SOW

1. My portrait of Aldrovandi is drawn from the following sources of biographical information: Lind, *Aldrovandi on Chickens,* Introduction, xvii–xxxvi; Castellani, "Ulisse Aldrovandi"; Giovanni Cristofolini and Annalisa Managlia, "Ulisse Aldrovandi," Scienza Giovani: Bologna University Web site for Science Communication, 2005, at www.scienzagiovane.unibo.it/English/scientists/aldrovandi-3.html; Richard S. Westfall, Department of History and Philosophy of Science, Indiana University, for the Galileo Project Web site, http://galileo.rice.edu/Catalog/NewFiles/aldrvndi.html; Michon Scott, "Ulisse Aldrovandi," from the Web site Strange Science: The Rocky Road to Modern Paleontology and Biology, www.strangescience.net/aldrovandi.htm.

2. This account combines information from the following sources: Jorg Adelberger, "Eduard Vogel and Eduard Robert Flegel: The Experiences of Two Nineteenth-Century German Explorers in Africa," *History in Africa: A Journal of Method* 27 (2000): 1–29; *Encyclopedia Britannica* eleventh edition (1910–11); Smith and Daniel, *The Chicken Book,* 36.

3. Laura Evans, "The House of Faberge, Russia, and the Imperial Eggs," Antiques & Collectibles department of *Garden and Hearth* Web site, www.gardenandhearth.com/AntiquesandCollectibles/House-of-Faberge.htm.

4. "Russian Buys Forbes Faberge Collection," *Jewelers Circular Keystone,* March 2004.

5. Smith and Daniel, *The Chicken Book,* 31, 34, 36.

6. John Pemberton, III, "Divination in Sub-Saharan Africa, Part 1: Azande," Art and Oracle: African Art and Rituals of Divination, Web site of the Metropolitan Museum of Art, New York, www.metmuseum.org/explore/oracle/essay1.html.

7. The account is related by Suetonius in *Life of Tiberius* 2.2 and by Cicero in *De Natura Deorum* 2.3.

8. Michael Page and Robert Ingpen, *Encyclopedia of Things That Never Were: Creatures, Places and People* (New York: Viking Studio Books, 1987).

9. Jones, *Credulities Past and Present.*

10. Patricia Leigh Brown, "Where the Spirits Feel at Home," *The New York Times,* December 31, 1998.

11. Associated Press, "CDC: Baby Birds Make Dangerous Gifts," March 29, 2007.

12. Matthew 23:37.

13. Information on rooster sculpture comes from Hopkins, *A World Full of Gods,* 178,

plate 23; Maj. Gen. J. G. R. Forlong, *Faiths of Man: A Cyclopaedia of Religions* (London: Bernard Quaritch, 1906), 2:202, with citation to Richard Payne Knight, *Essays on Ancient Worship* (1865), 10, plate ii; E. R. Goodenough, *Jewish Symbols in the Greco-Roman Period,* vol. XII (New York: Princeton University Press, Bollingen Series, 1965).

14. Percy, *The Complete Chicken,* 20.

15. Smith and Daniel, *The Chicken Book,* 120.

16. Percy, *The Complete Chicken,* 26.

17. Lezlie Laws Couch, " 'So Much Depends' . . . on How You Begin: A Poetry Lesson," *The English Journal* 76, no. 7 (November 1987): 35.

18. Information on early domestication is from the following sources: Kenneth F. Kiple and Kriemhild Conee Ornelas, *Cambridge World History of Food,* vol. 1 (Cambridge: Cambridge University Press, 2000), 496–99; Smith and Daniel, *The Chicken Book,* 10–13.

19. Smith and Daniel, *The Chicken Book,* 69–124.

20. Oklahoma State Courts Network, *Lock v. Falkenstine,* 1963 OK CR 32, 380 P.2d 278, case number A-13307, decided: 03/13/1963. Oklahoma Court of Criminal Appeals, www.oscn.net.

21. Smith and Daniel, *The Chicken Book,* 28.

22. Nicholas E. Collias and Elsie C. Collias, "A Field Study of the Red Jungle Fowl in North-Central India," *Condor* 69, no. 4 (July–August 1967): 360–86.

23. Smith and Daniel, *The Chicken Book,* 14.

24. Hans L. Schippers, *Chickens* (Zutphen, Netherlands: Roodbont, 2007); Schippers's essay "The Araucana Fowl" (1975) can be viewed at araucanabreeder.freeservers.com. See also Gavin Menzies, *1421: The Year China Discovered America* (New York: Morrow, 2003): 124.

25. Terra Madre 2006 Web site, Food Communities List, "Blue Egg Chicken Presidium," www.terramadre2006.org.

26. Brunson, *Araucanas.*

27. Jaime Gongora, Victor A. Mobegi, et al., "Mitochondrial DNA Sequences Reveal a Putative East Asian Ancestry for Old Chilean Chickens," *Proceedings of the 30th International Conference on Animal Genetics,* Porto Seguro, Brazil, 2006.

28. Alice A. Storey, José Miguel Ramirez, et al., "Radiocarbon and DNA Evidence for a Pre-Columbian Introduction of Polynesian Chickens to Chile," *Proceedings of the National Academy of Sciences of the United States of America,* June 2007.

29. "The Araucana Chicken," Kintaline Farm Plant and Poultry Centre, Benderloch, Argyll, Scotland. Historical notes on business Web site: www.araucanas.co.uk.

30. H. S. Babcock, "Chickens for Use and Beauty," *The Century: A Popular Quarterly* 40 (May 1890): 47–60.

31. Burnham, *The History of the Hen Fever,* 21–22.

32. Smith and Daniel, *The Chicken Book,* 233.

33. USDA, Economic Research Service, "Poultry Production in the United States," www.ers.usda.gov.

34. Jones, *Mama Learned Us to Work,* 36–39, 78.

35. Smith and Daniel, *The Chicken Book,* 236.

36. Ibid., 264–68.

37. Roger Horowitz, "Making the Chicken of Tomorrow. Reworking Poultry as Commodities and as Creatures, 1945–1990," in Schrepfer and Scranton, *Industrializing Organisms.*

38. USDA, Sustainable Agriculture Research and Education Program, www.sare.org.

39. National Chicken Council, U.S. Broiler Performance Historical Chart, 2006.

40. Jean Buzby, "Chicken Consumption Continues Longrun Rise," *Amber Waves,* April 2006, www.ers.usda.gov.

41. William Boyd and Michael Watts, "Agro-Industrial Just-in-Time," in Goodman and Watts, *Globalising Food.*

42. USDA, Food Safety and Inspection Service, "Meat and Poultry Labeling Terms," www.fsis.usda.gov.

43. Suzanne Hamlin, "Free Range? Natural? Sorting Out Labels," *The New York Times,* November 13, 1996.

44. L. Hegelund, J. T. Sorensen, et al., "Use of the Range Area in Organic Egg Production Systems," *British Poultry Science* 46, no. 1 (February 2005): 1–8.

45. E. Zeltner and H. Hirt, "Effect of Artificial Structuring on the Use of Laying Hen Runs in a Free-Range System," *British Poultry Science* 44, no.4 (September 2003): 533–37.

46. Lydia Oberholtzer, Catherine Greene, and Enrique Lopez, "Organic Poultry and Eggs Capture High Price Premiums and Growing Share of Specialty Markets," USDA, Outlook Report from the Economic Research Service (December 2006), www.ers.usda.gov.

47. Michael Pollan, "Naturally: How Organic Became a Marketing Niche and a Multibillion-Dollar Industry," *The New York Times Magazine,* May 13, 2001.

48. Oberholtzer, Greene, and Lopez, "Organic Poultry and Eggs" (see n. 46).

49. USDA, "Meat and Poultry Labeling Terms" (see n. 42).

50. Center for Integrated Agricultural Systems, "Raising Poultry on Pasture," University of Wisconsin–Madison, College of Agricultural and Life Sciences (2004), www .cias.wisc.edu.

51. Michael Pollan, "No Bar Code: The Next Revolution in Food Is Just Around the Corner," *Mother Jones* 31, no. 3 (May 1, 2006): 36–46.

52. Ken Druse, "Scratch a Suburb, Find a Chicken," *The New York Times,* August 11, 2005.

53. Paula Bock, "Custom Coops: From Penthouse Perches to Covered Porches, City Chickens Are Sitting Pretty," *Seattle Times, Pacific Northwest Magazine,* January 20, 2002.

54. Jennifer Bleyer, "In the Land of Co-ops, Coops," *The New York Times,* October 1, 2006.

55. Mad City Chickens Web site, www.madcitychickens.com.

55. USDA, AMS Farmers Markets, "Farmers Market Growth, 1994–2006," www.ams.usda.gov.

57. Robyn Van En Center for CSA Resources, Wilson College, Chambersburg, Pennsylvania, www.wilson.edu.

58. Suzanne DeMuth, "Community Supported Agriculture (CSA): An Annotated Bibliography and Resource Guide," USDA, National Agricultural Library (September 1993), www.nal.usda.gov.

59. Jim Robbins, "Think Global, Eat Local," *Los Angeles Times Magazine,* July 31, 2005.

60. R. T. Pirog, K. Enshayan, Van Pelt, and E. Cook, "Food, Fuel, and Freeways: An Iowa Perspective on How Far Food Travels, Fuel Usage, and Greenhouse Gas Emissions," Leopold Center for Sustainable Agriculture, Ames, Iowa (2001). See also R. Pirog and Andrew Benjamin, "Checking the Food Odometer," Leopold Center (2003), www.leopold.iastate.edu.

61. For information on Terra Madre 2006, including complete list of food communities, see www.terramadre2006.org. For information on Slow Food International, see www.slowfood.com.

62. Interview: Carlo Petrini, *The Ecologist,* April 1, 2004.

63. For information on Label Rouge, see "The Label Rouge System" on Web sites for USDA's Sustainable Agriculture Research and Education program and National Sustainable Agriculture Information Service: www.sare.org/publications/poultry/poultry02.htm and www.attra.ncat.org/attra-pub/labelrouge.html.

64. National Sustainable Agriculture Information Service, www.attra.ncat.org/attra-pub/labelrouge.html.

SUMMER: A SEASON TO GROW

1. Information on predators is drawn from the following sources: Gail Damerow, "Poultry Predator Identification: The First Step to Deterrence," *Backyard Poultry* (August–September 2007); Aaron J. Ison, Sara J. Spiegle, and Teresa Y. Morishita, "Predators of Poultry," Fact Sheet VME-22-05, Ohio State University Extension;

Joe Berry, "Predators: Thieves in the Night," Fact Sheet F-8204, Oklahoma Cooperative Extension Service.

2. The Associated Press, "Man Accused of Biting Off Rooster's Head," July 29, 2006.

3. The Associated Press, "Cops: Chicken Dies, Wife Shoots Husband," September 6, 2006.

4. "Cheating Chooks," transcript of Jonica Newby with Chris Evans, *Catalyst,* Australian Broadcasting Corp., October 3, 2002, www.abc.net.au.

5. Ibid.

6. Suzanne T. Millman and Ian Duncan, "Do Female Broiler Breeder Fowl Display a Preference for Broiler Breeder or Laying Strain Males in a Y-Maze Test?" Col. K. L. Campbell Centre for the Study of Animal Welfare, Department of Animal and Poultry Science, University of Guelph, Ontario, Canada, *Applied Animal Behaviour Science* (October 25, 2000).

7. "Animal Behavior: Not All Females Like Macho Males," *The New York Times,* Life Science Weekly, August 18, 2003.

8. Bob Giuliano, "When Barnyard Genetics Turn Ugly," *Owen Sound Sun Times* (Ontario), October 13, 2006.

9. Suzanne T. Millman, "The Animal Welfare Dilemma of Broiler Breeder Aggressiveness," *Poultry Perspectives* newsletter 4, no. 1 (Spring 2002): 7–10.

10. Suzanne T. Millman and Ian Duncan, "Effect of Male-to-Male Aggressiveness and Feed-Restriction During Rearing on Sexual Behaviour and Aggressiveness Towards Females by Male Domestic Fowl," Department of Animal and Poultry Science, University of Guelph, Ontario, Canada, *Applied Animal Behaviour Science* (November 1, 2000).

11. Suzanne T. Millman and Ian Duncan, "Male Broiler Breeder Fowl Display High Levels of Aggression Toward Females," *Poultry Science* 79, no. 9 (September 2000): 1233–41.

12. Alan Stanford, "Aggressive Cocks," BrownEggBlueEgg Web site, www.browneggblueegg.com.

13. T. M. Widowski, D. M. Lo Fo Wong, and Ian Duncan, "Rearing with Males Accelerates Onset of Sexual Maturity in Female Domestic Fowl," Department of Animal and Poultry Science, University of Guelph, Ontario, Canada, *Poultry Science* 77, no. 1 (January 1998): 150–55.

14. Paul M. Hocking and R. Bernard, "Effects of the Age of Male and Female Broiler Breeders on Sexual Behaviour, Fertility and Hatchability of Eggs," Roslin Institute (Edinburgh), Midlothian, Scotland, *British Poultry Science* 41, no. 3 (July 2000): 370–76.

15. Smith and Daniel, *The Chicken Book,* 164.

16. Ibid., 181–83.

17. Nicholas E. Collias and Elsie C. Collias, "Seeking to Understand the Living Bird: The 1997 Margaret Morse Nice Lecture," Wilson Ornithological Society, *Wilson Bulletin* 110, no. N1 (March 1, 1998): 28.

18. Richard Smith, "Freaky . . . the Hen That Turned into a Cockerel," *The Mirror* Web site, www.mirror.co.uk, April 19, 2006.

19. C. H. Bigland and F. E. Graesser, "Case Report of Sex Reversal in a Chicken," *Canadian Journal of Comparative Medicine and Veterinary Science* (February 1955): 50–52.

20. Jacqueline P. Jacob and F. Ben Mather, "Sex Reversal in Chickens," Factsheet PS-53, Department of Animal Sciences, Cooperative Extension Service, Institute of Food and Agricultural Sciences, University of Florida, Gainesville (November 2000).

21. Singapore Science Center, "Do Male Birds Have a Penis?" ScienceNet/Zoology, Question No. 2230, www.science.edu.sg.

22. "Such Strange Behavior: Is It an Imprinting Issue?" *Backyard Poultry* 1, no. 3 (June–July 2006): 28–29.

23. Ibid.

24. Information on imprinting and Konrad Lorenz is drawn from the following sources: "The Man Who Walked with Geese," *Nature,* online companion to PBS broadcast, December 31, 2006, www.pbs.org/wnet/nature; obituary, "Konrad Lorenz, 85; Nobel Laureate Pioneered Study of Human Behavior," Associated Press, March 1, 1989, as published in *The Boston Globe;* Konrad Lorenz, *Civilized Man's Eight Deadly Sins* (London: Methuen Publishing, July 1974); "Lorenz, Konrad (1903–1989)," *Learning & Memory* second ed. (New York: Macmillan Reference Books, 2002).

25. Faye Flam, "Fatherly Types Make Females Swoon," *The Philadelphia Inquirer,* June 5, 2006.

26. Jeff Nesmith, "Chickens Groove on Music; a Point Well-Taken to Coop," Cox News Service, November 8, 1987, as published in *The Sunday Oregonian* (Portland).

27. Information on the headless chicken is drawn from the following sources: Steve Silverman, "Mike the Headless Chicken," Useless Information Web site, home.ny cap.rr.com/useless/headless_chicken; "Mike's Story," Mike the Headless Chicken Web site, www.miketheheadlesschicken.org/story.html; Thomas, *The Official Mike the Headless Chicken Book;* "Headless Rooster—Beheaded Chicken Lives Normally after Freak Decapitation by Ax," *Life* (October 22, 1945): 53–54; Nancy Lofholm, "Town Celebrates Headless Critter of the '40s," *The Denver Post,* May 11, 1999; "Longest Surviving Headless Chicken," Guinness World Records Web site, archived.

28. Tic-tac-toe chicken sources include "Fowl Play," *The Independent* (London), February 9, 2004; "Cross Out a Landmark on the Chinatown Tour," *The New York Times,* August 14, 1993.

29. Smith and Daniel, *The Chicken Book*, 10.

30. S. L. Davis and P. R. Cheeke, "Do Domestic Animals Have Minds and the Ability to Think? A Provisional Sample of Opinions on the Question," Department of Animal Sciences, Oregon State University, Corvallis, *Journal of Animal Science* 76, no. 8 (August 1998).

31. E. S. Paul and A. L. Podberscek, "Veterinary Education and Students' Attitudes Towards Animal Welfare," *The Veterinary Record* 146, no. 10 (March 4, 2000): 269–72.

32. Patrick H. Zimmerman, Stuart J. Pope, Tim Guilford, and Christine J. Nicol, "Navigational Ability in the Domestic Fowl *(Gallus gallus domesticus),*" Department of Clinical Veterinary Science, Division of Animal Health and Husbandry, University of Bristol, Langford House, Langford, Bristol, *Applied Animal Behaviour Science* 80, no. 4 (March 1, 2003).

33. "Smart Chicks," transcript of Robyn Williams interview with Christine Nicol, *The Science Show*, Australian Broadcasting Corp., October 19, 2002, www.abc.net.au.

34. S. Jackson and Jared Diamond, "Ontogenetic Development of Gut Function, Growth, and Metabolism in a Wild Bird, the Red Jungle Fowl," *American Journal of Physiology—Regulatory, Integrative and Comparative Physiology* 269, no. 5 (November 1995).

35. Smith and Daniel, *The Chicken Book*, 142.

36. "Chicken Talk," *Time*, January 24, 1964.

37. S. Milius, "Breaking the Code on Chicken Clucks," *Science News* 156, no. 9 (August 28, 1999): 135.

38. Roger Highfield, "So Who Are You Calling Bird Brain? Chatter of Chickens Proves They Are Brighter Than We Thought," *The Telegraph* (London), November 16, 2006.

39. *Bizarre* (January 1999): 63.

40. Zoe Gautier, "*Gallus gallus,* Red Junglefowl," Animal Diversity Web (animaldiversity .ummz.umich.edu), University of Michigan, Museum of Zoology. Article cites behavior studies by Limburg (1975) and Ponnampalam (2000).

41. Candace C. Croney, Nova Prince-Kelly, and Camie L. Meller, "A Note on Social Dominance and Learning Ability in the Domestic Chicken *(Gallus gallus),*" Department of Animal Sciences, Oregon State University, Corvallis, *Applied Animal Behaviour Science* (June 2006).

42. Stephanie Coontz, "A Pop Quiz on Marriage," *The New York Times*, February 19, 2006.

43. Bayard Webster, "Eggs Converse with Hens," *The New York Times*, July 1, 1980.

FALL: A SEASON TO COLLECT

1. Richard Gaines, "Long-missing Bracelet Turns Up in Chicken Gizzard," *Gloucester (Mass.) Daily Times,* December 1, 2007.

2. Ancient Roman accounts from Pliny and Suetonius: Pliny the Elder (A.D. 23–79), *The Naturall Historie of G. Plinius Secundus. Tenth Booke of the Historie of Nature,* Chapter LV: "The Auguries and Presages of Egges," translated into English by Philemon Holland, 1601; Gaius Suetonius Tranquillus (c. A.D. 69–130), *The Lives of the Twelve Caesars,* Book III: *Tiberius,* Chapter 14, Loeb Classical Library edition, 1913, with English translation by J. C. Rolfe. Both are presented online by University of Chicago's Lacus-Curtius: Into the Roman World Web site, penelope.uchicago.edu.

3. W. G. Waters, *Jerome Cardan: A Biographical Study* (London: Lawrence & Bullen, 1898).

4. Jacqueline P. Jacob, Richard D. Miles, and F. Ben Mather, "Egg Quality," Fact Sheet PS24, Department of Animal Sciences, Cooperative Extension Service, Institute of Food and Agricultural Sciences, University of Florida, Gainesville (April 1998).

5. Chicken genome information is drawn from the following sources: Dave Burt and Olivier Pourquie, "Chicken Genome—Science Nuggets to Come Soon," *Science* (June 13, 2003); Tom Hopkinson, "Chicken Genome 60% Shared with Humans," *Society of Chemical Industry* (December 20, 2004); International Chicken Genome Sequencing Consortium, "Sequence and Analysis of the Chicken Genome Provide Unique Perspectives on Vertebrate Evolution," *Nature* (December 9, 2004); Michael Purdy, "First Analysis of Chicken Genome Offers Many New Insights," Washington University in St. Louis, School of Medicine, Medical Public Affairs (December 2004), mednews.wustl.edu; National Institutes of Health, "Researchers Compare Human, Chicken Genomes," *NIH News* (December 8, 2004); Malcolm Ritter, "Cracked Genome Shows Chicken DNA a Lot Like Yours," Associated Press (December 8, 2004).

6. Jennifer Viegas, "Mutant Chickens Grow Teeth," *Animal Planet News,* February 22, 2006.

7. "Chicken Genome Analysis Will Benefit Human Health and Agriculture," Special Reports, Michigan State University, special.newsroom.msu.edu/chicken_genome/index.html.

8. Percy, *The Complete Chicken,* 17.

9. Xenophon, *The Symposium,* Chapter II, translation by H. G. Dakyns, Internet Ancient History Sourcebook (Fordham University, New York), www.fordham.edu.

10. Information on Martha Stewart's Bedford estate is drawn from the following sources:

Matt Tyrnauer, "The Prisoner of Bedford," *Vanity Fair*, no. 540 (August 2005): 110; Karen Thomas, "Stewart Feeling Confined," *USA Today*, July 5, 2005; Andrew Ritchie, Martha Moments blog, May 29, 2006, marthamoments.blogspot.com.

11. International Federation of Competitive Eating, New York, www.ifoce.com/home .php. Eater Profiles: Joey Chestnut.

12. Smith and Daniel, *The Chicken Book*, 34.

13. Marian Burros, "What the Egg Was First," *The New York Times*, February 7, 2007.

14. Alan Davidson, *Oxford Companion to Food* (Oxford: Oxford University Press, 1999), 166–67.

15. Paul Freedman, "How the Search for Flavors Influenced Our World," YaleGlobal Online, March 11, 2003, yaleglobal.yale.edu.

16. Andrew Jacobs, "Buddha and the Art of Raising Chickens; Family Caters to Chinese Market with Farm-Fresh, Whole Pullets," *The New York Times*, May 5, 1998.

17. Carlye Adler, "Colonel Sanders' March on China," *Time* Asia edition (November 17, 2003), www.time.com.

18. Calum MacLeod, "Obesity of China's Kids Stuns Officials," *USA Today*, January 9, 2007.

19. Kate MacArthur, "KFC Spells It Out: Chain Takes Pride in Being Fried," *Advertising Age* (April 25, 2005): 3.

20. "Designer Eggs to Hit Shelves in India," *World Poultry*, April 10, 2007.

21. Andrea Platzman, "Designer Eggs: An Excellent Idea—or More Hype Than They're Cracked Up to Be?" *Men's Fitness* (April 2004).

22. Jacqueline P. Jacob and Richard D. Miles, "Designer and Specialty Eggs." Fact Sheet PS-51, Department of Animal Sciences, Cooperative Extension Service, Institute of Food and Agricultural Sciences, University of Florida, Gainesville (November 2000).

23. Xinhua News Agency, "Chickens Control Grasslands Locust Infestation," August 25, 1998; Xinhua General News Service, "Starling 'Air Force' Set to Fight Locusts in NW China," August 2, 2007.

24. Smith and Daniel, *The Chicken Book*, 278.

25. Mike Moore, "Weed Eaters," *Mother Earth News* (March 1987).

26. Curt and Ginny Hoskins, "Chickens for Pest Control," *Mother Earth News* (February 2, 2003).

27. Thomas Ledbetter, "Country Lore," *Mother Earth News* (March 4, 2007).

28. Barry Gringrod, "The Marvelous Chicken-Powered Motorcar!" *Mother Earth News* (July 1971): 14–19.

WINTER: A SEASON TO REFLECT

1. Linda Wasmer Smith, "Bits and Pieces: Help for the Henpecked," *Mother Earth News* (February–March 1994).

2. Danny Penman, "Animals Torn to Pieces by Lions in Front of Baying Crowds," *Daily Mail*, January 5, 2008.

3. "Cockfighting for the Squeamish," *The New York Times*, January 28, 2005; Ron Jackson, "Senator's Plan Spurs New Debate," *The Oklahoman*, January 31, 2005.

4. Ian Duncan, "The Science of Animal Well-being," *Animal Welfare Information Center Newsletter* (January–March 1993): 5.

5. T. C. Danbury, C. A. Weeks, et al., "Self-selection of the Analgesic Drug Carprofen by Lame Broiler Chickens," *The Veterinary Record* 146, no. 11 (March 2000): 307–11.

6. M. Debut, C. Berri, et al., "Behavioural and Physiological Responses of Three Chicken Breeds to Pre-slaughter Shackling and Acute Heat Stress," *British Poultry Science* 46, no. 5 (October 2005): 527–35.

7. Society for the Advancement of Education, "Building a Kinder, Gentler Chicken," *USA Today Magazine* (June 1994).

8. BBC News (London), "Stop Grieving, It's Only a Chicken," October 24, 2005.

9. Stacey Burling, "Pet Care Extraordinaire," *The Philadelphia Inquirer*, September 3, 2006.

10. Dolores Harrington, "Nurse Resuscitates Drowned Chicken," *The Daily Siftings Herald* (Arkadelphia, Arkansas), February 7, 2006.

11. Ahmed S. Hussein, "Induced Moulting Procedures in Laying Fowl," *World's Poultry Science Journal* 52, no. 2 (July 1996): 175–87.

12. V. Luk'yanov, A. Baidevlyatov, et al., "A Study of Stress Associated with the Induction of Moult in Laying Hens," *Ptitsevodstvo*, no. 8 (1976): 17–19.

13. A. Rolon, R. J. Buhr, et al., "Twenty-four-hour Feed Withdrawal and Limited Feeding as Alternative Methods for Induction of Molt in Laying Hens," *Poultry Science* 72, no. 5 (May 1993): 776–85.

14. Norman Dunn, "New Restriction on German Battery Units Threatens the Country's Self-sufficiency in Eggs," *Better Farming* (December 2004), www.betterfarming .com/nov99/europe.htm.

15. A. A. Taylor and J. F. Hurnik, "The Long-term Productivity of Hens Housed in Battery Cages and an Aviary," *Poultry Science* 75, issue 1 (January 1996): 47–51.

16. Amanda Griscom Little, "The Whole Foods Shebang: An Interview with John Mackey, Founder of Whole Foods," *Grist* (December 17, 2004).

17. Elizabeth Weise, "Food Sellers Push Animal Welfare," *USA Today*, August 12, 2003.

18. Grandin, *Thinking in Pictures*; Grandin and Johnson, *Animals in Translation*.

19. Temple Grandin, "Poultry Slaughter Plant and Farm Audit: Critical Control Points for Bird Welfare (updated December 2006)," available on Grandin's Web site, www .grandin.com/poultry.audit.html.

20. Julian Brouwer, "Mechanical Chicken Catcher Causes a Flap," *The Scotsman,* June 19, 2000.

21. Weise, "Food Sellers Push Animal Welfare" (see n. 17).

22. Ron Schara, "Some Animal Rights Can Burn out of Control," *(Minneapolis) Star Tribune*, November 19, 1996.

23. Ibid.

24. "Cockfighting in Southeast Asia Harbors Avian Flu," *Anderson Cooper 360°,* CNN report, December 9, 2005, www.transcripts.cnn.com.

25. Gretchen Reynolds, "Our Lives in Their Hands," *The Independent* (London), November 15, 2004.

26. World Health Organization, "Cumulative Number of Confirmed Human Cases of Avian Influenza A/(H5N1) Reported to WHO," March 18, 2008, www.who.int/csr/ disease.

27. Gregory Juckett, "Avian Influenza: Preparing for a Pandemic," *American Family Physician* 74, no. 5 (September 1, 2006): 783.

28. "Backyard Farmers Give Resistance to AI Checks," *World Poultry* (March 23, 2007).

29. Neil Merrett, "Indonesian Agreement Targets Poultry Safety," MeatProcess.com, October 5, 2007, http://www.meatprocess.com.

30. USDA, "Indonesia Poultry Update," *International Egg and Poultry Review* 9, no. 37 (September 12, 2006), www.ams.usda.gov.

31. Ruth R. Faden, Patrick S. Duggan, and Ruth Karron, "Who Pays to Stop a Pandemic?" *The New York Times,* February 9, 2007.

32. Juckett, "Avian Influenza" (see n. 27).

33. Alan Sipress, "Bird Flu Adds New Danger to Bloody Game," *The Washington Post,* April 14, 2005.

34. "Bird Flu: UN Agency Urges Greater Support for Countries Struggling to Control Virus," UN News Centre, February 7, 2007, www.un.org.

35. John E. Lange, U.S. Ambassador, Special Representative, Avian and Pandemic Influenza, speech to National Chicken Council Annual Conference, Washington, D.C., October 5, 2006, transcript at www.state.gov/g/avianflu/73688.htm.

36. Melanie Warner, "Business Prepares for the Possibility of Avian Flu in the United States," *The New York Times,* March 21, 2006.

37. Libby Quaid, "Flock-Killing Planned if Bird Flu Found," the Associated Press, April 19, 2006.

38. Juckett, "Avian Influenza" (see n. 27).

39. L. H. Bailey, *The School-Book of Farming* (New York: Macmillan, 1920), 333–34.

40. "Poultry Virus Is Possible Cure for Cancer," *World Poultry* (April 11, 2007).

41. Jacob and Miles, "Designer and Specialty Eggs" (see *Fall*, n. 22).

42. Susan FitzGerald, "Noted Vaccinologist Whose Shots Saved Millions Dies," *The Philadelphia Inquirer*, April 12, 2005; Lawrence K. Altman, "Maurice Hilleman, Master in Creating Vaccines, Dies at 85," *The New York Times*, April 12, 2005.

43. Information on featherless chickens is drawn from the following sources: James Bennet, "Rehovot Journal: Cluck! Cluck! Chickens in Their Birthday Suits!" *The New York Times*, May 24, 2002; BBC, "Bald Chicken 'Needs No Plucking,'" May 21, 2002; Aaron Priel, "Featherless Chicken," *World Poultry* 18, no. 8 (2002): 26–28; "Naked Birds May Have Market Advantage," *World Poultry* (March 6, 2007); "Featherless—the Future or an Unsaleable Concept?" *World Poultry* (April 4, 2007).

44. Marjorie E. F. Bender, Robert O. Hawes, and Donald E. Bixby, *Counting Our Chickens: Identifying Breeds in Danger of Extinction* (Pittsboro, N.C.: The American Livestock Breeds Conservancy, 2004).

45. Janet Ott, "Java Chickens Back from the Brink," *Mother Earth News* (February–March 2002); Christine Heinrichs and Don Schrider, "Enjoy Heritage Chickens," *Mother Earth News* (February–March 2005).

46. "How Corporate Globalization Pushes Millions Off the Land and Into Desperation. An Interview with Anuradha Mittal," *Multinational Monitor* (July–August 2003); Carolyn Dimitri, Anne Effland, and Neilson Conklin, "The 20th Century Transformation of U.S. Agriculture and Farm Policy," USDA, Economic Research Service, Economic Information Bulletin No. EIB3, June 2005.

47. Ibid.

48. USDA, Census of Agriculture, National Agricultural Statistics Service, www.agcensus.usda.gov/Publications/2002/index.asp.

49. Stull and Broadway, *Slaughterhouse Blues*.

50. Horowitz, "Making the Chicken of Tomorrow" (see *Spring*, n. 37).

51. Ibid.

52. Don Comis, "Going Coo Coo for Chicken Feathers," USDA, Agricultural Research Service, Sci4Kids Web page, www.ars.usda.gov/is/kids/animals/story1/story1.htm.

Selected Reading

American Farmer's New and Universal Hand-Book. Philadelphia: Cowperthwait, Desilver & Butler, 1854.

Bement, Caleb N. *The American Poulterer's Companion.* New York: Harper and Brothers, 1852.

Brunson, Cathy. *Araucanas: Rings on Their Ears!* Pendleton, S.C.: Araucana Club of America, 2007.

Burnham, George P. *The History of the Hen Fever: A Humorous Record.* Boston: James French, 1855.

Castellani, Carlo. "Ulisse Aldrovandi." *Dictionary of Scientific Biography.* New York: Scribner, 1970, 108–10.

Chatterley, Cedric N., and Alicia J. Rouverol, with Stephen A. Cole. *I Was Content and Not Content: The Story of Linda Lord and the Closing of Penobscot Poultry.* Carbondale, Ill.: Southern Illinois University Press, 2000.

Dixon, Edmund Saul. *A Treatise on the History and Management of Domestic and Ornamental Poultry,* second edition. Philadelphia: E. H. Butler, 1851.

Ekarius, Carol. *Storey's Illustrated Guide to Poultry Breeds.* North Adams, Mass.: Storey Publishing, 2007.

Goodman, David, and Michael J. Watts, editors. *Globalising Food: Agrarian Questions and Global Restructuring.* Oxford, U.K.: Routledge, 1997.

Grandin, Temple. *Thinking in Pictures.* New York: Doubleday, 1995.

Grandin, Temple, and Catherine Johnson. *Animals in Translation: Using the Mysteries of Autism to Decode Animal Behavior.* New York: Scribner, 2005.

Greene, Jeffrey. *The Bird Flu Pandemic*. New York: Thomas Dunne Books, 2006.

Hopkins, Keith. *A World Full of Gods: The Strange Triumph of Christianity*. New York: Free Press, 1999.

Horowitz, Roger. *Putting Meat on the American Table: Taste, Technology, Transformation*. Baltimore: Johns Hopkins University Press, 2006.

Jones, Lu Ann. *Mama Learned Us to Work: Farm Women in the New South*. Chapel Hill, N.C.: University of North Carolina Press, 2001.

Jones, William. *Credulities Past and Present: Including the Sea and Seamen, Miners, Amulets and Talismans, Rings, Word and Letter Divination, Numbers, Trials, Exorcising and Blessing of Animals, and More*. London: Chatto and Windus, 1898.

Lamon, Harry M. *Practical Poultry Production*. St. Paul, Minn.: Webb Publishing, 1920.

Lewis, William M. *The People's Practical Poultry Book*. New York: D. D. T. Moore, 1871.

Lind, L. R., translator and editor. *Aldrovandi on Chickens*. Norman, Okla.: University of Oklahoma Press, 1963.

Manning, Richard. *Against the Grain: How Agriculture Has Hijacked Civilization*. New York: North Point Press, 2004.

Midkiff, Ken. *The Meat You Eat: How Corporate Farming Has Endangered America's Food Supply*. New York: St. Martin's Press, 2004.

Percy, Pam. *The Complete Chicken*. Stillwater, Minn.: Voyageur Press, 2002.

Perrins, Christopher, editor. *Firefly Encyclopedia of Birds*. Buffalo, N.Y.: Firefly Books, 2003.

Robinson, John Henry. *Poultry-craft*. Boston: Farm-Poultry Publishing, 1904.

Salatin, Joel. *Pastured Poultry Profits*. Swoope, Va.: Polyface, 1993.

Schlosser, Eric. *Fast Food Nation: The Dark Side of the All-American Meal*. Boston: Houghton Mifflin, 2001.

Schrepfer, Susan R., and Philip Scranton, editors. *Industrializing Organisms: Introducing Evolutionary History*. Vol. 5 of *Hagley Perspectives on Business and Culture*. New York: Routledge, 2004.

Smith, Page, and Charles Daniel. *The Chicken Book*. Boston: Little, Brown, 1975.

Stromberg, Loyl. *Poultry Oddities, History, Folklore*. Pine River, Minn.: Stromberg Publishing, 1992.

Stull, Donald D., and Michael J. Broadway. *Slaughterhouse Blues: The Meat and Poultry Industry in North America*. Belmont, Calif.: Wadsworth/Thomson Learning, 2004.

Thomas, Teri. *The Official Mike the Headless Chicken Book*. Fruita, Colo.: The Fruita Times, 2000.

Waters, W. G. *Jerome Cardan: A Biographical Study*. London: Lawrence & Bullen, 1898.

Index